SCENIC DRIVING

UTAH

SCENIC **DRIVING** SERIES

FOURTH EDITION

SCENIC DRIVING

UTAH

Exploring the State's
Most Spectacular Back Roads

CHRISTY KARRAS

Globe
Pequot

Guilford, Connecticut

Globe
Pequot

An imprint of The Rowman & Littlefield Publishing Group, Inc.
4501 Forbes Blvd., Ste. 200
Lanham, MD 20706
www.rowman.com

Distributed by NATIONAL BOOK NETWORK

British Library Cataloguing in Publication Information available

Library of Congress Cataloging-in-Publication Data available

ISBN 978-1-4930-3586-1 (paperback)
ISBN 978-1-4930-3587-8 (e-book)

∞™ The paper used in this publication meets the minimum requirements of American National Standard for Information Sciences—Permanence of Paper for Printed Library Materials, ANSI/NISO Z39.48-1992

Printed in the United States of America

Contents

The Scenic Drives

About the Author

Christy Karras is a Seattle-based writer and editor who finds adventure—sometimes intentionally—in various spots around the world. She has lived in Washington, D.C., Oregon, and England, but a love for the outdoors frequently draws her back to her beloved home state of Utah.

Acknowledgments

Travel is an adventure made richer by people who help along the way. The late **Joe Bensen,** the original author of this book, filled it with his abundant knowledge and infectious enthusiasm. Much of the voice in these pages is his. Many editors, cartographers, proofreaders, and designers make this and all books possible.

I am grateful to all those park rangers, BLM employees, visitor center staff members, and "dam tour guides" who enthusiastically lend information to me and all travelers and who look after our precious and irreplaceable public lands and community treasures.

I very much appreciate the long-suffering friends and family who gamely support my unorthodox career choice. I'm especially grateful to those who have joined me on research trips for this book, including my dear friend Jen; my mom, Marilyn; and my husband, Bill.

I'm glad for all the friendly folks I meet whenever I travel, especially those who love these special places as much as I do. You're one of the best things about being on the road. I'll see you out there.

—Christy Karras

Introduction

Utah is an extraordinary place, remarkable for its tremendous diversity of scenic grandeur as well as for the way it stands out as culturally different from its neighbors in the American West. Utah is certainly a place apart, topographically and culturally, a place that can sometimes seem, well . . . exotic.

Topographically and geologically, Utah exceeds our expectations for natural scenery. This is a photographer's paradise, a rock hound's nirvana, and a geologist's ultimate dream world. The entire state is a like a huge open-air geology textbook, and many of its lessons are visible right from the road. (Don't be surprised

Overlooks not far from the road lead to gorgeous vistas like this one at Cedar Breaks National Monument.

if you find yourself wanting to hop out for a closer look now and then, though—bring hiking shoes on these drives!)

Utah comprises three distinct regions: the **Colorado Plateau,** the **Middle Rocky Mountain,** and the **Basin and Range** regions.

Colorado Plateau Region

The Colorado Plateau includes more than half of Utah, along with parts of Colorado, New Mexico, and Arizona. Composed mainly of sandstone and limestone, the plateau has been broken and buckled by dramatic geological faults, then etched by running water into huge and complex canyon systems. The result is some of the most impressive scenery in the world, and Utah certainly got more than its share.

The southern and eastern parts of the state are world famous for fantastic rock formations and brilliant colors. These almost unbelievable hues are largely caused by oxidation of iron ores in combination with other minerals: iron-rich soil oxidizes brilliant red or orange. Without enough oxygen, iron turns green. When iron mixes with oxygen and hydrogen, it turns into deep yellow limonite.

All five of Utah's national parks, most of its eight national monuments, and the huge **Glen Canyon National Recreation Area** lie within the Colorado Plateau region, making this perhaps the nation's single greatest concentration of easily accessible scenic attractions. Predominantly an arid land of rock and sky, the region's lack of reliable water has kept most of it a desert unfit for any major human settlement. The remoteness and emptiness of the land contributes, in many ways, to its great appeal. Yet the Colorado Plateau also contains spectacular subalpine terrain, with towering, forested plateaus and lush green river valleys. Seventeen of the drives in this guide are devoted to this famous region.

Middle Rocky Mountain Region

The **Wasatch Range and the Uinta Mountains,** both of which occupy the northeast corner of Utah, are the state's connection to the Intermountain West and the Rocky Mountains. Though by far the smallest of the three topographic regions, Utah's northern mountain ranges pack in a lot of scenic grandeur.

The two ranges are distinct from one another, both geologically and visually, and offer different rewards to the visitor. The north-south-running Wasatch Range is crisscrossed by numerous good roads and filled with fertile valleys supporting mountain communities, farms, ranches, and recreation areas. The Uintas, in contrast, remain a relatively untouched wilderness. Seven of the drives in this guide are in Utah's northern mountain wonderland, including two that give a glimpse of the remote High Uintas.

Basin & Range Region

The Basin and Range region west of the northern mountains is, on first impression, a vast wasteland of dubious interest to tourists. This is a hard, rugged land of treeless vistas, cracked earth, sparse vegetation, and a huge mostly-dead sea. Generally overlooked by visitors, and certainly overshadowed by Utah's mountain and canyon wonders, the **Great Basin** is hardly scenic by conventional standards. But it has a primal power and a distinct personality that may surprise those who experience it firsthand, many of whom come to love its solitary beauty. Four of the drives in this book focus directly on Great Basin locales, and two others touch on this forbidding yet fascinating region.

Public Lands, Parks & Campgrounds

Utah is blessed (some would say cursed) with more than two-thirds of its land owned by the state or federal government, the second-highest proportion in the nation after next-door Nevada. From the earliest days of Mormon settlement, the good of the community trumped individual acquisition—a communal idea central to everyday life in early Mormon settlements. Despite more recent squabbles over who should manage what, this philosophy of communal land stewardship exerts its influence on present-day Utah as well—much to the traveler's benefit. With the exception of its few populated valleys, Utah has a "free and open" demeanor, a feeling that the land is here for us to explore and to enjoy.

There are hundreds of **public campgrounds** in Utah, many with toilets and other amenities. The most popular fill up quickly, so reservations are recommended. For state park camping reservations, visit utahstateparks.reserveamerica .com. For national forest or national park campgrounds, go to recreation.gov or call (877) 444-6777. While the most coveted national park campsites have traditionally been of the first-come, first-served variety, the National Park Service now allows reservations for many of its sites, so always check in advance to see if that's possible where you're headed.

The abundance of public lands also makes for ample opportunities to camp outside of established campgrounds. When doing so, make every effort to use the numerous established primitive sites, especially if you intend to build a campfire; this will help limit the number of fire rings. Remember that gathering firewood in these areas is not allowed, so if you want a fire, bring your own fuel.

Before building a campfire in summer or fall, inquire at a local ranger station or visitor center about current fire restrictions. Due to high risk of wildfire, campfires are often prohibited altogether at those times, and violators face not only citations but also the prospect of being forced to foot the bill if a wildfire results. Given the restrictions, many backcountry campers simply bring portable stoves and forgo the fire.

When you use these undeveloped sites, the **Bureau of Land Management** (referred to as **BLM** in this guide) also requires that you responsibly dispose of all of your waste. In some areas, this requires that you bring and use a portable toilet system. Either way, if you pack it in, please pack it out.

In an era of increasing conflict between those who would restrict commercial use of public land and those who view the land as a resource for development, the BLM, the US Forest Service, and other government agencies charged with carrying out public-lands policy are caught in the middle, stuck in a no-win situation, as they struggle to preserve and sensibly manage these tremendous natural resources we all own.

These federal agencies appear to have been good about overseeing public lands in Utah despite an often severe shortage of funding. Unfortunately, many local residents have expressed their displeasure with government oversight by vandalizing or stealing road and trail signs and other federal property (or worse, irreplaceable natural and cultural sites), which only hinders travelers in the state. Drivers who want to help stop this destruction can call and report such activity (the BLM tip line number is 800-722-3998), including helping identify culprits if they see it happen.

The **National Park Service** oversees a relatively small portion of Utah's public land: five national parks, six of the state's eight national monuments, and two national recreation areas. Each of these renowned sites is highlighted in at least one of the drives in this book, with the sole exception of remote **Rainbow Bridge National Monument,** which cannot be reached by any paved road. In addition to these very important sites, Utah has forty-five state parks.

While the majority of the National Park Service areas lie in the southern part of the state, even those within the same geographical region have their own distinct "personality." Zion is nothing like Bryce, which is nothing like Capitol Reef, which is distinct from Glen Canyon, which looks little like Canyonlands, and so on through the list. The variety of amazing wilderness scenery in this state is truly outstanding.

For information about national parks, monuments, and historic sites, visit the park service's information-packed and well-organized website, nps.gov. State

Many of Utah's roads climb into steep canyons, as Highway 153 does east of Beaver.

park information, including campsite reservation information, is at stateparks
.utah.gov. The **US Forest Service** maintains a comprehensive but somewhat less
user-friendly website at fs.fed.us. Most of the parks require an entrance or use fee;
given what those fees pay for, they are totally worth the money. If you intend to
visit many national parks and other federal fee areas, it might make sense to buy
an annual America the Beautiful pass, which grants admission to more than 2,000
recreational sites across the nation. Similarly, an annual state parks pass might be
a good option if you want to visit more than a few.

History

Culturally, Utah has managed to maintain much of its individuality in an ever-
changing American West. The state is well known for its unity of heritage and for
the distinct social cohesion born of patterns clearly established in pioneer settlements. Utah began its modern period as a **Mormon** enclave 160 years ago, and
those beginnings are still manifest in the way the state looks and feels today.

Before Utah became the Mormon Zion, it was a sort of paradise for the various waves of Native peoples who roamed and settled throughout the Intermountain and desert West. (A note about names for Native peoples: The issue of what
to call Native peoples of the Southwest, both modern and ancient, is a complicated
one. The term "Indian" has fallen out of favor, but while some members of Native
tribes prefer "Native American," for others, "American Indian" or just plain
"Indian" works fine. Many now use the term "Ancestral Puebloan" for ancient settlers previously known as "Anasazi," since Anasazi is actually an old Navajo term
meaning "enemy people" or "ancient people who are not us." While many landmarks, including rivers and canyons, still bear the "Indian" name, it and other,
more offensive, terms are being changed over time. We have tried to keep things
clear, avoid repetition, and use specific names wherever possible.)

The earliest Utah **Paleo-Indians** were entirely hunter-gatherers. Flint tools
dating back 11,000 years, left by descendants of the nomadic bands who migrated
across the frozen Bering Strait, have been found in caves in Utah. During the
Archaic period, over thousands of years, these nomadic people gradually settled
down. Now known as the **Ancestral Puebloans**, they cultivated the land, wove
baskets, and built substantial stone constructions throughout the Southwest,
including what is now southern Utah.

*Theft or vandalism of rock art, dinosaur tracks, and other
artifacts is not only disrespectful—it's a crime.*

TRACKS AND TRACES

This large rock slab was first discovered in 1963. The block had fallen from the hillside directly in front of you and tilted outward, resting these dinosaur tracks that had been hidden from view for 190 million years. Most of the tracks preserved belong to the theropods *Dilophosaurus* and *Grallator*, but this is also the type locality for *Anomoepus minimus*, a small ornithopod, most likely a plant-eating dinosaur. These tracks are in the Navajo Sandstone and over 24 theropod tracks of various sizes are preserved here.

The vandalism on the cliff wall to the right of this block is so deeply scratched into the rock surface that it cannot be removed. Vandalism to petroglyphs and pictographs sites like these destroys the experience for future visitors. Please help preserve these tracks, petroglyphs and pictographs so future visitors can experience these traces of the past. By treading softly and leaving things as we find them, we show respect for those who came before us and those who will visit these places after us.

At about the same time, the **Fremont Culture** developed to the north; some of this group's pit houses and rock-wall art panels are still visible throughout central Utah.

These two cultures flourished for more than a thousand years, until they suddenly disappeared around AD 1200. Severe drought may have driven them to abandon their farms and dwellings. The Hopi and Pueblo people are modern-day descendants of the Ancestral Puebloans. It's unclear what happened to the Fremont people, though they may have been absorbed by a new incursion of nomadic hunters. The current Native American residents of central and northern Utah are largely descended from those nomadic bands of horse-centered **Ute, Paiute,** and **Shoshone** hunters who moved into well-watered parts of the state in relatively recent times.

The **Navajo,** an Athabascan people from the north whose language links them to tribes in the northwestern United States and Canada, still occupy their traditional lands in the Four Corners area and Monument Valley.

Some of the drives in this book will take you through sovereign Native lands; keep in mind that they sometimes have their own laws, including speed limits.

As you travel throughout the state, the physical record of Utah's ancient people is a recurring point of interest, a graphic reminder of those who have enjoyed this special place over the centuries. Native American rock art falls into two categories. Pictographs are painted, usually in deep red, and always found in caves or under ledges. Petroglyphs are incised in stone, often by pecking at the dark patina left by rainwater (sometimes called "desert varnish"), which stands out from the lighter surrounding rock. Early European-American explorers later added their own names and dates to the long "visitors register" of Native peoples. Ancient people also built dwellings on mesa tops or under rock ledges, and remnants of their craftsmanship survive, as do pottery shards and other evidence of rich and diverse cultures.

Many of the drives in this guide feature such attractions, and trail hikes throughout the state lead to lesser-known sites. A word of warning and advice: Much has been lost to vandalism and "souvenir collection" (aka theft). But today an equally dangerous threat is posed by the increasing numbers of visitors to these sites. While the damage caused is largely unintentional, it has been suggested that the public may be "loving to death" its natural resources and historic treasures. It is ever more important that we practice low-impact strategies when visiting historic sites. Never touch rock art or artifacts. Chalking, tracing, and rubbing all cause damage. We owe this consideration to future generations. Besides, these days we have plenty of other ways to communicate with our fellow humans.

Besides, protecting these sites is the law, specifically the Antiquities Act of 1906 and the Archaeological Resources Protection Act of 1979. The ARPA

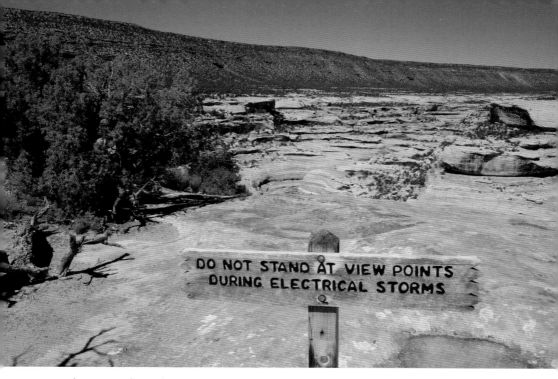

Hiking in Utah can be very rewarding, but do heed warning signs.

provides penalties up to $250,000 and five years' imprisonment for damaging sites or removing artifacts. The BLM requests that you report, as quickly as possible, any violations you might observe. Beyond the legalities, keep in mind that no jail term or fine can replace the loss of these treasures for future generations—once gone, they are lost to all of us, forever.

Modern exploration of the region began with Spanish expeditions from New Mexico, searching for a route that might connect the New Mexico colonies with Spanish outposts in southern California. The most notable of these efforts took place in 1776, when two Franciscan priests, **Francisco Dominguez** and **Silvestre Velez de Escalante,** led a party from Santa Fe all the way to central Utah before turning back in fear of the approaching and dangerous winter. The American mountain man and adventurer **Jedediah Smith** pushed through to California from northern Utah in 1826.

For the next 20 years, large caravans passed along the **Old Spanish Trail,** leading mules laden with woolen goods from the sheep-rich hills of New Mexico to the garrisons and ranches of California. The woolens were traded for mules and horses, and as many as 2,000 animals were herded back to New Mexico in the spring. The trail was described as "the longest, crookedest, most arduous pack mule trail in the history of America."

The **Treaty of Guadalupe–Hidalgo** in 1848 ended Mexico's colonial ventures in the American West, dramatically altering territorial alignments and regional trade patterns. With the dissolution of the New Mexico–California relationship, the importance of trade between the two regions declined and the Spanish Trail was no longer of major importance. The trail had, however, established the routes by which later pioneers would travel, as well as the paths of many of today's highways. Four National Historic Trails, designated and administered by the BLM and National Park Service, run through Utah: **Old Spanish, California, Mormon Pioneer,** and **Pony Express Trails.** Drives in this book touch on all of these and in some cases follow them; download maps from the NPS website and look for related informational plaques along your drives.

The subsequent history of Utah is tied inextricably to the story of the **Church of Jesus Christ of Latter-day Saints** (often shortened in local lingo to Latter-day Saints, or LDS), more widely known as the Mormons. Utah is one of the last places in America to still exhibit a cohesive regional culture, a place where the land and the people are still tied to one another in ways quite different from the rest of American society. This is still very much Mormon country.

Joseph Smith founded the church in upstate New York in 1830. Its tenets included a new work of scripture, the **Book of Mormon,** and the practice of polygamy or plural marriage. By the time they set off for Utah, the church's adherents had already fled progressively westward from one home to another, and Smith was killed by a mob in Illinois, a long way from their destination. **Brigham Young** took the helm as the church's second president and oversaw the march toward what was then Mexican territory.

On July 24, 1847, a bedridden Young was carried out to a point above the Salt Lake Valley where, according to legend, he declared, "This is the place." The Mormons were looking for an unpopulated wilderness where they could build their modern Zion (in a view typical of their time, they did not count the Native people who were already living there—an attitude that led to the same kinds of disputes that erupted all over the West between settlers and aboriginal people). The Mormon pioneers carved out—first in the Salt Lake Valley, then in far-flung valleys throughout the region—a true pioneer empire for themselves, establishing new colonies of fresh immigrant converts, sent out into the territory's remotest corners by the Church elders.

There was never in Utah the sense of the wholly independent pioneer, one who made it purely on individual accomplishment. Pioneer life here was a communal affair, connected by the community ward (church parish) with broader connections to regional temples and the church headquarters in Salt Lake City. It would be difficult to fully comprehend the achievement of the Mormon pioneers without an understanding of the philosophies and patterns of Mormon settlement and an appreciation for what it meant to colonize the far-flung desert and mountain corners of this topographically diverse state. Some advance reading about their fascinating history will enhance your trip, helping explain why the towns are located where they are and even why they still look the way they do.

One of the visual features that most distinguishes old LDS settlements from their counterparts in other regions of the rural West is the number of old brick houses. Brick was very much a part of the Mormon village aesthetic, and most of these communities established a brickyard early on. This may have been a heritage transported from their eastern hometowns. With their red brick, white fences, and tidy gardens, some of these towns have an almost back-East look, yet they are very much part of the Western frontier—sort of like Norman Rockwell gone "yippee-aye-o-kaiyay."

At any rate, they built their towns to last, which leaves us much to admire today. In most towns of any size, the local chapters of the Daughters of Utah Pioneers (DUP) maintain community museums that give an excellent glimpse into the pioneer past. The standard visiting procedure is to call one of the several numbers displayed on the front door, and a volunteer will come down to not only give you a tour but also tell you everything of note that's ever happened in that part of the county and the stories behind objects that are now on display, often heirlooms carted across the plains.

In 1890, the church officially disallowed polygamy, paving the way for statehood in 1896. Even before then, mining and the railroad had brought diversity to much of Utah, especially in the north.

Utah Today

In general, modern Utah ranks almost as low on the urban excitement scale as it does high on the scenery scale. With the exception of community arts venues and the National Basketball Association's Utah Jazz, entertainment is scarce, especially in smaller or more far-flung towns. Statewide, Mormons make up about 60 percent of the population. Some counties are almost entirely Mormon, especially along the Highway 89 corridor (sometimes called the "Morridor") through central Utah, but adherents make up less than half the population in Salt Lake City or recreation meccas like Moab and Park City.

But things are changing. Spurred partly by the 2002 Winter Olympics, Salt Lake City has gone in recent years from a sleepy crossroads to a cosmopolitan oasis with its fair share of good restaurants and bars, a healthy counterculture, and a world-class arts scene. The state has largely normalized its once-Byzantine liquor laws, bringing them more in line with those in the rest of the country and vastly reducing tourist confusion (beers on tap still can't have more than 4 percent alcohol by volume, and you still can't get wine in a grocery store. But progress doesn't happen all at once). Utah does have its vices, namely dessert: you'll find excellent ice cream throughout the state, homemade pie is a regional specialty, and do try what the locals call "scones" (chunks of fried dough covered in sugar).

A handful of remote towns have successfully blended tourism, history, and culture to create unique locales brimming with good food and other amenities. They are often near national parks and make good choices for a night's stay or a meal. Among them are Moab, near Arches and Canyonlands; Torrey, near Capitol Reef; and Springdale, just outside Zion. College towns like Logan and Cedar City offer vibrant arts scenes and decent restaurants. Alas, a good cup of coffee is still hard to find outside Salt Lake City.

Salt Lake City itself is still not a massive tourist destination, unless you're skiing, doing genealogy, or are interested in Mormonism. But the surrounding scenery—especially the *roadside* scenery—is arguably the best in the West and some of the best in the world. In fact, Utah appears to have been custommade for the driving tour. There may be other places on Earth that have grander mountains or denser forests or wilder desert country than Utah, but it's doubtful that any other place of this size encapsulates such spectacular scenic diversity, and certainly none that can be viewed from the family sedan!

Deciding which drives to include as "scenic drives in Utah" presents a real dilemma, because few roads outside the major corridor of I-15 are not scenic. Many drives deserve mention, in addition to those included here. Highway 20, between I-15 and US 89, is

Many Utah towns are full of well-preserved pioneer architecture.

attractive. The entire corridor of US 89 is both scenic and culturally interesting. US 40 from Heber to Vernal fails to warrant a scenic designation on the state road map, but you notice when you head east out of Heber just how beautiful this drive really is. Highway 35, just to the north of it, is even better—a hidden gem.

The 28 selected drives represent the many different kinds of roadside attractions in the state. Some are almost purely scenic, featuring mile after mile of gorgeous or dramatic landscape. Others involve a cultural component, featuring picturesque small towns and historic sites. Many of these drives provide access to very appealing hiking trails. Canyon and alpine drives are good opportunities to let your vehicle gain all the elevation you might otherwise have had to work hard for. Plan to combine hikes with these drives—this is a place to be savored, not rushed through.

Utah has perhaps the best developed tourist infrastructure of any state between the two coasts—one reason it won the first Michelin three-star designation ever awarded to a state in 2018. Indeed, tourism (including the ski industry) is one of the state's top industries. Visitors come from all over the world to marvel at Utah's wonders. Consequently, it is a state of visitor centers and tourist information offices. Between the state and national parks, the various ranger districts, and all of the community, regional, and state travel information offices, Utah has an awful lot of proud, friendly folks eager to help you enjoy your stay. Take advantage of all this assistance; always make the visitor center your first stop in any new region or national park.

Practical Considerations

If you're in a hurry and really need to do the "scenic blitz," most of these roads are fine for speed-limit driving. But you will miss a lot. Allow for plenty of 10-minute stops at viewpoints—longer if you're into history, hiking, or photography. While all of these drives can be completed as day trips (a very long day for one or two of them), whole days and more can be spent exploring individual parks and wilderness areas. A look at the drive locator map will indicate how easy it is to link several drives together as a multiday excursion. Allow yourself some flexibility in determining precise routes and touring strategies.

Keep an eye out for rubbernecking tourists whose eyes are on the scenery rather than the road. This is especially a problem in places like Arches National Park, where you may actually see drivers with their heads stuck out the window! On some of the narrow canyon and mountain drives, there are few places to pass. If you find a traffic buildup developing behind you—either because you are in a slow-moving vehicle or simply because you are enjoying the scenery—take advantage of the pull-outs to let traffic pass you. Bicyclists are plentiful in Utah, both as

Be sure to build in time to take in sights away from the road, such as Corona Arch near Moab.

day-trippers in the canyons above urban centers (Provo Canyon, the Cottonwood Canyons, Logan, Ogden) and on longer tours—especially on Highway 12 and Highway 95. Keep alert and don't ruin their day (or their lives).

Most of the drives described in this guide are on good, paved roads, free of extreme grades that might cause problems for any vehicle. The state of Utah has designated Scenic Byway and Scenic Backway drives, and the BLM has named a number of National Backcountry Byway drives in the state. In general, a Scenic Byway is on paved road (usually a major two-lane artery), while Scenic Back-ways are smaller (usually unpaved) back roads of varying surface quality. A BLM Backcountry Byway is usually the same as a Utah Scenic Backway. Many of these twenty-eight drives follow state-designated byways, sometimes combined with an adjacent backway of reasonable road quality, and often with recommended side trips that sometimes require a more rugged vehicle.

Many of Utah's unpaved roads are crucial for recreation and industries such as mining, so they're generally kept in good condition. However, unpaved roads can also be neglected, and their conditions can vary greatly from year to year—even from day to day—depending on weather and level of maintenance. It is espe-cially important to determine whether these roads are practical for passenger cars, recreational vehicles, or trailers. If a local says your car won't handle the road in question, take his or her word for it. In some cases you may just have to make a note to return next year in your new 4x4.

If you plan on taking any of these suggested backcountry drives, always inquire locally as to current road conditions. Your best bet is usually a BLM office, Forest Service office, or ranger station (these are often located in the same building). Agency staffers know these roads intimately, have often driven them recently, and are aware of washouts and other weather-related hazards.

When you're on a dirt or gravel road, drive slowly and avoid hitting the brakes any more than necessary, because it's easy to skid. If it's raining today or rained yesterday, don't attempt unpaved roads, especially in southern Utah, where clay soil turns to a gooey, glue-like muck that may be impossible to escape. Rain can also lead to dangerous flash floods in canyons. If a dirt road gets rough, turn around, because chances are it won't get any better farther from civilization.

In *every* case where you opt to stray from the main routes, be sure your vehicle is in good working order, that you are carrying at least one good spare tire, that you have plenty of emergency food and water, and that you know where the heck you are going. Bring a detailed paper map or road atlas, because much of rural Utah is outside cell phone range. Recreational maps are especially helpful, including the regional ones you can often find at or download from tourism offices (listed at the back of this book). Be prepared, be informed, and enjoy your driving adventure.

With so much topographic diversity, it's no wonder Utah's climate varies so much from north to south and from high elevation to low. The desert country can be blistering hot in the daytime, yet chilly at night. Experienced Utah travelers know to keep spare clothes in the car, especially when traveling in the mountain regions. After heavy-snow years or cool springs, many of the higher elevation roads can be closed until late June. Many of the higher campgrounds, even along main roads, may also be snowed in.

Despite the snow, Utah is a desert state. Dry conditions, often combined with high elevation, mean dehydration happens quickly. The rule of thumb is to drink at least a gallon a day, more if you're hiking. Most hikes don't have water along the way, and most water you will find won't be fit to drink, so bring refillable water containers and fill them at visitor centers, campgrounds, or restrooms with potable water.

Additional Reading

The following resources may help you to enjoy more fully your travels through this most extraordinary state. Read these resources, and Utah's fantastic geological/historical/cultural patchwork will begin to come together as the most fascinating sort of human and topographical quilt.

Alexander, Thomas G.: *Utah: The Right Place.* A reader-friendly overview of the state's history.

Baars, Donald L.: *A Traveler's Guide to the Geology of the Colorado Plateau.* An informative look at the forces shaping this region.

Bagley, Will: *Blood of the Prophets: Brigham Young and the Massacre at Mountain Meadows.* An exhaustively researched account of a tragedy that won't go away.

Bennett, Cynthia Larsen: *Roadside History of Utah.* A region-by-region description of the state's most interesting events.

Chronic, Halka: *Roadside Geology of Utah.* The definitive inside look at a geological wonderland.

Cuch, Forrest: *A History of Utah's American Indians.* An overview of the many people who inhabited the state before white settlers and whose descendants still live there today.

Gearey, Edward: *The Proper Edge of the Sky: The High Plateau Country of Utah.* This is a must-read for anyone with a real interest in Utah's southern plateauland.

Griggs, Brandon: *Utah Curiosities: Quirky Characters, Roadside Oddities & Other Offbeat Stuff.* A guide to the wackier side of the state.

Nelson, Lowry: "Boyhood in a Mormon Village" in *In the Direction of His Dreams: Memoirs.* This is a fascinating scholarly analysis of the hows and whys of community structure and construction in rural Utah.

Ostling, Richard, and Ostling, Joan: *Mormon America: The Power and the Promise.* Widely regarded as a fair and detailed look at the Mormon religion.

Stegner, Wallace: *Mormon Country.* Another classic. A carefully observed and beautifully written set of essays on life in Utah.

Williams, David B.: *A Naturalist's Guide to Canyon Country.* Gives richly illustrated details about the flora and fauna of the Colorado Plateau.

geology.utah.gov. The Utah Geological Survey site presents richly detailed information on geological forms and features, arranged by location, as well as mile-by-mile descriptions of some roads.

heritage.utah.gov. The Utah Department of Heritage & Arts has links to articles, interactive maps, roadside markers, and other ways to delve into Utah's history and culture.

utahindians.org/archives. A digital trove of information about Utah's Native American people.

Now, get out there and experience it.

Overview

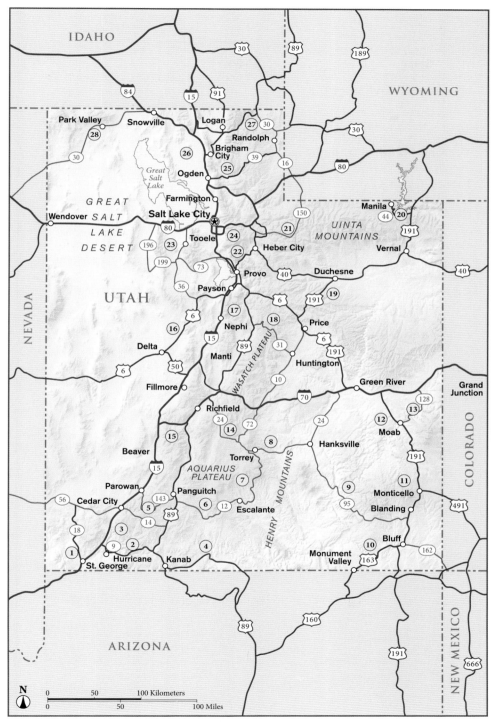

Map Legend

Interstate Highway/ Featured Interstate Highway	———(15)——— / ———(15)———
US Highway/ Featured US Highway	———(40)——— / ———(40)———
State Highway/ Featured State Highway	———(12)——— / ———(12)———
Paved Road/ Featured Paved Road	——————— / ———————
Unpaved Road/ Featured Unpaved Road	- - - - - - - / - - - - - - -
Railroad	+—+—+—+—+—+—+—+
Trail	- - - - - - - - - - - - -

Visitor, Interpretive Center	?	Small State Park, Wilderness or Natural Area	♠
Ranger Station	👫	Point of Interest	▫
Campground	▲	Ski Area	🎿
Building or Structure	■	Historic Site	🏛
Trailhead	🚶	Pass	)(
Picnic Area	⛱		
Mountain, Peak, or Butte		▲ *Deseret Peak 11,031 ft.*	
Spring		⌕	
River, Creek, or Drainage		~~~~~~~~~~~	
Reservoir or Lake		⬭	
State Line		— · — · UTAH — · — ·	
National Park State Park, or other Federal Area		▭	
National Forest		▭	
Wilderness Area		▭	
Indian Reservation		▭	
Primitive/Refuge Area, Wildlife Management Area		▭	

Utah's Desert Southwest

St. George to Littlefield, Arizona, Loop

General Description: A 100-mile loop tour that combines redrock canyon and dry Mojave Desert scenery.

Special Attractions: Snow Canyon sandstone formations, volcanic cinder cones, Mojave Desert/Joshua Tree Road Scenic Backway, hiking, and rock climbing.

Location: The extreme southwest corner of Utah.

Drive Route Numbers: Highways 18 and 3184, Old US 91.

Travel Season: Year-round. Fall and spring are the most comfortable. Summers can be hot; start early in the day and carry plenty of water.

Camping: Snow Canyon and Gunlock State Parks, public campgrounds at Baker Reservoir and Pine Valley, commercial campground at St. George.

Services: All services at St. George; limited services at Veyo, Ivins, and Littlefield, Arizona.

Nearby Attractions: Mountain Meadows, Pine Valley, Lytle Reserve, gaming in Nevada.

The Drive

Mormon pioneers were sent to Utah's southwest corner by the LDS Church in 1861 to investigate the possibility of growing warm-climate crops. The region's southern location, its climate, and the temporary success of its cotton industry earned it the nickname "Utah's Dixie."

As you might expect, this is a warm spot, with summer temperatures often exceeding 100 degrees. The landscape tends toward dry, rocky desert, with a couple of exceptions. One is the pleasant, narrow valley carved by the little Santa Clara River (through which part of this drive runs). To the north of St. George, the forested Pine Valley and Bull Valley Mountains provide a cool, green, and much needed refuge from the often blistering temperatures down here in Utah's lowest and warmest corner.

The total distance of this drive is approximately 100 miles, depending on which options you choose to follow. All roads on this drive are well maintained and drivable in all vehicles, with the exception of the unpaved Joshua Tree Road Scenic Backway. The basic St. George to Veyo to Littlefield and back to St. George drive, though relatively short, is packed with enough scenic attractions to warrant spending at least 4 hours. Add a Snow Canyon hike and a short side trip or two, and this can easily be stretched into a full day's outing. The short diversion into Snow Canyon should not be considered a mere side trip option; the scenery in Snow Canyon is the real must-do highlight of this drive.

Utah's Desert Southwest

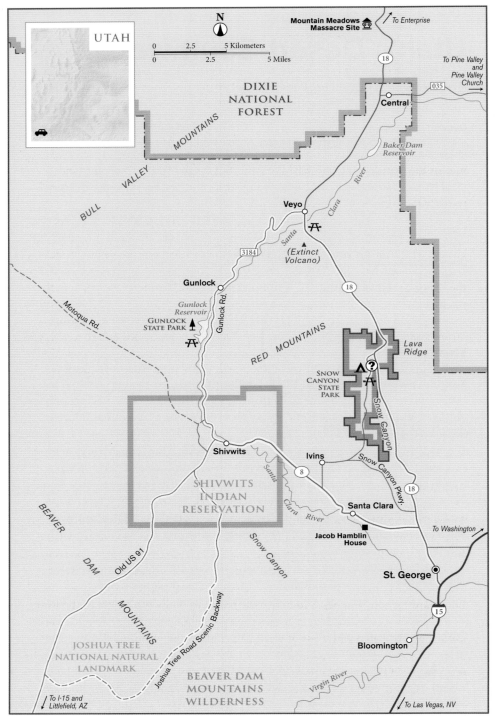

N

UTAH

0   2.5   5 Kilometers
0   2.5   5 Miles

Mountain Meadows Massacre Site

To Enterprise

DIXIE
NATIONAL
FOREST

18

To Pine Valley
and
Pine Valley
Church

035

Central

Baker Dam
Reservoir

MOUNTAINS

VALLEY

BULL

Veyo

Santa Clara River

3184

(Extinct
Volcano)

18

Gunlock

Gunlock
Reservoir

GUNLOCK
STATE PARK

Gunlock Rd.

Motoqua Rd.

RED MOUNTAINS

Lava
Ridge

SNOW
CANYON
STATE
PARK

Snow Canyon

Shivwits

SHIVWITS
INDIAN
RESERVATION

Ivins

8

Santa Clara River

Snow Canyon Pkwy.

18

Santa Clara

BEAVER

DAM

Old US 91

Joshua Tree Road Scenic Backway

Snow Canyon

Jacob Hamblin
House

To Washington

St. George

MOUNTAINS

JOSHUA TREE
NATIONAL NATURAL
LANDMARK

BEAVER DAM
MOUNTAINS
WILDERNESS

Virgin River

15

Bloomington

To I-15 and
Littlefield, AZ

To Las Vegas, NV

This drive begins in **St. George,** the regional capital of Dixie. St. George is one of the country's fastest-growing urban areas, largely due to the popularity of the weather (and nearby Nevada casinos) among retirees. The city's population grew by about 50 percent between 2000 and 2010, and about 165,000 residents called the metro area home by 2017.

Given its attractiveness, this location could evolve into a miniature Phoenix. Fortunately, much of the country in this corner of Utah is public land, which should somewhat limit the coming sprawl. St. George was named, incidentally, not for the British saint who killed dragons but for the Latter-day Saint (and apostle) George A. Smith, who selected the original families called by the church to settle the region.

Apart from tennis courts, golf courses, and RV parks, there is not a great deal to see in St. George itself. The town is clearly designed to be moved to, rather than visited, which means restaurant and entertainment selections are generally lacking for a locale of its size. Two St. George attractions that really should be seen are the historic (and very beautiful) Mormon temple and Mormon tabernacle in the center of town. The **St. George Temple,** completed in 1871, is the oldest Mormon temple still in use and the first built west of Ohio. The brilliant white building is visible from nearly everywhere in the city. The freshly renovated tabernacle, a type of large meeting house, is one of the finest examples of pioneer-era construction in the entire West. On the corner of Main Street and Tabernacle Avenue, it is open to visitors Mon through Sat from 9 a.m. to 5 p.m.

Gem of Sandstone

Highway 18, north from St. George, is signed for Veyo/Enterprise. (From I-15, take the exit signed for Bluff Street, which becomes Highway 18 north of town.) Stay northbound on Highway 18 past the turn for Sunset Boulevard, an artery that heads off to the west and makes its way through sprawling subdivisions toward **Snow Canyon State Park**'s south entrance. It is a relatively pristine 8-mile desert drive from here to the turnoff (on the left) for the park's north entrance, with a couple of new developments scattered along the hillsides. It remains to be seen, considering St. George's rapid growth (and the fact that this is mostly privately held land), how long this remains undeveloped. About 5 miles north of the Sunset Boulevard turnoff, you begin to notice the red walls of Snow Canyon to the west.

Snow Canyon is a real gem, a very impressive mix of red and white Navajo sandstone blanketed with beds of black lava. This is one of the most convenient places to see, in a small and encapsulated area, the landscape that has made southern Utah world famous. And what of the snow? While the thought of this redrock wonderland covered in a blanket of winter white is certainly appealing, this area seldom receives snow. Instead, Snow Canyon was named for one of the prominent Mormon families that settled this region.

The entrance fee is $10 per vehicle, payable at kiosks near each entrance. There are plenty of scenic pull-outs, and several moderate trails leading to overlooks and other canyon features make this an ideal spot to get out of the car to stretch your legs. The **Lava Flow Lookout trail** leads to several viewpoints and a couple of lava tubes formed during and after volcanic flows, while the short and easy **Jenny's Canyon walk** includes a slot canyon (a deep and extremely narrow canyon formed by water flowing through and wearing away rock). A few of the trails are accessible for wheelchair users, making this a great recreation spot for a wide range of abilities.

It is 2 miles from Snow Canyon's north entrance to the **park campground and visitor center.** The visitor center has a useful booklet on Snow Canyon geology, as well as guides to some of its popular hiking trails and rock climbs. The modern campground has 35 sites, including 14 trailer sites with electrical hookups and showers. It's very popular with RV travelers, so book in advance if you're bringing a trailer.

Keep an eye open for a distinctive species of bipeds that roam freely along the roadside in the park. Ivins, the town at Snow Canyon's southwest entrance, is home to the **Red Mountain Resort**, a major-league health spa that arranges for its clients to use the park as an exercise ground. Do be careful of the fitness walkers.

Ivins is hardly worth visiting unless you have a desperate urge to purchase a second home. In the throes of massive residential subdivision development that reaches all the way to the public-land border, this is a fine example of how man and development encroach on the natural beauty of the desert West.

Hard-core western history buffs might want to make a quick side trip from the Ivins end of Snow Canyon down to **Santa Clara** to visit the **Jacob Hamblin House.** Hamblin was one of the most interesting and dynamic figures in Utah's early pioneer era. He was a missionary, a colonizer, and one of the most effective and respected Indian agents in the entire West. His Santa Clara house is a classic example of a substantial pioneer home of the 1860s. Located at the north end of town (on the left), the house is fascinating—and tours are free!

With or without the Santa Clara diversion, retrace your route through Snow Canyon (hardly a chore, as the scenery is great and the perspectives appear different in either direction) back to the highway. The route to the park is a little harder to find from this direction; look for small brown government signs amid all the brightly colored signage leading to various developments and the **Tuacahn Amphitheatre,** which must be one of the world's warmest musical-theater venues.

A ranger leads a group of hikers on an interpretive hike in Snow Canyon State Park.

A final note as you retrace the canyon drive: Snow Canyon was the location for some of the filming of Robert Redford's *Jeremiah Johnson*. The filming here of an earlier movie may have been ultimately responsible for the death of the Duke, John Wayne. During the 1956 filming of *The Conqueror* (an excruciatingly bad movie starring Wayne as Genghis Khan), the government tested a nuclear bomb in the Nevada desert, upwind from Snow Canyon. Wayne, director Dick Powell, and several other members of the cast and crew later died of cancer. Perhaps a coincidence, perhaps not . . .

Black Mark in Mormon History

Leaving the state park, continue north on Highway 18 for 8 miles to **Veyo.** Approximately 5 miles north of the Snow Canyon turnoff, notice a prominent steep butte on your left, clearly an extinct cinder cone. Veyo features a couple of mom-and-pop restaurants and is your last chance for gas and provisions until Santa Clara; Enterprise; or Littlefield, Arizona (depending on your choice of route). This drive hooks to the south and west on Highway 3184 at the only intersection in town, well-marked for Gunlock.

A short side trip north from Veyo takes you to the site of the infamous **Mountain Meadows Massacre,** the blackest mark against Utah's Mormon settlers—a wound that, generations later, is still healing. This northern diversion also presents a nice glimpse of the lovely forested hill country of the Pine Valley and Bull Valley mountains.

The incident at Mountain Meadows is one of the most thoroughly discussed and written-about affairs in Utah history. A brief summary will suffice here. In 1857, 10 years after the often-persecuted Latter-day Saints finally found their own Zion in the American West, hostile forces once again threatened their way of life. A government expeditionary force was on its way to quell what was perceived as a Mormon rebellion. Brigham Young declared a state of martial law in the territory, in preparation for a war that seemed likely.

Enter into this tinderbox a large party of emigrants from Arkansas and Missouri, bound for California. Under the circumstances, the Mormon settlers would not have been well disposed to any Americans passing through their new land, but the origin of this particular wagon train was perhaps especially significant, given the rough treatment the Mormon pioneers had received in their earlier home in Missouri. The emigrants were angered at their inability to secure provisions from the Utahns (either because of the Mormons' preparations for war or out of simple animosity), and there had reportedly been unpleasant exchanges *before* the party reached the popular camping place at Mountain Meadows, the last well-watered camp before the long haul across the Mojave Desert.

A group of Mormon leaders in Cedar City persuaded a band of Paiutes to attack the wagon train. After the emigrants beat back the Indians in a five-day siege, Mormon militia arrived on the scene on September 11, 1857. They convinced the emigrants to lay down their weapons and accept militia protection and an escort out of the territory, then proceeded to murder 120 men, women, and children. Eighteen very young children, believed too young to remember and testify, were spared and given over to Mormon families, including Jacob Hamblin's, to be raised.

Twenty years after the tragic affair (the federal investigation was held up by the Civil War), the important and highly respected Mormon pioneer John D. Lee was convicted in a trial in Beaver for his part in the massacre. Lee was returned to Mountain Meadows and executed. Others were excommunicated from the church for their roles, but no one else was prosecuted.

It is a disturbing and complex story, and one that much of Mormondom seemed anxious to forget completely until 1950, when intrepid Mormon historian Juanita Brooks published *The Mountain Meadows Massacre.*

You can reach this now-peaceful site by driving about 12 miles north from Veyo and taking a left turn at the sign. In 1990 descendants of both the victims and their murderers dedicated a monument listing the names of the dead in an expression of closure to an incident painful to both sides. Various groups have built a series of monuments at the spot where US Army agents interred the bodies they found when they arrived on the scene in 1859. In 1999, the LDS Church put up the current memorial there, down a short gravel road into the valley from the 1990 monument. In 2011, the year Mountain Meadows was designated a National Historic Landmark, a Men and Boys monument was installed just off Highway 18 a half mile to the north, in a spot where many of the male victims were buried.

From Mountain Meadows you might continue this attractive hill-country drive another 8.5 miles north to the community of **Enterprise,** or return to Veyo. The mountains between Mountain Meadows and Enterprise are rough and wild, with occasional vistas across lovely green valleys. Beyond Enterprise, the Legacy Loop Highway, which loops east to Cedar City, is fairly uninspiring unless you are into alfalfa farms and ranches. But it's an easy and pleasant jaunt if you're headed north or east anyway.

On your return to Veyo from Enterprise, you may want to take a 7-mile side trip up to the forest hamlet of **Pine Valley**, with its very pretty old LDS chapel. Watch for the road on the left at the town of Central. The forests around Pine Valley supplied timber for early settlers, and this became a popular summer retreat. The Pine Valley Chapel was built in 1868 by Ebenezer Bryce, who later moved farther east and herded cattle in what is now Bryce Canyon National Park.

THE BURIAL SITES

The Baker-Fancher emigrants buried the bodies of ten men killed during the siege somewhere within the circled wagons of the encampment located west of the current monument in the valley. Most of the Baker-Fancher party died at various locations northeast of the encampment. In May 1859, Brevet Major James H. Carleton, commanding some eighty soldiers of the First Dragoons from Ft. Tejon, California, gathered scattered bones representing the partial remains of thirty-six of the emigrants, interred them near the wagon camp, and erected a stone cairn at the site. Before Carleton's arrival, Captains Reuben T. Campbell and Charles Brewer along with 207 men from Camp Floyd, Utah, collected and buried the remains of twenty-six emigrants in three different graves on the west side of the California road about one and one-half miles north of the original encampment. Brewer reported that "the remains of [an additional] 18 were buried in one grave, 12 in another and 6 in another."

Since the erection of the memorial by Major Carleton, several local families, including the Platts, Lytles, and Burgesses, have preserved and protected the graves in this area from being desecrated by souvenir hunters, land developers, curiosity seekers, and other intruders. In 1999, the Mountain Meadows Association collaborated with The Church of Jesus Christ of Latter-day Saints in erecting the new monument over the spot of the original 1859 grave. On August 3rd, 1999, workers excavating for the footings for a wall around the new monument accidentally uncovered the Carleton grave. On September 10th, 1999, the remains recovered from that grave were reinterred in a burial vault inside the new wall. The monument was dedicated the following day, September 11th, 1999.

Sites just east of Pine Valley and at **Baker Dam Reservoir,** just off Highway 18, provide cooler hiking and camping opportunities than you'll find near St. George.

From Veyo, continue our loop by heading southwest on Highway 3184. A steep descent 2.5 miles from town brings the road down into the lush, narrow gorge cut by the Santa Clara River. A few miles farther is the sprawling **Eagle Mountain Ranch,** with what seems like miles of perfect white fences.

From State Parks to Joshua Trees

The quiet little village of **Gunlock** has just about everything a small Mormon ranching community could need: a post office, an LDS church, one of the cutest little tree-shaded rodeo arenas you'll see anywhere, and not much else. Gunlock was named after Jacob Hamblin's brother, William "Gunlock" Hamblin. Evidently, he was extremely conscientious in the care of his firearms. There are no services in Gunlock—not even a gunsmith.

The road south of Gunlock follows the Santa Clara River until the valley opens up at Gunlock Reservoir, 2 miles south of town. **Gunlock State Park** has picnic areas, camping sites, and outhouses, but no drinking water and very little shade. There are nicer camping spots (undeveloped, with no facilities) another mile or so farther south alongside the river and better protected by trees from the wind that whips across the reservoir. South of Gunlock State Park the road passes through more glorious Utah redrock. Five miles south of Gunlock, you enter the **Shivwits (Paiute) Indian Reservation.** Mining-company trucks may be your only companionship on this lonely road.

A little more than 7 miles south of Gunlock, watch for a DANGEROUS INTER-SECTION sign, then a good paved road that angles sharply back to the right. This is Old US 91, formerly the main route west from St. George. The road is unmistakable—the first paved road to intersect Highway 3184. This is the access to the final segment of this drive: the Mojave Desert/Joshua Tree Road Scenic Backway.

If you choose to skip the Joshua Tree tour and return to St. George, continue south and east on Highway 3184. The road runs through an attractive narrow valley and past several ruined cabins, one or two of which are quite picturesque. Two miles south of the US 91 turnoff is the small cluster of reservation housing that constitutes the community of Shivwits, and 8 miles farther is the turnoff (on the left) well marked for Ivins and Snow Canyon.

For the **Joshua Tree Road Scenic Backway,** take the hard right turn on US 91. The old highway climbs out of the Santa Clara River Valley and winds through

A short gravel road leads to the burial sites of victims of the Mountain Meadows Massacre.

The Joshua Tree Road Scenic Backway travels through desolate territory and gives "top-down" views of the scenery around St. George.

the desert hills. Just at the top of the first hill, where the road turns back slightly to the left, is a good dirt road on the right, signed for Motoqua. A little more than a mile farther is a paved road on the left that soon turns to gravel: This is the northern entrance to the Mojave Desert/Joshua Tree Road Scenic Backway.

Named by the early Mormon pioneers, who were reminded of "Joshua in the wilderness" with arms upraised to heaven, these distinctive plants that look like a cross between a cactus and a tree are actually members of the lily family. This is the northernmost point where Joshua trees grow, and their existence here is perilous. A number of wildfires over the past 20 years have devastated much of the vegetation along both the highway and the unpaved backway, giving the whole place an even more desolate atmosphere.

The Mojave Desert/Joshua Tree Road Scenic Backway is a 16-mile loop on gravel and dirt road that comes back out on Old US 91 about 2 miles north of the Arizona state line. The road is generally well maintained, depending on weather and how recently it's been graded. If you go, views of the **Mojave Desert** to the south and west are superb, and the Joshua trees finally appear at the southern end.

If you do not care to drive 16 miles of gravel road, the Joshua viewing is fine from the southern section of the paved Highway 91. There are also numerous dirt roads down below on the desert floor that pass through denser stands of the plants. Despite ongoing efforts to preserve the population, many of these are burned-out shells of their former selves. Other Joshua trees are succumbing to attacks by rodents and encroachment of nonnative plants.

The old highway descends onto the desert floor and continues south. After about 10 miles, watch on the left for the BLM sign for WOODBURY DESERT STUDY AREA. This is also the southern access to the Joshua Tree Road Scenic Backway. Here, you get an idea of what things farther north looked like before the fires. A few miles up and back this end of the unpaved backway should suffice to get you in the midst of plenty of Joshua trees.

From here you can either retrace Old US 91 back to St. George via Santa Clara or continue south for 10 miles on fast, straight road across the flat desert to join I-15 at **Littlefield, Arizona.** The I-15 option is faster and (though the best part is not in Utah) gives the opportunity to drive through the steep-walled **Virgin River Gorge**—some of the most dramatic 8 miles or so of interstate driving in America. From St. George, it's easy to reach Zion National Park (Drives 2 and 3) or Highway 89 to Kane County (Drive 4).

From Littlefield, you may also opt for the 9-mile drive southwest to the Nevada casino town of Mesquite for a little of the sort of entertainment and recreation you really will not find in Utah.

Zion Park Scenic Byway

Hurricane to Mount Carmel Junction

General Description: A 60-mile drive highlighted by Zion National Park, one of the Southwest's landscape showcases.

Special Attractions: Zion National Park, Grafton ghost town.

Location: Southwestern Utah.

Drive Route Number & Names: Highway 9, Zion Park Scenic Byway, and Kolob Reservoir Road Scenic Backway.

Travel Season: Year-round.

Camping: Limited. Three national park campgrounds at Zion (two near the visitor center and one free primitive campground at Lava Point); public campgrounds at Sand Hollow State Park near Hurricane; commercial campgrounds (mainly RV parks with few tent sites) at Hurricane/La Verkin, Springdale, Mount Carmel Junction. Tenters with backpacking equipment can camp in the backcountry of Zion Park (at least 1 mile from roads) with an overnight permit from the visitor center.

Services: Most services at Hurricane/La Verkin, Springdale, and Mount Carmel Junction.

Nearby Attractions: Kolob Reservoir Road Scenic Backway/Lava Point, Smithsonian Butte Scenic Backway, Coral Pink Sand Dunes State Park, Kane County Scenic Drive.

The Drive

This route follows Highway 9 from its western terminus at exit 16 on I-15 to its eastern junction with US 89 at Mount Carmel Junction. The most important scenic features of this drive center on the dramatic landscape within the confines of Zion National Park, although the scenery along the length of Highway 9 is consistently good.

In addition to the 6.2-mile Zion Park Scenic Drive, there are two other notable scenic backways departing from Highway 9: Smithsonian Butte Scenic Backway and Kolob Reservoir Road Scenic Backway. Both are highly recommended side trips you should take.

You reach the town of **Hurricane** (pronounced "HUR-i-can") and its little sister **La Verkin** 9 miles from the interstate along Highway 9. (An alternate approach for this drive, if coming from the north, is via Highway 17 from I-15 exit 27.) Follow Highway 9 right through Hurricane, cross the Virgin River, and you are in La Verkin. (Hurricane and La Verkin are sort of like the Hungarian towns of Buda and Pest, except they are considerably smaller and the food is not as good.)

Just beneath the Virgin River bridge is a now-closed commercial spa called **Pah Tempe Hot Springs** that once featured seven hot mineral pools, a swimming pool, a campground, and a bed and breakfast.

Zion Park Scenic Byway

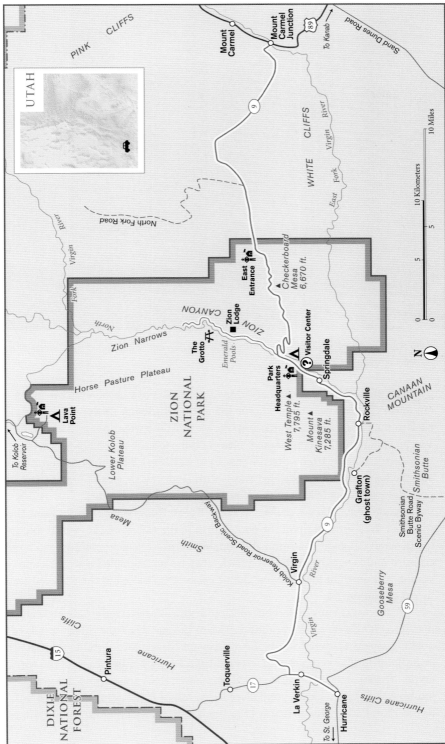

UTAH

PINK CLIFFS

Mount Carmel

Mount Carmel Junction

To Kanab

Sand Dunes Road

89

9

WHITE CLIFFS

East Fork

Virgin River

North Fork Road

Virgin River

North Fork

East Entrance

Checkerboard Mesa 6,670 ft.

ZION CANYON

Zion Lodge

Zion Narrows

The Grotto

Emerald Pools

Visitor Center

Springdale

Horse Pasture Plateau

Park Headquarters

West Temple 7,795 ft.

Mount Kinesava 7,285 ft.

ZION NATIONAL PARK

Rockville

CANAAN MOUNTAIN

2

N

Lava Point

To Kolob Reservoir

Lower Kolob Plateau

Grafton (ghost town)

Smithsonian Butte Road Scenic Byway / Smithsonian Butte

Gooseberry Mesa

59

Mesa

Smith

Kolob Reservoir Road Scenic Backway

Virgin

9

Virgin River

DIXIE NATIONAL FOREST

Cliffs

15

Pintura

Hurricane

Toquerville

17

La Verkin

To St. George

Hurricane

Hurricane Cliffs

0   5   10 Kilometers

0   5   10 Miles

Zion National Park gives chances to see both "bottom-up" and "top-down" views of its colorful canyon.

East of La Verkin, the scenery along the drive becomes increasingly more attractive. The highway climbs to the top of the **Hurricane Cliffs,** with a fine view back to the Pine Valley Mountains to the west. At the wide spot in the road called Virgin, watch for the well-marked turnoff on the left for the Kolob Reservoir Road (a member of Utah's State Scenic Byway system). This highly recommended 45-mile backway drive links Highway 9 with Highway 14, east of Cedar City, and provides exceptional views of the west side of Zion National Park. The road is paved and suitable for all vehicles as far as **Kolob Reservoir** (27 miles from Highway 9) at the northern tip of the park. North of the reservoir, the road is unpaved but generally in good condition and suitable for most vehicles, though the northernmost end is narrow, with switchbacks that are not suitable for trailers, and the section just north of the reservoir can be rocky. Don't attempt the unpaved section in wet conditions.

The backway runs in and out of Zion through forests and lovely high-alpine meadows. It's an especially beautiful drive in the fall, when the bright stands of quaking aspens scattered across the plateau are particularly vibrant. There is a beautiful primitive campground (free) at **Lava Point,** 5 miles south of the reservoir. The six first-come, first-served sites have tables, toilets, and fire grates, but no water. This makes a good place to overnight if you want to spend a full day in Zion Park. If you arrive at Lava Point in the early evening, you will more than likely see large numbers of deer in the open areas near the turnoff to the campground.

Even if you don't plan to camp, it's worth making the short drive on gravel to the point itself, which offers a rare top-down view into **Zion Canyon.** (Vehicles longer than 19 feet are not allowed on the narrow Lava Point access road.) Numerous roadside trailheads along the backway give you more chances to explore, if you're so inclined.

Ghost Town

It is 9 miles from Virgin to the tidy little community of **Rockville.** At Rockville, you might want to take half an hour to visit the site of old Grafton or an hour or so to drive the 9-mile Smithsonian Butte Scenic Backway.

The peaceful little ghost town of **Grafton,** first settled in 1859 by settlers hoping to grow cotton, is semi-famous as the filming location for many of the scenes in the classic Newman/Redford film *Butch Cassidy and the Sundance Kid.* Today it makes a nice picnic spot. To find Grafton, watch for Bridge Road on the right. Cross the narrow bridge over the Virgin River. The dirt road takes a jog to the right and runs 3.5 miles to the old town site. A handful of buildings remain, some of them partly restored. Note the interesting old cemetery, about half a mile before the town, where people keep swiping the grave markers for the colorfully named Native Americans in the back row.

This same road, across the Virgin River bridge, is the start to the **Smithsonian Butte Scenic Backway.** This drive offers spectacular panoramas of Zion Park, a short distance to the north, as well as closer encounters with Smithsonian Butte and **Canaan Mountain,** now popular mountain-biking spots. It is recommended that you drive the 9-mile-long backway in both directions, as the views change from either direction. The entire drive should take an hour. The well-marked dirt road is suitable for most vehicles, although one short, steep section might pose problems for larger vehicles. Inquire in Virgin or Rockville about current road conditions.

One mile east of Rockville is the start of 3 miles of commercial development at **Springdale,** the west entrance to Zion. The sprawling concrete **O.C. Tanner Amphitheater** hosts concerts near the national park entrance. Springdale has an abundance of bed-and-breakfasts and hotels—all of which fill up early during the tourist season—a handful of good restaurants, and a number of art galleries.

Park of Grandeur

At Springdale you enter Zion, and the world begins to look a little different. The evocative names of some of the more famous landmarks—the Great White

Throne, Angels Landing, Temple of Sinawava, Mountain of the Sun—suggest something of the grandeur of the place. But **Zion National Park** really must be seen to be believed.

Ancestral Puebloans and Paiutes probably used the canyon as a year-round refuge, as did some of the early white settlers. Among the first homesteaders here in 1861 was Isaac Behunin, who remarked: "A man can worship God among these great cathedrals as well as in any man-made church—this is Zion."

Utah's first national park, Zion was established in 1909 by President William Howard Taft, though it took roughly 250 million years to create. After millions of years of tilting, cracking, and layering, the little Virgin River did most of the fine finish-work in carving the rocky canyon—but it did take her a little while. What you see today is the product of more than 13 million years of persistent erosion.

On calm, blue-sky days it is hard to imagine how this peaceful stream could have had such a profound effect on the rocky landscape. But if you have the opportunity to see the Virgin in a wilder mood, swollen by thunderstorm or spring snowmelt, sweeping full-grown trees and massive boulders along in her torrent, the geology here begins to make sense.

The weather is almost always warm in Zion Park, with hot days and pleasantly cool nights in summer. Afternoon thunderstorms are common in July and August. It rarely snows in the canyon itself, though the higher plateaus usually receive a fair accumulation, making winter an especially scenic (and crowd-free) time to visit.

Summer crowds are, in fact, the only drawback to a Zion visit. This is one of the single greatest tourist attractions in the American West, on everyone's must-see list. A $35-per-vehicle entrance fee is good for seven days in the park. Because of increasing traffic, pollution, and safety problems, the park instituted a free shuttle system for the Zion Canyon Scenic Drive, mandatory March through November. Visitors can park in Springdale or the visitor center parking lot and board buses that run frequently and stop at all major attractions. There is no shuttle service in winter.

One other note on driving in Zion Park: Many recreational vehicles and trailers are too big to pass safely in two-way traffic through the mile-long **Zion–Mount Carmel Tunnel.** For vehicles wider than 94 inches (including mirrors) or higher than 11 feet 4 inches, an escort (required) is provided for a small fee ($15 in 2018). You must arrange for the escort in advance at a park entrance or at the visitor center. During the height of the summer tourist season, large vehicles may face parking restrictions within the park. Be sure to check on this at the visitor center.

Hikers prepare for the final ridge at Angels Landing, one of Zion National Park's most popular—and scary—ascents.

Options for Exploration

The visitor center is just under 1 mile from the Springdale entrance. Close to it are two park campgrounds (no hookups and no showers), one of which is open year-round. Given the limited number of spots, it's wise to reserve yours via recreation .gov well in advance. For those with overnight backpacking gear, a backcountry permit allows you to camp in primitive campsites along the many trails in the park as long as you are at least 1 mile from the road. Remote primitive campsites allow for several fine overnight backpacking trips in the park, and technical rock climbing is also popular here.

With backcountry use skyrocketing, the park instituted new fees, quotas, and a lottery system to limit the number of people using sensitive backcountry areas. Call (435) 772-0170 or go to nps.gov/zion for permit information before you go, or stop by the backcountry desk at the visitor center as soon as you arrive—the day before you intend to camp, if possible. Fees for permits range from $15 to $25, depending on the number of people in your party, plus another $5 online reservation fee. Keep in mind that pets are not allowed on unpaved trails or in backcountry areas in national parks.

Just east of the visitor center is the turnoff (on the left) for **Zion Canyon.** This is the part of the park you'll encounter by shuttle most of the year. Sheer cliffs of brilliant red and orange hues tower 2,000 to 3,000 feet above the canyon floor, giving this remarkable 6.2-mile tour along the North Fork of the Virgin River its well-deserved reputation as perhaps the most dramatic of all National Park drives. Along the river, stands of cottonwood, willow, and ash provide shady spots to stretch your legs and picnic. Where the water runs, Zion is a fairly lush place, with almost 800 native plant species and a tremendous variety of fauna.

The park has an abundance of hiking paths of varying lengths and degrees of difficulty. Inquire for detailed trail information at the visitor center. Two highly recommended (easy) hikes are the **Middle Emerald Pool Loop** and **Canyon Overlook.** From late March until November, there are scheduled hikes with park naturalists as well as informative evening programs. **Zion Lodge**, the park's only hotel, provides rooms, cabins, a restaurant, and other amenities and is open year-round. Room reservations are necessary and need to be booked six months in advance. Call (888) 297-2757 or visit zionlodge.com for reservation information.

The road east from Zion to Mount Carmel Junction, completed in 1930, was considered one of the great road-building accomplishments of its time. As you climb switchbacks from the canyon floor to the two high plateaus to the east, passing through two narrow tunnels blasted through the cliffs, you will understand why it created such a sensation.

A sudden rainstorm can turn Zion's steep walls into waterfalls.

When you exit the second of these tunnels, you find yourself in a very different sort of landscape. No longer amid towering sandstone cliffs, you are now in classic Utah "slickrock" country—a strange moonscape of rounded, molded, weather-sculpted rock. This multicolored sandstone, eroded and etched with grooves and cracks, presents a fantastic geologic complexity. Checkerboard Mesa, near the east entrance to the park, is particularly impressive, with its almost surreal cross-bedding of grooves.

Nothing like the commercial development at Springdale awaits you outside the park's east entrance. Thirteen miles east of Zion, at **Mount Carmel Junction,** is a small cluster of travelers' amenities, including a well-maintained golf course.

The end of this drive leaves you in the heart of some very scenic country. From Mount Carmel Junction you have several options: turn right or left or return to Hurricane and I-15. A left at the intersection with US 89 takes you north into scenic Long Valley. Right takes you south to Kanab, along the start of Drive 4.

Kolob Fingers Scenic Byway

Zion National Park's Kolob Canyons

General Description: A 5-mile mini-tour of dramatic, colorful cliffs and deep-cut gorges.

Special Attractions: Redrock cliffs, picnic spots, hiking trails.

Location: Southwestern Utah, in the northwest corner of Zion National Park.

Drive Route Name: Kolob Fingers Scenic Byway.

Travel Season: Year-round.

Camping: None in this section of the park, except by backcountry permit; BLM campground at Leeds/Red Cliff; commercial campground at Kanarraville.

Services: All services at Cedar City and St. George, limited services at Kanarraville.

Nearby Attractions: Markagunt Scenic Byway, Cedar Breaks National Monument.

The Drive

Kolob Canyons, the northwestern section of Zion National Park, features the same dramatic landscape associated with the main section of the park: towering colored cliffs, narrow winding canyons, forested plateaus, and wooded trails along twisting side canyons. What you probably will not find here are the crowds of visitors for which Zion is also famous. This place is a real find off the well-worn tourist tracks of southern Utah.

The Kolob Fingers scenic drive is only 10 miles round-trip and can be done in 40 minutes. As short as it is, this excursion may not be long enough or substantial enough to warrant a special trip, but if you are passing through this part of Utah, it would be a huge mistake to overlook this gem of a drive. Combined with a short trail walk, and perhaps lunch at the upper picnic area, this is a very pleasant afternoon project.

This is definitely best done as a late afternoon/early evening drive. In the morning you will generally be looking directly into the light, and the steep canyon walls and narrow ravines (mostly viewed from the west) lose their visual impact. The morning or midday views can seem ordinary, and the light is dull; in the late afternoon this place is completely spectacular, with the sharply defined orange cliffs contrasting dramatically with the green of the forest. Sunset from the upper parking area is sublime.

Kolob Canyons is about 18 miles south of Cedar City, conveniently just off I-15. Whether you are coming from south or north, watch for exit 40. Leave the interstate and head east, and immediately on the right is the **Kolob Canyons Visitor Center,** which should be your first stop (open daily 8 a.m. to 5 p.m. in

Kolob Fingers Scenic Byway

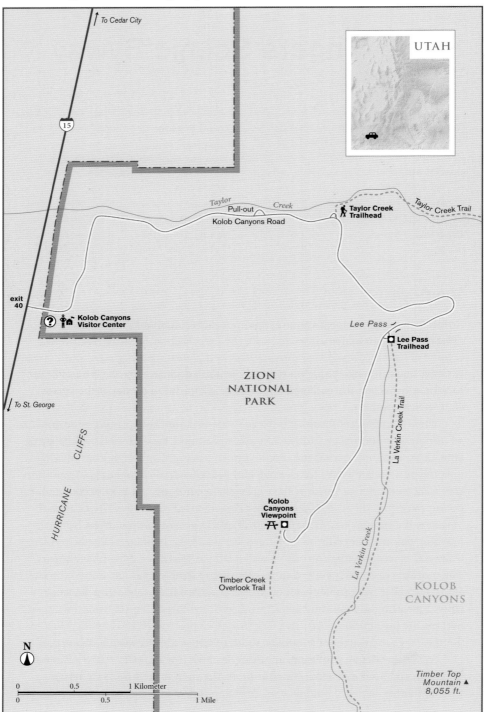

To Cedar City

15

UTAH

Taylor Creek

Pull-out

Kolob Canyons Road

Taylor Creek Trailhead

Taylor Creek Trail

exit 40

Kolob Canyons Visitor Center

Lee Pass

Lee Pass Trailhead

To St. George

ZION NATIONAL PARK

CLIFFS

HURRICANE

La Verkin Creek Trail

Kolob Canyons Viewpoint

Timber Creek Overlook Trail

La Verkin Creek

KOLOB CANYONS

N

0   0.5   1 Kilometer

0   0.5   1 Mile

Timber Top Mountain ▲ 8,055 ft.

A sign at the top of the Kolob Canyons drive gives names and elevations of the surrounding red rock mountains.

summer and until 4:30 p.m. in winter). Your $35 entrance fee gets you into both Kolob Canyons and the park's lower portions. Get drinking water at the visitor center, because there is none along the drive. A water pump near the parking area works whether the visitor center is open or not and produces drinkable water.

There are few facilities and no developed camping areas. All you will find here, between the visitor center and the summit, are a couple of picnic areas (without water), a few trailheads, and plenty of scenic pull-outs. Backpacking-equipped visitors can secure an overnight backcountry permit from either visitor center, park at a trailhead, and camp at a designated trailside site. Check with the ranger at the visitor center for specific rules and site recommendations.

The well-maintained road, which was entirely repaved and slightly recon-figured to improve accessibility and add toilets in 2018, climbs from the visitor center, ascending 1,100 feet in 5 miles, with fairly steep grades and many curves. Pulling a trailer will probably not be practical on this road, and larger RVs may wheeze a bit on the long climb.

On the lower part of the drive there are fine and typically Zion-like views—the same "we're down here, looking up" sort of perspective as in the main part of Zion. **Taylor Creek trailhead,** at just under mile 2, is the start of the moderate hike along Taylor Creek to Double Arch Alcove. The trail passes **two ruined**

settler cabins en route to the beautiful, mossy alcove. This highly recommended hike is 5.4 miles round-trip and takes approximately 4 hours.

Just past mile 3 of the drive is a large parking area with excellent views of the narrow canyon ahead, and here it really starts to look "Zion-esque." **Lee Pass trailhead** and viewpoint are at mile 3.7. This is the departure point for the long and fairly strenuous hike to **Kolob Arch.** Spanning 310 feet, Kolob Arch is thought to be perhaps the largest freestanding arch in the world. This is a serious walk, sometimes done as an overnight; the round-trip distance is 14.4 miles.

Canyons Through Time

The views from the upper end of the drive are outstanding, and you get a real sense of the complex little wonderland that lies among these narrow canyons and spires. Directly across from **Kolob Canyons Viewpoint** is a perfect example of a hanging valley: a small green cove isolated from the rest of the forested terrain by cliffs on all sides, above and below, creating its own microenvironment. The viewpoint makes an excellent picnic spot; it's also the only stop after the visitor center with a toilet.

The half-mile each way **Timber Creek Overlook Trail,** which leaves the viewpoint parking lot, is a relatively easy and level hike out to a spur of rock with even more expansive views of the mountains and canyons to the south. It's a great hike for families.

These canyons are home to much wildlife. A wide range of high desert and alpine creatures inhabit the area, and eagles or other birds of prey can often be seen riding the wind currents above the canyons.

This must have seemed the perfect environment for the earliest human inhabitants of this region: a paradise of cool, protected canyons, running water, and abundant game. The Ancestral Puebloans hunted and farmed here until their general disappearance from Utah around AD 1300. The Paiute Indians were well established here at the time of the earliest expeditions by white explorers.

In 1776 the Dominquez-Escalante party, having just decided to abort their attempt at finding a route to California, passed just to the west of the canyon mouth, following the approximate line of the interstate on their way south. An interpretive panel near the hamlet of **Kanarraville,** a few miles to the north of Kolob Canyons and just off I-15, commemorates a low point in the Spanish expedition: Having hoped to get to California, the party got caught in a blizzard, gave up, and headed south instead. Subsequent blizzards forced the explorers to eat their mules. Jedediah Smith passed these canyons 50 years later on what proved to be the first successful traverse of the Old Spanish Trail.

The Timber Creek Overlook Trail leads to expansive views.

During the 1850s, Mormon settlers spread south from the Cedar City area. They found these canyons a good source of timber and water and useful for raising livestock. Though it may sound like a Native American name, Kolob was named by the early Mormon settlers for the star closest to Heaven in the Book of Mormon—a most appropriate name.

The Kolob Fingers drive is one of the best short scenic drives in Utah, and probably the most convenient national park visit in the country. There is no finer scenery in Utah than Kolob's, and certainly none so easily reached from the interstate.

Kane County Drive-About

Long Valley Junction to Glen Canyon Dam

General Description: Desert and canyon driving for 115 miles, offering glimpses of geographic features along the southern part of US 89.

Special Attractions: Coral Pink Sand Dunes State Park, Moqui Cave, Kanab, Vermilion Cliffs, Grand Staircase–Escalante National Monument.

Location: Extreme southern edge of Utah, between Zion and Glen Canyon.

Drive Route Number: US 89.

Travel Season: Year-round.

Camping: One state park campground, several public campgrounds, commercial campgrounds at Kanab and Big Water.

Services: All services at Orderville, Kanab, and Page, Arizona; basic services at Glendale, Mount Carmel Junction, and Big Water; gas at Long Valley Junction.

Nearby Attractions: Johnson Canyon/ Alton Amphitheater Scenic Backway, Paria River Valley Scenic Backway, Paria Canyon hikes, Cottonwood Canyon Scenic Backway, Glen Canyon National Recreation Area, Lake Powell excursions, the Grand Canyon to the south.

The Drive

This 115-mile drive is perhaps more notable for its several important and highly recommended side trips than for the scenery along the main drive itself. There's nothing wrong with the scenery along US 89. In fact, the first 40-mile stretch, from Long Valley Junction to Kanab, is part of a designated state scenic byway. The stretch of US 89 between Kanab and Big Water is characterized by sagebrush flats and expansive views across a seemingly limitless desert landscape, broken only by dramatic sandstone cliffs. This is definitely rough land, appealing to folks who like wide-open spaces. Beyond Big Water is the dramatic country of Glen Canyon National Recreation Area and Lake Powell.

In order to catch some of the most interesting sights and beautiful landscapes in this part of Utah, you need to explore beyond the highway. Take advantage of the highlighted side trips appropriate for your vehicle. The two main attractions are the extraordinary landscapes at Coral Pink Sand Dunes State Park and side trips to ghost towns and former movie sets in spectacular settings. It would be a real shame to do this drive and *not* visit these sites.

Kane County Drive-About

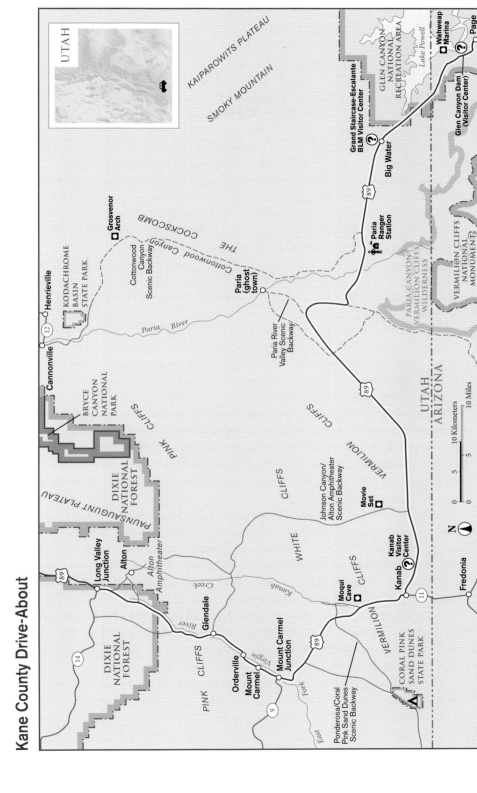

Getting Started

Begin this drive either at **Mount Carmel Junction,** for those coming out of Zion National Park's east exit, or at **Long Valley Junction,** for those coming in from the north on US 89. Either start puts you north of this drive's first main attraction.

From Long Valley Junction the road descends along the east fork of the Virgin River in one of Utah's prettiest valleys. Thirteen miles south of Long Valley Junction is **Glendale,** a quiet farm hamlet settled in 1871 by a group of Mormons who had lost their western Nevada farms when they couldn't pay their taxes. Three years later, members of the settlement at Glendale established a new community a few miles down the valley and called it **Orderville,** after the movement then under way in Utah called the United Order.

The United Order was a system of Christian communism and community self-sufficiency practiced in various parts of Utah during the latter part of the 19th century. Brigham Young encouraged the start of the United Order here in 1874, and it lasted until the mid-1880s. All property was communal, and all members worked toward what was perceived to be the common good. The entire village awoke to a bugle call at 5 a.m. and shared all meals in a communal hall. Polygamy was the familial norm. The townsfolk eventually tired of the strict regimen and of the bickering that ensued from such close living, ultimately reverting to more traditional patterns of property ownership and community life.

Today nothing but its name hints at Orderville's unique history. To the casual visitor it is a perfectly ordinary town. The **Daughters of Utah Pioneers Museum,** with mementos of Orderville's intriguing past, is worth a visit. As with most DUP museums, call one of the phone numbers on the door and a volunteer will be happy to open the building and show you around. The little brick museum is right on US 89.

At Mount Carmel Junction (13 miles east of Zion's east entrance) is a cluster of tourist-oriented facilities, including a well-maintained golf course, but not much of interest. At this point the road climbs up out of the Virgin River drainage while the river flows west along the southern boundary of Zion Park. As you exit Long Valley, you'll notice the color of the sandstone changing to delicate shades of orange and pink, hinting at the visual treat over the next rise.

Four miles southeast of Mount Carmel Junction, watch for a turnoff on the right, signed for **Coral Pink Sand Dunes State Park.** This is a must-do side trip. The 12-mile drive to the park is on a paved but narrow road, suitable for all vehicles. There is an $8-per-vehicle entrance fee.

The dunes at Coral Pink—more coral orange than pink—are created (the process is ongoing) by thousands of years of high winds blowing through a notch between Moquith and Moccasin Mountains. A Venturi effect increases the wind velocity through this notch. The wind deposits grains of eroded, iron-rich Navajo sandstone on the plain. At an elevation of 6,000 feet, Coral Pink receives enough moisture to support stands of ponderosa pine, dune grasses, and many beautiful wildflowers, making its appearance less desertlike.

Were these delicately colored dunes in any other spot, they would be hugely famous. As it is, this place gets somewhat lost among all of southern Utah's more renowned natural wonders. Still, those who have been here will list Coral Pink among their favorite "surprise finds" in Utah. The park was established in 1963 to preserve the unique environment—the most significant dune area on the Colorado Plateau. There are hundreds of miles of ATV trails, along with a more limited choice of hiking trails. Backdrops of juniper/pinyon, steep red cliffs, and dramatic rock outcroppings make Coral Pink a visual treat.

The wide expanses of dunes hold many trails open to off-road enthusiasts: Dune buggies, ATVs, and dirt bikes go wild here. There is also excellent hiking in the **Moquith Mountains,** which form the east boundary of the park, with views as far as the North Rim of the Grand Canyon. Four miles northeast of the park is the trailhead for **South Fork Indian Canyon,** where there are interesting pictographs. Park facilities include a 22-unit campground with hot showers, an easy boardwalk overlook trail, a half-mile nature trail, and a small visitor center with information on area walks.

From Caverns to Kanab

The fastest way to return to US 89 is to take the right turn just to the north of the park, called the Hancock Road. This is also the **Ponderosa/Coral Pink Sand Dunes Scenic Backway,** and there is a primitive camping site in the ponderosa pine grove on the left as you climb the hill. Dune-buggy enthusiasts can make it noisy here, especially on the weekend. This 12-mile backway connects to the highway and is meant for those who want an even better view of the dunes and surrounding country. The paved road is suitable for all vehicles and comes out on US 89 just south of the main road to the park.

Just south of Coral Pink, you might want to visit **Moqui Cave,** a roadside attraction 5 miles north of Kanab. This is, of course, a tourist trap and not an authentic Native American cave at all, but it's enough beyond simple to make it worth seeing. Assembled in this cleaned-up ancient cave are various exhibits of general interest, mostly relating to the region. There are dinosaur tracks, a huge (and quite impressive) display of fluorescent minerals, a display of Native American artifacts, and a replica of nearby cliff dwellings. There are no two-headed calves, no snake pit, and no Elvis wax replicas. But it could be worth a stop anyway. Their ads used to proclaim: "The coolest stop on Highway 89—Never over 70° on the hottest days."

Just down the road is the turnoff for **Best Friends Animal Sanctuary,** a sprawling no-kill animal shelter. Sign up online in advance at bestfriends.org if you'd like to volunteer there during your trip.

Kanab was first settled in the mid-1860s, abandoned during the Black Hawk Indian War, then resettled for keeps in 1870. Its geographic position, ideal for the burgeoning tourism industry of the 1920s, and Wild West landscapes, perfect for the booming Hollywood film industry, brought Kanab to its current status as a quintessential tourist town of the desert West.

In 1922 Tom Mix starred in *The Deadwood Coach*, the first in a string of more than 100 films (and hundreds of TV programs) that gave Kanab the nickname "Little Hollywood." The first outdoor talkie, *In Old Arizona*, was filmed here. Other films made near Kanab, and in the Johnson and Paria Canyon areas east of here include *Billy the Kid, How the West Was Won, Mackenna's Gold, The Outlaw Josey Wales, Buffalo Bill, Fort Yuma*, and *Maverick*. And it hasn't all been Westerns. Other films that used locations in this part of Utah were *The Arabian Nights, Ali Baba and the Forty Thieves, Octopussy, Galaxy Quest*, and the 2001 remake of *Planet of the Apes* as well as episodes of the television shows *Lassie* and *Route 66*.

Filming largely dried up here by the 1970s for various reasons, including the rise of air travel (which made it easy to shoot farther from Hollywood) and the decline in the popularity of Westerns. Still, townspeople, many of whom acted as stunt riders, crew members, and small-time actors during Kanab's movie heyday, have action-packed stories to tell. The town celebrates its heritage each August during its **Western Legends Roundup** (which also features a "cowboy poetry rodeo") and with occasional public screenings of old films. There's a small museum dedicated to the region's movie history in the Kanab visitor center on the main drag, where volunteers can direct you to shooting locations. You don't even have to leave town to find some of them: The still-operational **Parry Lodge** (parrylodge.com) has played host to casts and crews since the 1930s, and an interactive old movie set beside the museum lets you imagine you're in a Western of your own. Both are in the middle of town.

In many ways, Kanab defines the classic southwestern tourist town, with its tour buses, steady streams of traffic, and rows of "Indian Trading Post" souvenir shops. And yet this place still manages to retain a sense of character. Before tourism became the driving force in the local economy, Kanab grew as a service community for the ranches of southern Kane County. It's still a great place to see a traditional small-town rodeo.

The Parry Lodge hosted movie stars during the area's filmmaking heyday.

On to the main section of this drive, heading east on US 89.

Cliffside Views

It is about 8.5 miles across sagebrush desert flats to the well-marked paved road on the left signed for Johnson Canyon. This is the start of the **Johnson Canyon/ Alton Amphitheater Scenic Backway,** a 32-mile drive that loops back north to join US 89, 28 miles north of Kanab. This scenic drive traverses the very colorful country of the Vermilion and White Cliffs and provides fine views to the north of the Pink Cliffs, marking the southern edge of Bryce Canyon. The first 15 miles of this backway are paved; the rest is well-maintained gravel, suitable for passenger vehicles. The backway might be a nice return route if you're heading back north at the end of this drive.

Five and a half miles up Johnson Canyon, on the right, is a once-famous, though now fairly dilapidated, **movie set** that was featured regularly on the television series *Gunsmoke, Have Gun Will Travel, Death Valley Days,* and *Wagon Train.* There is also a telegraph and Pony Express station from the 1953 Charlton Heston movie *Pony Express.* The set is on privately owned land, so you'll have to view it from a distance unless you can get the owners to give you a private tour (ask at the visitor center in Kanab for details). The unpaved north end of the backway splits into two options: straight toward Glendale (the faster option) or right to Alton on the Amphitheater Scenic Backway, which connects with US 89 a few miles farther north. Or you can just turn around when the pavement ends.

The landscape east of Kanab is pristine, wide-open, and scenic, though unspectacular—mostly sagebrush flats and grazing land. About 20 miles east of Kanab, the landscape begins to get more dramatic, with striking redrock cliffs ahead and the very rugged Vermilion Cliffs to the left.

At mile 32 is the turnoff on the left for "Old Paria" and the start of the **Paria River Valley Scenic Backway.** The well-maintained 5-mile gravel road is suitable for all vehicles—even larger RVs and trailers, if driven slowly. As always, stay off it when it's wet.

The short drive to the town site passes truly remarkable geological formations: sandstone cliffs banded in the most lovely and delicate hues. It used to give a fine view of deserted wooden buildings, part of a set built in 1963 for the movie *Sergeants Three* and later used for Clint Eastwood's *The Outlaw Josey Wales.* The buildings were moved to a safer spot after they were damaged in a 1998 Paria River flood, but that couldn't save them from vandals who burned them down

A movie set in Kanab lets visitors pretend they're starring in a Western.

in 2006. Now, the striated cliffs are the main attraction. There's still a small BLM campground with outhouses, tables, grills, and fire pits, but no water.

The original, real-life town of **Paria** (also called "Pahreah") was established in 1870 as an agricultural community. As many as 47 families lived here during the town's one-decade existence. Severe flooding of the Paria River washed away most of the farmland, and the town gradually dwindled and died.

The remnants of the old town are on the west bank of the Paria River. While you may not opt to cross the river to visit the town site, the short drive beyond the campground is very nice, on a dirt road that gets a little steep and rough at the end (just park and walk the rest of the way if the sand gets too deep for your vehicle). A memorial about 0.3 mile past the campground indicates the site of the town cemetery. It's about a mile farther to the bank of the Paria River. To find the town site, cross the river on foot (it's usually ankle-deep at most). About all you'll find is one old chimney stack and a couple of stone foundations—unless you're a hard-core archaeo-tourist, it's hardly worth the effort.

Continuing east on US 89, you pass through a short stretch of red and gray sandstone, a fascinating jumble of shapes and colors known as the Carmel formation, which suggests a sort of mini-Canyonlands zone. On the right, 10 miles past the Old Paria turnoff, is a nice ranger station and BLM visitor center with information on the hikes and bike trails in the nearby **Paria Canyon Wilderness** and throughout the Grand Staircase–Escalante region. The ranger station is the best place to check on the current status of the **Cottonwood Canyon Scenic Backway,** which departs US 89 just past the BLM office, on the left.

The Cottonwood Canyon drive runs 46 miles north to Kodachrome Basin and Highway 12, making this the most direct route, but not the fastest, to Bryce Canyon and the many sights along Highway 12 (see Drives 6 and 7). The road is passable for most vehicles when it's dry (though in extremely dry periods it can also be very dusty). Do not attempt it after rain, because the road's fine sand turns to something more like quicksand when it's wet. The lower part of this drive, along the Paria River and Cottonwood Creek, provides excellent views of wildly eroded sandstone formations.

The **Paria Canyon–Vermilion Cliffs Wilderness,** south of the highway, was one of the country's very first designated primitive areas. The full 35-mile length of Paria Canyon is one of the premier hikes in the desert Southwest, a three- to five-day excursion through the most incredible canyon country imaginable—some of it far beyond imagination. Permits are required to hike overnight in the canyon, and only 20 people are allowed to camp in it at any time. It's not a hike to take

Drives around Grand Staircase-Escalante National Monument lead to many slot canyons.

without plenty of advance planning, but there are numerous less demanding hikes in the wilderness area. The BLM office has full information and helpful brochures.

East of the BLM office, the landscape along US 89 reverts to scenic but unspectacular wide-open sagebrush flats with desert hills and sandstone formations. Thirteen miles east of the office you reach **Big Water,** a 1-mile scattering of mobile homes along the highway. You will have to continue on to Page, Arizona, to find a real town.

Man-made Splendor

Even if you plan to return to Kanab, you might want first to continue on to Glen Canyon Dam in **Glen Canyon National Recreation Area.** If you don't want to retrace US 89 back to Kanab, the most obvious option would be to complete a large southern loop from Page back to Kanab via Marble Canyon, Jacob Lake, and Fredonia, an attractive drive along US 89A on the Arizona side of the line. That route also gives you access to the Grand Canyon's north rim.

Past Big Water the views open up over the southern region of Glen Canyon National Recreation Area. The landscape here looks a bit like the Monument Valley area of southeastern Utah: flat, open desert dotted with eroded mesas and spires, much different from the narrow, twisting canyons to the west. After 3 or 4 miles you will see the very blue water of Lake Powell off to the left.

The Arizona state line is 6 miles beyond Big Water; 2.5 miles farther is **Wahweap Marina,** the largest marina and lodging in Glen Canyon recreation area. Most services are available here (including laundry and showers). Wahweap is also the most active center for boat excursions on Lake Powell, including the popular trip to **Rainbow Bridge National Monument.** These are half-day excursions at least, so you should check on details here, then head to Page for the night.

It is 5 miles from Wahweap to the **Glen Canyon Dam visitor center,** next to the dam and the **Glen Canyon Bridge.** The visitor center is open and $5 tours are given daily except Thanksgiving Day, Christmas Day, and New Year's Day. Call (928) 608-6200 for information, including exact hours the visitor center is open (they vary seasonally).

At 710 feet, this is the fourth-tallest dam in the country. The story behind the building of the dam and creation of **Lake Powell** is one of the more interesting and controversial examples of Man's attempts at controlling Nature. Construction began in 1959 and was completed in 1964 (it took three years of round-the-clock work just to pour the concrete). Two years later the power plant began generating electricity.

Above the dam is the much-widened 200-mile stretch of the Colorado River now known as Lake Powell. This is the second-largest man-made lake in America after Lake Mead, which is downstream. Lake Powell was full by 1980, although levels have risen and dropped dramatically over the years since then. The lake was named for Major John Wesley Powell, the most important explorer of the Colorado River Basin, who had named this rough stretch of the Colorado Glen Canyon.

Page was built as a service center during the construction of the Glen Canyon Dam. Today Page is the headquarters for tour companies offering air and boat excursions to the many sights along the shores of Lake Powell, including the popular trip to Rainbow Bridge and rafting trips down the Colorado River below the dam. A good place to orient yourself on Glen Canyon attractions and the dam construction story is the very fine **Powell Memorial Museum,** also home to a regional visitor center, at the corner of Lake Powell Boulevard and Navajo Drive. It's free and open from 9 to 5 daily.

For more details on the fascinating story of Glen Canyon and Lake Powell, see the description in Drive 9.

5

Plateau Playground

Cedar City to Parowan

General Description: A high-elevation mountain and plateau drive, this loop is composed of three separate designated scenic byways, giving two major options to complete either a short (39-mile) or long (123-mile) loop. The scenery is a terrific combination of alpine forest, aspen groves, and southwestern sandstone.

Special Attractions: Cedar City, Cedar Canyon, Cedar Breaks National Monument, lava fields, wildflowers, Panguitch Lake, Brian Head Ski Resort, old Parowan.

Location: Southwest Utah, mostly in the Dixie National Forest. This drive traverses the Markagunt Plateau from west to east, then back from east to west.

Drive Route Numbers & Names: Highways 14, 148, and 143, and US 89. Markagunt Scenic Byway (Highway 14, Cedar City to US 89), Cedar Breaks Scenic Byway (Highway 148), Brian Head-Panguitch Lake Scenic Byway (Highway 143, Panguitch to Parowan).

Travel Season: Mostly year-round. The Cedar Breaks Scenic Byway is closed by snow from mid-October until early summer (depending on snowpack). All parts of this high-elevation drive are subject to winter-driving hazards and temporary snow closures. The Markagunt Plateau presents fine opportunities for viewing autumn colors.

Camping: One National Park Service campground (Cedar Breaks); at least 10 national forest campgrounds on or near the route; commercial campgrounds and RV parks at Cedar City, Parowan, Panguitch Lake, and Panguitch.

Services: All services in Cedar City, Panguitch, and Parowan; basic services at Duck Creek Village, Long Valley Junction, Hatch, and Panguitch Lake.

Nearby Attractions: Kolob Reservoir Road Scenic Backway (to Zion National Park/Lava Point), Red Canyon, Highway 12 Scenic Byway, Dry Lakes/Summit Canyon Scenic Backway, old Paragonah, Parowan Gap pictographs.

The Drive

This can be either a very long drive or just a short outing, depending on which option you choose. The full circuit is a 123-mile loop, including Cedar City–Cedar Breaks–Long Valley Junction–Panguitch–Panguitch Lake–Parowan. The short loop of Cedar City–Cedar Breaks–Parowan is just 39 miles, but you'll still want to plan a significant amount of time for the shorter loop's many viewpoints and attractions. In either case, this drive should give a good introduction to the fascinating high country of the Markagunt Plateau.

The **Markagunt Plateau** is the chief water source for southwestern Utah and the birthplace of the Virgin and Sevier Rivers. Indeed, the name "markagunt" means "highland of trees" in Paiute. Here alpine terrain combines with south-western sandstone to give the traveler the best mix of Utah's most famous scenic

Plateau Playground

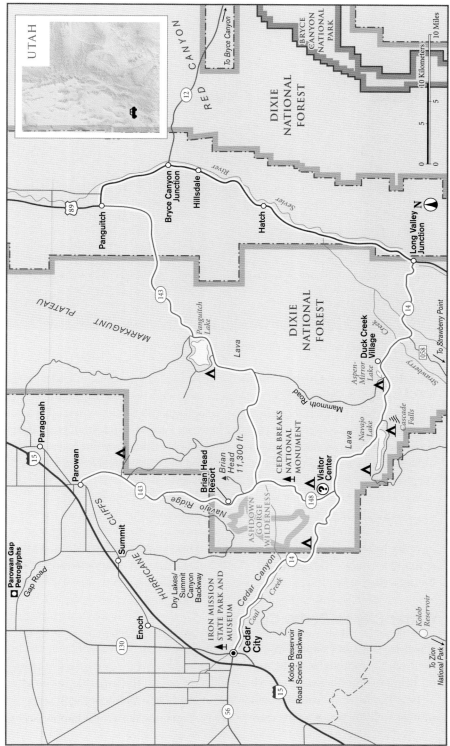

UTAH

Parowan Gap
Petroglyphs

Gap Road

Paragonah

Parowan

15

Summit

Enoch

130

CLIFFS

HURRICANE

Dry Lakes/
Summit
Canyon
Backway

IRON MISSION
STATE PARK AND
MUSEUM

Cedar
City

15

56

Kolob Reservoir
Road Scenic Backway

To Zion
National Park

Kolob
Reservoir

Coal Creek

Cedar Canyon

14

143

Navajo Ridge

Brian Head
Resort

Brian
Head
11,300 ft.

MARKAGUNT PLATEAU

143

Panguitch
Lake

Lava

ASHDOWN
GORGE
WILDERNESS

CEDAR BREAKS
NATIONAL
MONUMENT

Visitor
Center

148

Lava

Mammoth Road

Navajo
Lake

Cascade
Falls

Aspen-
Mirror
Lake

Duck Creek
Village

DIXIE
NATIONAL
FOREST

Creek

14

058

Strawberry

To Strawberry Point

Long Valley
Junction

N

Panguitch

89

Bryce Canyon
Junction

Hillsdale

River

Hatch

Sevier

12

RED CANYON

To Bryce Canyon

DIXIE
NATIONAL
FOREST

BRYCE
CANYON
NATIONAL
PARK

0   5   10 Kilometers

0   5   10 Miles

Highway 14 leads to views of Cedar Breaks from below.

offerings. This drive's highlight is the fantastic eroded sandstone of Cedar Breaks; this sculpted jewel sits in a lush setting of evergreen forest and aspen groves.

The drive's four main roads are paved and suitable for all vehicles. Traffic is generally moderate, except for the road between Parowan and Brian Head during ski season. The Markagunt Plateau receives ample snowfall, making parts of this drive sometimes difficult in winter and closing the Cedar Breaks Scenic Byway (Highway 148) from the first major snowfalls until as late as the end of June. Definitely carry chains in winter and check on current road conditions.

A special danger to the long version of this drive must be pointed out: As long as it is, and with so many attractions warranting frequent stops, what may have started as a day trip might end up as an overnighter. If you plan to do this entire drive in one day, get an early start from Cedar City . . . or else bring your toothbrush.

Cedar City to Cedar Canyon

The drive starts in **Cedar City.** Coal from the canyons to the east of town and iron ore from the mountains to the west were responsible for the marginally successful Iron Mission smelting enterprise established here at the suggestion of Brigham Young. While the industrial basis for the town was only partly successful, the community endured and is today second only to St. George in regional importance.

Today Cedar City is a pleasant community of nearly 28,000. The town has a small university (Southern Utah University) and is well known for its **summer Shakespearean festival.** Higher and much colder in winter than nearby St. George, Cedar City has not experienced the much-too-rapid growth that has transformed its southern neighbor into a sprawling mini-metropolis of apartment complexes, trailer parks, and subdivisions. Cedar City, while growing faster than many of its residents care to see, still clings to its small-town look and sense of community.

The spiffy **Cedar City–Brian Head Tourism Bureau & Visitor Center,** at 581 North Main in Cedar City, is a great starting point for exploring the region. Since many businesses and offices in the ski town of Brian Head are closed in summer, it's a good idea to ask Brian Head–related questions here.

Highway 14 (called Center Street in town) leaves Cedar City from its intersection with Main Street. Turn east and note immediately on the left the attractive LDS church in an unusual Tudor style. Just a few blocks past the church you will be out of town and in the mountains.

The mouth of **Cedar Canyon** is one of the few breaks in the geologic formation called the **Hurricane Cliffs,** which run from north of Parowan all the way south into Arizona. The Hurricane Fault caused the terrain to the east to lift thousands of feet above the flat desert floor to the west and also exposed the colorful layers of sandstone and elaborate formations you see as you ascend Cedar Canyon. Like Utah towns to the north that lie at the base of the west slope of the Wasatch Mountains, Cedar City has rugged alpine terrain to the east and rough, dry, Great Basin desert and scrub-covered hills to the west. Thus, the area offers a broad diversity of recreational and scenic possibilities.

The highway gains elevation quickly, with Coal Creek flowing swiftly on the right, in a series of giant switchbacks. The first few miles up the canyon may seem like a grunt in an RV or dragging a trailer. It's about 5 miles to the turnoff on the right for the **Kolob Reservoir Road Scenic Backway** described in Drive 2. A sign gives details on the coal mines established here in 1851. Mines in this area operated until the 1960s.

The mostly unpaved 45-mile Kolob Reservoir Road Scenic Backway runs from here to the town of Virgin, near the west entrance of Zion National Park. The first 22 miles, to Kolob Reservoir, are the steepest and most difficult, though passable in most passenger cars in dry conditions. Beyond the reservoir, views into Zion Park become most impressive, with an especially fine view from Lava Point. From Kolob Reservoir to Virgin, the road is paved. This backway is closed in winter and early spring.

About 12 miles from Cedar City on Highway 14, the canyon opens up a little and the views, especially to the left, become very dramatic. During the spring and early summer, this canyon is alive with waterfalls. You should begin to see the first examples of the black lava that will become common along this drive. It is assumed that about 30 million years ago, the upthrusting action that created the Hurricane Cliffs also created vents through which molten volcanic rock escaped. The lava from that activity is hundreds of feet thick. But most of the surface lava flows and cinder cones you will see on this drive are from a very recent era, when small vents spat molten rock and rose to form cones just 2,000 to 5,000 years ago.

At around mile 15 you pass the **Southern Utah University Mountain Center,** and a mile or so later **Cedar Canyon Campground** and the entrance to **Dixie National Forest.** Half a mile farther, the road rises up above the end of the canyon, quite steeply for about 2 miles. There are many nice pull-outs, with an especially attractive view from Zion Overlook. From here the views to the south, toward Zion National Park, have opened up splendidly.

Visiting the Breaks

At just under mile 18 (from Cedar City) is the intersection (on the left) with High-way 148, the 6-mile-long **Cedar Breaks National Monument Scenic Byway.** At this point, you may choose to shorten this long loop by driving north, past Cedar Breaks National Monument, to join Highway 143 above Brian Head and make the descent to Parowan. The total drive from Cedar City to Parowan via this route is 39 miles. Regardless of which version you choose, you really should drive up to the national monument visitor center.

I recommend doing a quick trip from here up and back the Cedar Breaks byway, then continuing east along Highway 14 to Long Valley Junction and around to Parowan via Panguitch.

Because of heavy snows, the Cedar Breaks road doesn't open until late spring and sometimes remains closed right through June. It generally closes for the winter in mid-October. It is 3.5 miles to the Cedar Breaks visitor center, where visitors must pay a $6 fee to enter the park. Note that the speed limit within the monument boundary is 35 mph, sometimes lower.

Cedar Breaks is highly reminiscent of its more famous relative, Bryce Canyon: It contains a huge amphitheater, more than 3 miles in diameter and more than 2,000 feet deep, filled with the most exquisitely formed hoodoos, spires, and twisting canyons. Less expansive, intricate, and complex than Bryce, at 10,350 feet it is higher, airier, and has a sort of deeper look. The panorama to the west stretches out across the Great Basin, while the view to the north is defined by Brian Head, at 11,307 feet the highest point on the Markagunt Plateau.

As with Bryce, Cedar Breaks is best viewed from above; you must park and walk out to overlooks to really get a view. The very nice, easy 2-mile Wasatch

The Point Supreme Overlook in Cedar Breaks National Monument lets visitors look deep into the carved-out mountainside.

Ramparts Trail departs from the visitor center. Essentially a rim overlook walk, the trail offers fine views into the amphitheater. The terminus of the walk is **Spectra Point,** with a small stand of ancient bristlecone pines, one of which is 1,600 years old. One attractive thing about Cedar Breaks is the relative absence of crowds compared to the national parks. This is a frequently overlooked attraction.

The rock colors vary greatly here, depending on the oxidation of the combinations of iron and manganese present. There are pale tans and yellows, a dull salmon pink, various shades of brick red, and even some extraordinary shades of purple. Early Native Americans named this place "Circle of Painted Cliffs." The name "Cedar Breaks" comes from the regional use of "cedar" for the juniper tree, and the common term "breaks" for eroded badlands at the top of a watershed (remember that great old Nicholson/Brando film, *The Missouri Breaks*?).

A 25-spot developed campground (generally open mid-June through mid-September) and picnic area are near the visitor center. Keep in mind that nighttime temperatures are brisk at this elevation, even in summer.

From the visitor center at Cedar Breaks, you have a major route decision to make. For the long version of this drive, you will return to the intersection with Highway 14, turn left, and continue the loop through Long Valley Junction and Panguitch. To make a short trip of it, continue along Highway 148 to the intersection with Highway 143 just above Brian Head, then descend to Parowan.

In either case, the 3 miles from the visitor center to the north end of Highway 148 is a pleasant and beautiful drive. You gain most of your elevation en route to the visitor center, so this is mostly level driving through gorgeous high meadowland (road elevation is approximately 10,000 feet). The drive takes you past three terrific overlooks, spaced about 1 mile apart, before intersecting with Highway 143. Each overlook (all pull-outs are on the left) gives a slightly different perspective of the Cedar Breaks amphitheater. The rock up here is very crumbly, so stay behind the viewpoint fences and keep a close eye on the kids. Due to frequent lightning strikes, it is best to avoid the overlooks during thunderstorms.

At the third overlook is the trailhead for the 2-mile **Alpine Pond Loop,** a very pleasant trail that leads to a picturesque pond in a lovely grove of Engelmann spruce, fir, and aspen, with commanding views of the amphitheater. Pick up an interpretive brochure at the beginning of the hike. It gives you a better sense of the plants, animals, and formations you're seeing and makes this a great diversion for families. About 1 mile past this overlook is the intersection with Highway 143, which comes in on your right. Continue straight here for Brian Head and Parowan, skipping ahead in this route description if you do.

Taking the Long Loop

So, back to the long loop. The junction with Highway 148 marks the high point of the Highway 14 drive, so the drive is mostly downhill from here to Long Valley Junction. About 3 miles from the Cedar Breaks road is a great example of the region's recent volcanic activity, with both a lava flow and cinder cone.

The extensive meadow area called **Deer Valley** is ablaze with wildflowers from late July until the middle of August. The cool, clean air, abundant water, bright sunlight, and good soil of the Markagunt make this plateau land a terrific place to view wildflowers: Mountain bluebell, larkspur, lupine, penstemon, columbine, and Indian paintbrush all flourish here in great abundance.

About a mile beyond the meadows is the Navajo Lake Overlook. **Navajo Lake** has no surface outlet; it drains subterraneously through lava tubes and percolation through porous limestone to resurface later as springs. A mile or so past the lake is a road on the right (FR 053) providing access to Navajo Lake trails, three national forest campgrounds, and **Navajo Lake Lodge**'s marina and rustic log cabins. A branch to the left of FR 053, just after the turnoff, takes you to **Cascade Falls,** one of the major drainages from Navajo Lake. Here the headwaters of the Virgin River gush forth from a rocky cavern, seemingly out of nowhere, then drops down the falls. A half-mile, self-guided trail leads to the waterfall.

Highway 14 continues to descend, past some interesting lava flows, to pretty **Aspen Mirror Lake** with its campground, pleasant trails, and prime picnic sites. One mile farther is the private enterprise called **Duck Creek Village,** which will strike you as either an eyesore or a welcome return to civilization and amenities, including gas, lodging, food, and other basic services. Duck Creek occupies a small island of private land within the public confines of Dixie National Forest. Once past this development you return to the most lovely mountain drive, immediately passing through another wide meadow alive with beautiful ponds and streams.

On your right, just after reentering **Dixie National Forest,** is the turnoff to Strawberry Point (several miles on unpaved FR 058), where views of the Pink Cliffs and south toward Zion National Park are very fine. Meadows along the way are filled with wildflowers. Across the road is the turnoff for FR 064, which leads to **Mammoth Cave,** accessible to the public and home to bats, birds, and mammals. It's actually a lava tube formed during a volcanic event. Don't explore it without lights, sturdy shoes, and warm clothing.

As you continue the descent from the Markagunt Plateau on Highway 14, you should begin to see, straight ahead on the eastern horizon, the pink sandstone cliffs of the **Paunsaugunt Plateau,** site of Bryce Canyon. At 22 miles past the turnoff for Cedar Breaks you reach the junction with US 89 at Long Valley Junction, which is mostly just a gas station and convenience store.

While no longer a spectacular mountain drive, the 26-mile drive north through the valley of the **Sevier River** (pronounced "severe") is a real scenic pleasure. As you drive through Long Valley, you will just see on your right the little stream that marks the headwaters of the Sevier River. The stream meanders lazily northward through this valley, picking up more volume from flows off the Markagunt and Paunsaugunt Plateaus until it turns into a proper river. The valley is a great place to see farms and ranchland of unrivaled bucolic beauty.

The Sevier progresses all the way to central Utah, eventually tires of running north, makes a pronounced direction change to the southwest, then flows out into the desert wastes of the Great Basin, where it runs out of energy and dies.

It's 11 miles to **Hatch,** where you will find most basic services. Note the splendid red, white, and blue antique shop on the left as you pass through this otherwise nondescript town. The rustic beauty of Long Valley is somewhat diminished by the garish billboards just north of Hatch. Eight miles north of Hatch is the intersection with Highway 12, on the right, where you may be tempted to jump ahead to Drive 6, a truly great scenic drive. You can get a hint of Highway 12's wonders by making a short diversion here to visit the mouth of **Red Canyon,** about 3 miles east. This side trip is especially recommended if you reach this point late in the afternoon, when the late light gives the red rock a brilliant, almost surreal glow.

Panguitch to Parowan on the Patchwork Parkway

Panguitch means "big fish," which is what the Paiutes called nearby Panguitch Lake. The first white settlers came here from Beaver and Parowan in 1864. Like most of the other towns in this valley, Panguitch was abandoned during the Black Hawk War (1865–68), then resettled in 1871. Early residents worked together in the community brick factory, where they were paid in bricks—most were able to build their homes of brick, and many of those survive today.

Panguitch is the largest community in and the county seat of Garfield County. The **Daughters of Utah Pioneers Museum** is on Center Street just as you come into town. Panguitch is a real cowboy town (as reflected in the beef-centered menus of restaurants here) and hosts rodeos throughout the year.

Highway 143, signed for Parowan, is the left turn at the only real intersection in town. Just as the road leaves Panguitch, climbing back up into the foothills of the Markagunt Plateau, note the prominent sign on the right indicating that you are *not* on US 89 (which continues north through the Sevier River Valley).

Highway 143 is also called the Patchwork Parkway to honor an inventive group of pioneers. During their first winter in Panguitch, they needed to get to Parowan for food and supplies but found the snow too deep to negotiate in a wagon or on foot. They lay quilts on the snow, walked across them, then moved the quilts from back to front, repeating the process across the plateau. Even more remarkable than walking to Parowan this way was hiking all the way back carrying bags of food!

Once out of the valley, as you climb through pinyon-juniper growth, the character of the landscape changes dramatically. This becomes, once again, a mountain drive. Thirteen miles from Panguitch is **White Bridge campground,** the first of three in the vicinity of Panguitch Lake. The campground sits among the cottonwoods along Panguitch Creek, giving it a slightly different character from those close to the west edge of the lake. It's about 2.5 miles farther to the lake.

Panguitch Lake was a popular summer place for the Paiutes centuries ago. Early Mormon settlers established dairies and ranches here, taking advantage of the cool mountain air. Toward the end of the century, this became a popular recreation spot for miners who worked digging in the desert west of here, with saloons, gambling halls, and even a racetrack. By the 1890s there were also lodges and dance pavilions for more genteel entertainment. Unfortunately, all of these

19th-century attractions have disappeared, though the lake remains the major recreational draw for Panguitch-area residents.

Highway 143 follows the south edge of the big lake for about 2 miles. You'll find a gas station (closed in winter), two national forest campgrounds, and accommodations ranging from rustic cabins to homey lodges to an RV park at the west end of the lake. Once past the lake, keep your eyes peeled for golden marmots, large ground squirrels that abound in the meadows up here and make homes among the rocks.

About 3 miles past the lake, watch on the left for FR 069, signed for Birch Spring Knoll. Here you can drive (or hike, if the road conditions are too rough for your vehicle) through a vast lava field. A mile or so farther along the byway, a somewhat better road, also on the left (FR 067, signed for Mammoth Creek), offers terrific scenic views and more interesting geological encounters with Markagunt's volcanic past. It eventually connects with FR 064 (the road to

In the summer, Brian Head Resort's ski lifts are open for hikers and mountain-bike enthusiasts.

Mammoth Cave) and Highway 14. At this point about 5 miles west of Panguitch Lake, Highway 143 climbs through aspen groves and lava flows, which you may recognize as a northward continuation of those encountered along Highway 14 in the vicinity of Navajo Lake.

About 14 miles west of the lake you reach a T in the road, with the left (Highway 148) leading back to Cedar Breaks, the right continuing on to Brian Head and Parowan. Turn right, then watch immediately on the left for the large parking area at the terrific viewpoint that looks east toward Cedar Breaks.

One and a half miles from the intersection with Highway 148 the high point of this drive at 10,400 feet. From here, the drive is all descent—some of it steep. If you are towing a large trailer and feel nervous about very tight hairpin turns, another option is to drive back south past Cedar Breaks on Highway 148, then back down Cedar Canyon to Cedar City. When the snows have all disappeared, you may be able to drive the steep but graded gravel road to the 11,307-foot summit of **Brian Head Peak** for spectacular views of the Markagunt Plateau, Cedar Breaks, and to the west across the Great Basin all the way to Nevada. The well-marked turnoff is on the right, just past the Cedar Breaks overlook.

On Highway 143 you will soon pass about 2 miles of **Brian Head Resort** development, with scattered condo buildings, lodges, and shops and restaurants. In addition to fine powder skiing in the winter, Brian Head is a good place to rent bicycles for trail rides—an excellent way to explore this beautiful area. A ski lift stays open all summer to haul cyclists and their bikes up the mountain.

About 4 miles below the lowest limit of the Brian Head development, watch for a scenic backway sign on the left for Dry Lakes. This 19-mile backway winds through lovely meadows below Navajo Ridge and gradually snakes its way down the Hurricane Cliffs to the hamlet of Summit. The panoramic views of Ashdown Gorge, Cedar Breaks, and the Summit–Parowan Valley are well worth the hour-long descent. The unpaved road is generally passable by cars in dry conditions, though it's steep and narrow in places. Check with a local at Brian Head or inquire at the visitor center in Cedar City before you go.

After it leaves Brian Head, Highway 143 descends rapidly, with grades reaching 13 percent and some of the tightest hairpin turns you'll ever see. This part of the drive will be easy for most vehicles (though a lack of lighting can make it a bit of a thrill at night), but it could be a white-knuckler for those towing trailers.

This drive ends at the old Mormon settlement of **Parowan.** The Parowan Valley was inhabited by the people of the Fremont Culture from AD 750 to 1250. The Dominguez-Escalante expedition came through here in 1776, but it was another 50 years before the next white visitor, Jedediah Smith, arrived. In January of 1851 Brigham Young sent settlers who established Parowan as the mother colony for the southern frontier.

The steep road from Parowan to Brian Head is full of hairpin turns.

Unlike Cedar City and St. George, Parowan was passed by commercially. Partly for this reason, it retains the look and feel of a pioneer Mormon settlement, or at least a small town of decades ago. The old stone LDS church is a beautiful example of early church architecture. No longer used for services, the church now houses a Daughters of Utah Pioneers museum. Check the front door for the phone numbers of the ladies who maintain this facility; they will be happy to give you a tour. And, yes, the separate, identical front doors were originally meant as separate entrances for men and women.

If all the scenery and attractions haven't worn you out, an interesting short side trip from Parowan is the 12-mile drive to **Parowan Gap,** where extensive rock art, much of it visible from the road, dates from both the Desert Archaic and Fremont periods. Drive west on 400 North, pass under I-15, and continue out onto the desert.

From Parowan, Cedar City is 18 miles south on I-15; Salt Lake City is 232 miles north.

Highway 12 Scenic Byway Drive 1

Red Canyon to Escalante

General Description: A memorable 62-mile high-plateau and canyon drive featuring the redrock country of the Paunsaugunt Plateau and high desert canyons south of the Aquarius Plateau.

Special Attractions: Red Canyon, Bryce Canyon National Park, Kodachrome Basin State Park, Escalante Petrified Forest State Park.

Location: Southwest Utah, in western Garfield County.

Drive Route Number & Name: Highway 12 (Highway 12 Scenic Byway).

Travel Season: Year-round. Though winter is quite cold and snowy, Bryce Canyon National Park is extremely beautiful in snow.

Camping: National forest campground at Red Canyon, two national park campgrounds at Bryce Canyon, state park campgrounds at Kodachrome Basin and Escalante Petrified Forest, commercial campgrounds at Bryce and Escalante.

Services: Most services at Panguitch and Escalante; limited services at Red Canyon, Bryce Canyon, Tropic, Cannonville, and Henrieville.

Nearby Attractions: Sevier River Valley, East Fork of the Sevier Scenic Backway, Cottonwood Canyon Road Scenic Backway (Grosvenor Arch), Smoky Mountain Road Scenic Backway, Grand Staircase–Escalante backcountry drives and hikes.

The Drive

The most scenic highway in a state well known for its scenic drives, Highway 12 (also called, predictably, Highway 12 Scenic Byway) is arguably one of the most attractive drives in the nation, and certainly one of the most diverse. From Red Canyon in the west to its eastern terminus at Highway 24, just west of the entrance to Capitol Reef National Park, Highway 12 traverses a little more than 120 miles of ruggedly beautiful landscape. The constant succession of towering redrock, remote slickrock canyons, heavily forested alpine mountains, and rustic rural villages contribute to the uniqueness and diversity of the drive, which is split into Drives 6 and 7 in this guide.

Highway 12 traverses **Garfield County,** the home of two national parks, three state parks, and one national recreation area. The entire length of this road has been designated a Utah Scenic Byway and is nearly always described from west to east. Considering Red Canyon, Bryce's pink sandstone, Kodachrome Basin, and the landform just east of Henrieville called "the Blues," this first 62-mile section

Highway 12 Scenic Byway Drive 1

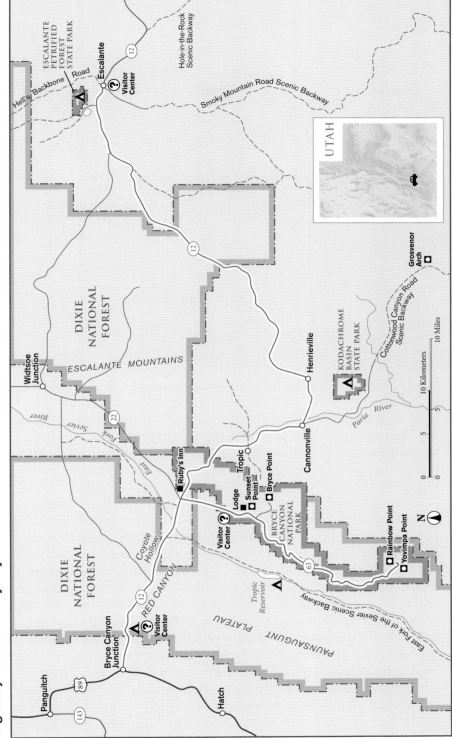

UTAH

ESCALANTE PETRIFIED FOREST STATE PARK

Hell's Backbone Road

Escalante

Visitor Center

12

Hole-in-the-Rock Scenic Backway

Smoky Mountain Road Scenic Backway

12

DIXIE NATIONAL FOREST

ESCALANTE MOUNTAINS

Widtsoe Junction

Sevier River

22

East Fork

Ruby's Inn

Coyote Hollow

Tropic

Lodge

Sunset Point

Bryce Point

Visitor Center

BRYCE CANYON NATIONAL PARK

Henrieville

KODACHROME BASIN STATE PARK

Parla River

Grosvenor Arch

Cottonwood Canyon Road Scenic Backway

Cannonville

10 Miles

10 Kilometers

5

5

0

0

Rainbow Point

Yovimpa Point

63

DIXIE NATIONAL FOREST

RED CANYON

12

Visitor Center

Bryce Canyon Junction

Panguitch

89

143

Hatch

PAUNSAUGUNT PLATEAU

Tropic Reservoir

East Fork of the Sevier Scenic Backway

N

Red Canyon starts off the Highway 12 drive with displays of bright red-orange rock.

of Highway 12 is a colorful drive indeed. Highway 12 is one of the West's most important tourist corridors. Expect the road to be well maintained throughout with moderate traffic, sometimes heavy from the Bryce Canyon turnoff and all through the park. This drive is suitable for all vehicles and is generally drivable year-round.

From its western terminus at US 89, 7 miles south of Panguitch, Highway 12 immediately cuts through the dramatic redrock formations of Dixie National Forest's **Red Canyon.** Gorgeous (and almost unbelievably brilliant) vermilion-colored formations and stands of ponderosa pines make the canyon a true gem of roadside beauty. Red Canyon is Mother Nature's original of all those "painted deserts" seen in amusement parks and old Warner Brothers cartoons. Here you will find perhaps the best scenery from the car of any drive in the entire country.

Definitely try to time your trip so that you drive with the light, or at least not against it. That means starting this drive no earlier than about noon (keep in mind that will make it difficult to do the whole 120-mile drive in one day). This could mean using the attractive Red Canyon Campground as a base and perhaps starting your day with one of the many short hikes in the area. Check in at the visitor center for information on recreating here.

Past Red Canyon, the highway crosses the top of the Paunsaugunt Plateau toward the northern part of Bryce Canyon National Park. Just outside the national forest, where the road crosses the East Fork of the Sevier River, is the turnoff on the right for the **East Fork of the Sevier Scenic Backway** (FR 087). You might wonder why you would need scenic side trips on this outstanding drive, and you are probably eager to get to Bryce, the region's top attraction. But you should consider driving at least the top part of this unpaved but well-maintained 30-mile scenic backway. The drive offers fine panoramas in all directions and plenty of interesting and beautiful redrock formations. **Tropic Reservoir,** about 8 miles south of the highway, has a national forest campground that makes a most convenient camping spot for Bryce visitors as well as anglers and off-roaders.

Near the backway's southern terminus is the creekside **Podunk forest guard station**. Like many old guard stations throughout the West (only a handful of which are in Utah), it may be available for rent from the Forest Service. Note that there's no running water, so fill up at the spring near Tropic Reservoir. Go to recreation.gov—also the site to reserve a spot at Tropic Reservoir—to check availability and make reservations for summer (mid-May through mid-October). For the rest of the year, contact the Forest Service office in Panguitch (435-676-9300). Trailheads and several primitive campsites are at the very end of the backway. The entire backway is good gravel (two-lane until the reservoir) with no steep grades and is suitable for all vehicles.

Hoodoo Heaven

Bryce Canyon National Park has some of the most stunning sandstone scenery in the American West and is especially famous for its pink and orange spires and hoodoos. A visitor center, campgrounds, scenic overlooks, hiking trails, and the most extraordinarily sculpted landscape on Earth are a short drive south of the highway.

Theodore Roosevelt recognized the importance of protecting the unspoiled character of the Bryce amphitheater, and he established a national forest there in 1905. Shortly after, a road was pushed through, and Bryce Canyon began to develop as a tourist attraction. Ruben "Ruby" Syrett built a homestead near the current entrance to the park and, in 1920, built his original lodge and cabins at the site of the current Bryce Lodge. As word spread of the scenic wonders here, Bryce was declared a national monument in 1923 and was elevated to national park status in 1928.

The cluster of commercial facilities at the intersection of Highway 12 and the park road (Utah Highway 63) are the descendants of Ruben Syrett's pioneer tourist development. Here you will find food, lodging, and RV facilities as well as concessions for park trail rides and helicopter flights. There is also a nightly rodeo at 7 p.m. (Wed through Sat, Memorial Day to Labor Day). The park entrance is 3.5 miles south of **Ruby's Inn.**

Just after passing the park boundary but before the entrance/fee station, watch on your left for the road to **Fairyland Canyon.** Many visitors, in their eagerness to enter the park, miss this viewpoint just 1 mile off the main road that allows you an up-close view of the redrock spires. It's also the trailhead for the 8-mile **Fairyland Loop hike,** which allows you to walk among them. The fantastic "hoodoos" you see below you here, and for which Bryce is so famous, were explained by the Paiutes as "legend people" who had been turned to stone. As you study the twisted maze of canyons below, consider the words of early Mormon pioneer (and park namesake) Ebenezer Bryce, who described it as "a hell of a place to lose a cow."

Fees for the park are $35 per vehicle. As always, your first stop after the entrance station should be the visitor center, where you will find a wealth of information on both the park in general and its many daily programs. The park brochure describes in fair detail the many overlooks and trails along the park's 18-mile scenic drive. This is also where you must apply for backcountry permits ($5 per person) for all overnight hikes. The visitor center is open daily from 8 a.m. to 8 p.m. during the summer tourist season (May through Sept) and until 6 p.m. in spring (Apr) and fall (Oct). From Nov to Mar, the visitor center closes at 4:30 p.m. It's closed on Thanksgiving, Christmas Day, and New Year's Day.

Due to congestion on the park road in summer, trailers are only allowed in certain areas, and there is no parking for vehicles longer than 25 feet beyond the visitor center parking lot. A free, voluntary (for now) bus system, operating May through Sept, 8 a.m. to 8 p.m. daily, will take you from the visitor center or the hotel area outside the park to all the park's overlooks and trailheads and save you a battle with traffic. The easiest option at busy times is to leave your car at one of the outside parking lots and use the shuttle until you leave the area rather than fighting for precious parking spots inside Bryce. Buses also act as shuttles for a number of hikes that start at one trailhead and end at another.

From late fall to early spring, driving in Bryce is easy. All of the overlooks lie to the east of the park road (left, as you head south). To avoid cutting across traffic, it is recommended that you drive all the way south, then stop at the overlooks on your way back. As always on these popular drives, park only in designated areas and stop only at pull-outs.

Actually, gawking drivers are less of a problem at Bryce than in some parks, as the best scenery cannot be seen from inside the car. Unlike Red Canyon, Zion,

Bryce Canyon is known for its bright red hoodoo spires.

and Capitol Reef, where you drive along the bottoms of steep canyons mostly looking out and up, and unlike the northern entrance to Canyonlands National Park, where tremendous pull-outs allow you to overlook the canyons right from your car, the Bryce road is up on the mostly forested rim of a great amphitheater, with no clear views of the dramatic scenery below. Here (as with smaller-scaled Cedar Breaks) you use the road to reach parking areas that access overlooks and elaborate trail systems that descend into the fantastic jumble of pink and orange sandstone formations.

If you never leave your car in Bryce, you will see a lot of nice trees . . . and not much else.

Trails on the Edge

I recommend stopping not far from the visitor center, at the **Sunrise Point** parking area, to hike the very easy and pleasant Rim Trail at least from Sunrise Point to Inspiration Point. If your party has two cars, you can leave one at the far end of the walk so you only have to walk the trail in one direction. Otherwise, Bryce Canyon Lodge makes a good starting point, walking in either direction, to **Sunrise or Sunset Points.** Taking the shuttle bus, of course, allows you to hike as long as you feel inclined and be picked up wherever you wish.

These trails are designed for easy strolls: well maintained, wheelchair accessible, and paved, with lots of beautiful overlooks and plenty of benches. Views here are especially impressive to the east and north. Clarence Dutton, a Civil War soldier turned explorer and eminent (and eloquent) geologist, described Table Cliff Plateau (the southwestern tip of the grand Aquarius Plateau), to the northeast of Bryce, as "a vast Acropolis crowned with a Parthenon." For a more strenuous hike, numerous trails (50 miles in all) descend into the amphitheater or follow just beneath the rim.

Bryce has most amenities, including a coin-operated laundry and showers (at the general store near Sunrise Point parking area). The two park campgrounds are first-come, first-served and fill quickly in season; Sunset Campground is closed in winter. Your other camping options are at commercial campgrounds near the Highway 12/park road or via hiking (with backcountry permit) to one of several primitive sites in the park.

Bryce Canyon Lodge is definitely worth a look. Built in 1924–25 of local stone and timber, it is one of those classic, timeless artifacts of rustic elegance from the early days of automobile tourism in America. Rooms and cabins are available Apr to mid-Nov. Go to brycecanyonforever.com or call (877) 386-4383 for reservations, but be advised that you may have to book a year or more before your trip.

A visit to Bryce can occupy a few hours or a few days. An overnight stay is highly recommended because the end and beginning of day are especially spectacular. The pink-orange sandstone goes through a dramatic transformation of light, shadow, and color. Because of its elevation and lack of surrounding development, Bryce is also one of the best places in the nation for stargazing. A view of Bryce by full moon is an experience you will never forget. But at some point you will have to tear yourself away and continue the drive east. More of Utah awaits you.

Continuing east on Highway 12, it is 7 miles to the village of **Tropic.** Though Ebenezer Bryce had a homestead here in the early 1870s, the town did not really come into being until 10 years later. Today it is a pleasant place with a surprising abundance of flowers and fruit orchards as well as a handful of decent restaurants (which makes it a nice break from the less appealing options around Bryce).

Striking Formations

Kodachrome Basin State Park, with its fascinating multicolored formations, is a highly recommended 18-mile (9 each way) diversion to the south from Cannonville, a couple of miles down the road from Tropic. Kodachrome Basin was named by a *National Geographic* author doing a story on the Escalante region in 1949. The 2,200-acre park, with an entrance fee of $8 per vehicle, has a campground nicely equipped with showers, a laundromat, and plenty of picnic tables. Two rustic bunkhouses can each accommodate up to 6 people. The park also has six excellent hiking trails. Most recommended is the Panorama Trail: 3 miles of gentle terrain, interesting rock formations, and fine vistas.

The striking formations you see at Kodachrome Basin are variations of a sort of petrified geyser sometimes called a "sandpipe." The theory is that Kodachrome Basin once was something like Yellowstone. Millions of years ago the geysers and mineral springs filled with debris and hardened into a cementlike substance of calcite and sandstone. When softer materials eroded, these structures were exposed.

Either return to Cannonville and Highway 12 or continue southeast from Kodachrome Basin on the **Cottonwood Canyon Road Scenic Backway** (unpaved but passable in most vehicles when dry; inquire first about conditions). Along this rock-flanked backway, it is about 10 miles to **Grosvenor Arch,** a natural arch of delicate pastel-colored stone, named for a founder and past president of the National Geographic Society, Gilbert Grosvenor. The 46-mile Cottonwood Canyon Road continues south to the Paria River and intersection with US 89 just west of Glen Canyon National Recreation Area (Drive 4).

Continuing east, Highway 12 passes through the pretty little town of **Henrieville,** climbs past colored clay cliffs called "the Blues," and enters the rugged sandstone and shale country of the Escalante area. There is nothing for the next

Highway 12 (sometimes literally) cuts through sections of colorful rock.

30 miles except for some of the finest, most unspoiled high desert scenery you will ever see from a paved road.

Last Stop: Escalante

One mile west of the old pioneer town of Escalante is **Escalante Petrified Forest State Park.** To appreciate the many interesting sights here, you will have to get out of the car and hike one of the excellent interpretive trails describing the park's many examples of petrified wood and dinosaur bones. The park has two main trails: the 1-mile Petrified Forest Trail and a 0.75-mile branch called the Sleeping Rainbows Loop. To see the really good views and petrified trees, do the Sleeping Rainbows Loop. Even more petrified stuff is on display at the visitor center. The park has two well-appointed campgrounds with showers and a few RV hookups. An $8 park entrance fee is also good for launching a boat at the nearby **Wide Hollow Reservoir.**

    Escalante is a classic Mormon village that retains the aura of the pioneer West. Not settled until 1875–76, it was most prosperous right around the turn of the 20th century, as confirmed by the number of larger brick buildings from this period. Limited farmland made this primarily a ranching community. You may still see livestock grazing on town lots.

In Escalante, a few "backhouses" remain on residential lots. Not to be confused with "outhouses," backhouses were common in the 19th century as summer kitchens, wash houses, guest cottages, studios, and workshops. Many of these began as the original house and were retained when the larger house was built. Some residents still use theirs for storage or as art studios or guest cottages.

The **Daughters of Utah Pioneers Museum** is in the old LDS Bishop's Tithing Storehouse at 40 South Center St. This rock building was constructed in 1894 to store the eggs, bushels of wheat, woolens, and other goods contributed to the church by every good Mormon. These were distributed to the needy and helped contribute to the common wealth of church and community. DUP museums of older Mormon towns are often housed in the old tithing offices, and this is one of the state's best.

One odd item about Escalante is its name. If there is one place in southern Utah the Dominguez-Escalante expedition of 1776 did not get to, it was Escalante. In fact, the closest the fathers came to the town named for Silvestre Escalante was somewhere north of Panguitch, on the other side of the Paunsaugunt Plateau.

Book early if you want to stay in Escalante—lodging is relatively scarce here. While this is roughly the midpoint of the Highway 12 scenic drive, the Bryce Canyon area and Torrey have more options.

A side-trip drive from Escalante, for those with vehicles suitable for rough terrain, is the **Smoky Mountain Road Scenic Backway,** highlighted by tremendous views of the rugged Kaiparowits Plateau. Much of this remote 78-mile drive is passable for passenger cars in good conditions, but high clearance is helpful in the inevitable rough spots. You'd also want to have plenty of water, food, and time, as well as at least one spare tire and the wherewithal to drive on an occasional knife's-edge ridge. Check in at the BLM office on Highway 12 at the west end of Escalante for details.

Now that you've gotten yourself out here to the back of the beyond and the rather arbitrary end of this drive, the quickest way out of this fantasy land and back to the real world would be to retrace the route back to US 89. This may not be a bad prospect, as scenic as the drive was; but now that you've come this far, why not just continue with the second half of the Highway 12 Scenic Byway? You will not be sorry if you do.

Highway 12 Scenic Byway Drive 2

Escalante to Torrey

General Description: Put simply, 57 miles of the most spectacular desert and mountain landscape in the entire state.

Special Attractions: Slickrock country of the Escalante River, Calf Creek Falls, Anasazi Indian Village State Park, Boulder Mountain, Capitol Reef and Henry Mountain views.

Location: South-central Utah.

Drive Route Number & Name: Highway 12, Highway 12 Scenic Byway.

Travel Season: Year-round, though the road north from Boulder can be difficult in

winter conditions and has been known to close after a heavy snow.

Camping: State park campground at Escalante, BLM campground at Calf Creek, four national forest campgrounds on Boulder Mountain and one on the Burr Trail, commercial campgrounds at Escalante and Torrey.

Services: Most services in Escalante, Torrey, and Boulder.

Nearby Attractions: Escalante backcountry hikes and drives, Hole-in-the-Rock Road, Hell's Backbone Ridge, Burr Trail Scenic Backway.

The Drive

This is the second installment of a 120-mile drive on perhaps the most scenic highway in the nation, Highway 12. We are now deep in the heart of slickrock country, in a part of Garfield County that still looks like a wilderness. Until relatively recently, the red rock drive on Highway 12 from Escalante to Boulder and the alpine drive across Boulder Mountain were journeys into some of the most remote places in the entire country. Begun as an ambitious Civilian Conservation Corps building project of the late 1930s, this stretch of Highway 12 was opened in 1940 and was not entirely paved until 1971 (the stretch north of Boulder to Torrey was finally fully paved in the late 1980s).

The pioneer settlement of Escalante was described briefly at the end of the previous drive. Five miles east of Escalante is the turnoff on the right for the **Hole-in-the-Rock Road.** This very scenic, often rough dirt/gravel road traces the original route of the Mormon pioneers sent from Escalante in 1879 to colonize the remote southeast corner of Utah. The party made its way to a crossing of the Colorado River below Hole-in-the-Rock, a steep, narrow defile through which they amazingly blasted, cut, and fabricated a rough road, then lowered their wagons

Highway 12 Scenic Byway Drive 2

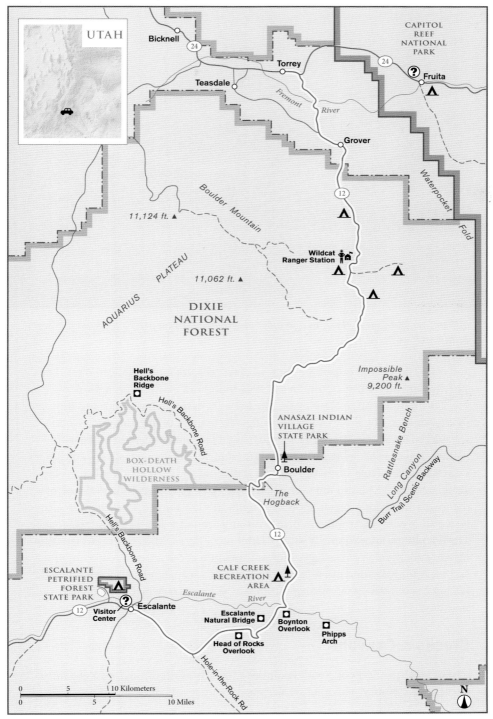

Miles of surrounding mountains and other geographic features are visible from the Burr Trail.

and teams down it in one of the truly great travel epics in the pioneer West. The story was memorialized in film in the 1949 John Ford classic *Wagon Master*.

The 62-mile trip to Hole-in-the-Rock is a bit easier today than it was for those pioneers. The drive can be done in a few hours, but the round-trip is best considered an all-day adventure. Though highly recommended for those with high-clearance vehicles and plenty of time (some of the very finest views of Lake Powell are from Hole-in-the-Rock), this is definitely not for RVs, trailers, or low-slung vehicles. The last 5 miles, over slickrock, are even more difficult. Some of the road's attractions, picnic spots, and trailheads are along the first half, so it may be worth driving a few miles in before turning around when things get too rough. The **Escalante Interagency Visitor Center** at 755 West Main Street is a fantastic resource for scenic-route suggestions, information about current road conditions, and ideas for hikes and other forms of recreation throughout south-central Utah. It's open seven days a week except from late Nov to Mar, when it's open only on weekdays.

Creeks & Canyons

East of Hole-in-the-Rock Road, Highway 12 trends north through vast expanses of slickrock country. The road skirts south of a huge fold of white sandstone, then drops into the **Escalante River Canyon.** Just on the downside of a low pass 10 miles east of Escalante is a spectacular overlook where (as the sign matter-of-factly states) you really can see forever on a clear day. As you look north toward the Aquarius Plateau, you get a good sense of what Wallace Stegner meant when he described this high plateau country as "remarkable mountains that are not mountains at all but greatly elevated rolling plains."

With all this geologic diversity, it's easy to see why this road is sometimes called the Journey Through Time Scenic Byway. The descent from this pass is a terrific driving and scenic experience. While the road is certainly drivable in any vehicle (with good brakes!), it is narrow and quite steep. If you are in a large RV or pulling a trailer, it will tax your driving skills a bit.

At about mile 14 is yet another outstanding viewpoint, **Boynton Overlook,** on the left. And here the thought may occur: If a person were to stop at every single scenic overlook along Highway 12, it might take a week to drive from Red Canyon to Torrey. And it would probably be worth the time.

At the bottom of this long descent are the trailheads for some of the many renowned Escalante Canyon backpacking and river trips. When you cross the Escalante River and start the climb up the other side, the first mile or so passes through a very narrow canyon of typical Utah redrock. At just under a mile of ascent from the river is the turnoff for **Calf Creek Campground.** It is a sandy 3-mile hike each way from the campground to Lower Calf Creek Falls, a 126-foot cascade of ice-cold water.

The **Calf Creek trail** is a fine example of the great diversity of attractions to hiking in southern Utah. En route to the falls you will walk through groves of Utah junipers (locally called "cedars") and pass between steep, pastel-colored cliffs of Navajo Sandstone. Interpretive signs along the way point out ancient rock art left by members of the Fremont Culture and a thousand-year-old Native American granary. Though the hike can be hot and somewhat strenuous, its numerous attractions and the shady, cool reward of the falls area make it well worth the effort. Pick up a guide to the numbered interpretive trail at the trailhead, bring plenty of water, and wear clothing suitable for pool wading.

If Highway 12 to this point has been impressive, beyond Calf Creek the road is extraordinary. The road appears to have been blasted through solid rock, climbing to a hogback ridge so narrow that in places you can enjoy views of 1,000-foot drops on either side (sadly, the narrow ridge doesn't allow for pull-outs). From the end of this high-level drive you catch your first glimpse of the green Boulder Valley below.

In the Shadow of Aquarius

Just at the end of the long hogback ridge and just before the final descent to Boulder is the turnoff on the left for **Hell's Backbone,** one of a few dirt roads that crisscross Boulder Mountain's flanks. This mostly alpine road is rough and may require a high-clearance vehicle, but it makes a dramatic backcountry adventure drive—especially if you are into steep switchbacks and long dropoffs. Head just a little way up the road to get an idea of the obstacles the road builders faced. Amazingly, this was the original route between Boulder and Escalante until Highway 12 was completed. Local legend has it that milk and cream, carried by mules from Boulder to Escalante over Hell's Backbone, sometimes turned to butter from the rough trip. (Well, sour cream most likely . . .)

Boulder was used by cattlemen in the late 1870s, but no permanent settlement evolved until 10 years later. This was one of the last communities in the lower 48 to be connected by road to the outside world. Boulder was so isolated that mail came by packhorse until the mid-1930s. Pickup trucks carried in by mule were reassembled and run on packed-in fuel. The original road from Escalante to Boulder over Hell's Backbone was pushed through in 1933.

Today, despite well-traveled Highway 12, Boulder still appears absolutely and stunningly remote. The wooded wilderness of the **Aquarius Plateau** dominates the northern and western horizons, the colorful canyons and roughlands of the Escalante River lie to the south, while the valley is defined in the east by forbidding desert cliffs. In the valley where the town sits, white hills rise amid green farms and ranches—an unusual color palette in this part of the world.

In recent years, Boulder and Torrey have seen an influx of artists, writers, and others seeking respite from everyday life. Surprisingly, the towns' remoteness has bred more great restaurants that you'll find anywhere outside the Wasatch Front, many of them using locally sourced ingredients including beef. Those cows you see grazing on the foothills of Boulder Mountain might end up being steak on your next trip. Boulder's internationally renowned **Hell's Backbone Grill** was the first such establishment, and the town now has three good restaurants (though, inexplicably, little lodging). The symbiotic relationship between chefs and local farmers and ranchers has helped the newcomers and old-timers coexist relatively peacefully. For travelers, it's made Boulder and Torrey great places to stop for lunch or dinner.

The **Burr Trail Scenic Backway** begins in Boulder. The paving of this route through the Waterpocket Fold area of Capitol Reef was a huge controversy and the source of spirited debate between environmentalists who did not wish to see traffic increase through the desert wilderness and state and local officials who

Unpaved switchbacks on the Burr Trail twist their way down a cliff face.

viewed the paving as a solution to critical road travel difficulties in the area. As a sort of compromise, the Burr Trail remains unpaved in a 17-mile section where it crosses Capitol Reef National Park.

You can follow this route all the way to Bullfrog Marina on Lake Powell or use it to connect with the mostly unpaved Notom Road Scenic Backway drive (see Drive 8). Switchbacks on these unpaved sections will cause problems for larger rigs; otherwise, the route is passable for most vehicles unless it's been raining. If you have time, or if plans or conditions prohibit driving the Burr Trail from Bullfrog or Notom Road, you should drive from Highway 12 at least to the very dramatic Burr Trail switchbacks, just past the end of the pavement. The Burr Trail descends a cliff face in a series of very tight switchbacks that are much easier to navigate going up than down. It may be more fun to watch someone else negotiate them than do it yourself.

At the north end of Boulder, **Anasazi Indian Village State Park,** with some well-preserved ruins and a museum, offers a glimpse into Utah's very interesting early Native American culture (admission is $5). This was the site of a 1958–59 University of Utah archaeological dig that uncovered a total of 87 rooms in an 800-year-old dwelling.

As Highway 12 leaves Boulder, it enters **Dixie National Forest** and begins to climb steeply onto the side of the Aquarius Plateau. Within 4 miles of Boulder, this is a true mountain drive, really terrific in autumn. A few miles farther and you

Views from Highway 12's Homestead Overlook stretch all the way to the Henry Mountains, with the rocky uplift of the Waterpocket Fold in between.

come into beautiful groves of aspen. Watch for deer on the road, especially in the evening.

The names Boulder Mountain and Aquarius Plateau both apply to the same landform; both names appear on current maps. Aquarius, the "waterbearer" of the zodiac, seems most appropriate for this vast alpine upland. Source of the Escalante River and major tributaries of the Fremont and Sevier, the Aquarius Plateau spills its waters down upon the desert.

Though by now you have probably realized the impracticality of stopping at every single scenic overlook, do not fail to stop at the truly incredible **Homestead Overlook** about 11 miles past Boulder and close to the 9,400-foot apex of this drive. It was a view like this that prompted the poetic explorer and geologist Clarence Dutton to remark: "It is a sublime panorama. The heart of the inner Plateau Country is spread out before us in a bird's-eye view. It is a maze of cliffs and terraces lined off with stratification, of crumbling buttes, red and white domes, rock platforms gashed with profound canyons, burning plains barren even of sage—all glowing with bright color and flooded with blazing sunlight. Everything visible tells of ruin and decay. It is the extreme of desolation, the blankest solitude, a superlative desert."

Dutton recorded these sentiments in approximately this same location, high up on the southeastern flank of the Aquarius Plateau. The view still lives up to his description.

On to Torrey

The road stays high for several miles, with especially spectacular views off to the right across the Waterpocket Fold and Capitol Reef and toward the Henry Mountains. At about mile 8.5 past Homestead is another not-to-be-missed overlook, called Larb Hollow, with even better views of the Henrys. Just past this overlook is a steep 5-mile descent. You leave Dixie National Forest just north of **Grover** in some of the most beautiful high ranch country you will ever see, covered with sage and juniper. Grover is not a town but a handful of ranches nestled in the valley.

Highway 12 ends at the intersection with Highway 24 just east of Torrey. Here you have the option of turning left/west to Loa to join Drive 14, the Fishlake Scenic Byway, or make the quickest return to I-15. If you wish to continue with Drive 8 through Capitol Reef and on to points east, turn right. In either case, you really ought to take a few minutes to visit the small residential community of **Teasdale** (about 4 miles west of Torrey and 1.5 miles south of Highway 24 at a well-marked intersection). This quiet little town with its lovely LDS church is a perfect example of why the Mormon pioneers, kicked out of town after town across America and just looking for some unwanted place to call their own, didn't get such a bad deal after all. Wouldn't you rather live in Teasdale?

Torrey is a pretty little town with tree-lined Highway 24 as its main street. This is increasingly a community of artists and retired academic types, with a couple of excellent restaurants and concerts or lectures presented on many weekend evenings. Just west of the modern LDS church, note on the right the small original church building, usually open for visitors. Across the street there is a cute little community picnic area with a bandstand. You will find all services in Torrey, including many friendly and inexpensive hotels and several RV parks. Combined with its proximity to Capitol Reef National Park, those amenities make this a popular overnight stop for visitors touring the area.

8

Highway 24 Scenic Byway

Loa to Hanksville

General Description: This 75-mile drive leaves a farming/ranching valley and quickly enters classic Utah canyon country, highlighted by the many scenic attractions of the Waterpocket Fold.

Special Attractions: Attractive agricultural communities along the Fremont River, Capitol Reef National Park, views of the Henry Mountains, outstanding geological formations.

Location: South-central Utah.

Drive Route Number & Name: Highway 24, Highway 24 Scenic Byway.

Travel Season: Year-round. Summers are hot.

Camping: One developed national park campground at Capitol Reef; undeveloped sites in the national park and on BLM land; state-park campground at Goblin Valley; commercial campgrounds at Bicknell, Torrey, Caineville, and Hanksville.

Services: Most services in Loa, Torrey, Hanksville, and Green River; limited services at Caineville.

Nearby Attractions: Fishlake Scenic Byway, Escalante–Torrey (Highway 12) Scenic Byway, Notom Road Scenic Backway, Cathedral Valley Scenic Backway, Goblin Valley State Park.

The Drive

It is approximately 75 miles along Highway 24 from Loa to Hanksville. Make that 75 extraordinary miles. This drive is almost nonstop knockout scenery, from the green valley of the Fremont River through the dramatic geologic upheaval of the Waterpocket Fold to the wild shale and sandstone high desert mesas and buttes that spread out to the north of the rugged Henry Mountains.

Plan on a full day for this entire scenic drive, including the 25-mile Capitol Reef National Park Scenic Drive, allowing at least half a day to poke around Capitol Reef and longer if the park grabs your interest. Several excellent side trips might extend this drive to multiple days.

Unless you've already arrived at Highway 24 from a previous drive, start this journey in the farm community of **Loa,** which is briefly described at the end of Drive 14. From the north, Highway 24 to Loa is easy to reach from I-70 near Richfield in the Sevier Valley. Highway 24 from Loa to Torrey is scenic in a peaceful, bucolic way, following a pretty river in a verdant valley. The land along the Fremont River here is all private and mostly farm and ranchland. It is easy to understand why early settlers found this valley so attractive. There is a small national forest campground, called **Sunglow,** just east of Bicknell on the left. Five miles east of Bicknell a paved road on the right leads a mile or so to the

Highway 24 Scenic Byway

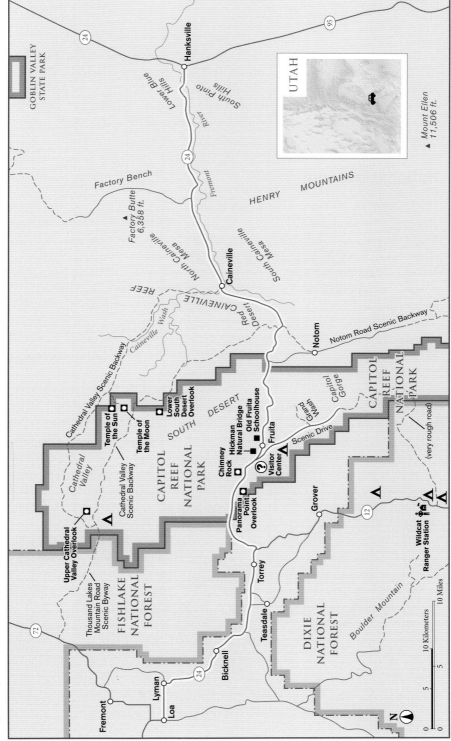

lovely little hamlet of **Teasdale,** a worthwhile diversion to see a fine example of a classic Mormon farming community. Keep an eye open for deer all along Highway 24.

Torrey is described at the end of Drive 7. This is the gateway to Capitol Reef National Park as well as to the mountain wilderness of the eastern flank of the Aquarius Plateau.

National Treasure

Driving east, past the intersection with Highway 12 on the right, you pass through classic Utah redrock for 4 miles to the boundary of **Capitol Reef National Park.** Established as a national monument in 1937 and made a national park in 1971, Capitol Reef is one of America's greatest natural treasures. The park preserves the 100-mile **Waterpocket Fold,** a mammoth buckling of the earth's surface ("waterpocket" refers to the potholes that dot the sandstone and fill with rainwater). The park's name combines the popular term for an uplifted landmass, "reef," with a visual resemblance of the park's many white Navajo Sandstone domes to that of the nation's Capitol Building. Capitol Reef is an incredible mixture of the finest elements of Bryce and Zion Canyons in a less crowded park that is more relaxing to visit than either of those more famous attractions.

This is an evocative world of spectacular colored cliffs, hidden arches, massive domes, and deep, twisting canyons. Of all of Utah's many impressive national parks and monuments, only Canyonlands National Park and the endless wildlands of Glen Canyon rival Capitol Reef's sense of expansiveness; of broad, sweeping vistas; of a tortured, twisted, seemingly endless landscape; of limitless sky and desert rock. While Bryce and Zion are like encapsulated little fantasy lands of colored stone and soaring cliffs, Capitol Reef is almost like a planet unto itself. Here you get a real feel for what the earth might have been like millions of years before life appeared, when nothing existed but earth and sky.

The Waterpocket Fold was created relatively recently, at about the same time and by the same forces as the entire Colorado Plateau. 65 million years ago (give or take a few millennia), when the uplift of the Colorado Plateau began, rock strata here were bent into a huge broken fold. Wind and water gradually eroded the ancient fold into the landforms and canyon systems we see today.

Due to the low humidity year-round, there is really no "wrong" season for visiting this park; while the frequent thunderstorms of late summer sometimes cause flash floods, they're fun to watch—from a distance. They also provide dramatic skies and some of the best lighting of the year. And while this may seem a lifeless, barren place, a surprising wealth of flora and fauna makes its home here. You just have to look sometimes to see it.

Red cliffs rise all around the scenic drive in Capitol Reef National Park.

There is no fee for travel directly through the park on Highway 24. If pressed for time, you can get a good taste of Capitol Reef from the highway—and informational roadside signs interpret what you see—but it would be a real tragedy to miss the park's attractions just to the south. It is easily possible to spend three days or more exploring this park. A basic introduction (including the park scenic drive, drives to the ends of Grand Valley Wash and Capitol Gorge, and perhaps one short hike) should occupy at least 3 hours.

Views in Capitol Reef are more "open" than those in Zion, which is rather confined by the narrow canyons. The highway is lined with pull-outs that let you stop and take it all in. One highly recommended stop is the **Panorama Point/ Goosenecks view area,** on the park's west end.

About 7 miles after the park boundary on Highway 24 is the well-marked turnoff on the right for the park visitor center and **Capitol Reef National Park Scenic Drive.** The visitor center is open daily (except certain federal holidays) year-round from 8 a.m. to 4:30 p.m., with extended hours spring through fall. This is a good place to get information on the many unpaved routes in and around the park, including road conditions.

The National Park Service suggests about 90 minutes for the 25-mile scenic drive, but plan on more time if you want to stretch your legs a bit (which you should—much of the best scenery is only visible on foot). Be sure to pick up literature on the park and on the old Mormon community of Fruita. At the fee station (passing through Capitol Reef is free, but there's a $15 fee per vehicle for activities in the park, including the scenic drive), pick up the free and very handy park driving brochure, which contains detailed descriptions of the numbered interpretive stops along the way as well as useful geological information.

Side Trips

From the scenic drive, several nice, short side drives on well-maintained dirt/gravel roads can be negotiated in virtually any vehicle. The first of these, **Grand Wash,** is sort of like taking a Disneyland ride in your own car. The hike through the Narrows, from the trailhead at the end of the Grand Wash drive, is highly recommended. You can either take the entire 2.5-mile walk through the canyon, which ends at Highway 24, or just go about 0.25 mile to a somewhat steep cutback trail on the left to visit **Cassidy Arch,** where the ubiquitous Butch is said to have hung out. The 1.7-mile (each way) hike, which skirts the edge of a cliff en route to the massive arch, is highly recommended for those without a fear of heights.

You should definitely drive out to the end of the unpaved but well-maintained **Capitol Gorge spur,** a few miles farther along the scenic drive. This 2.4-mile road is a little narrow for RVs, and nothing you would want to pull a trailer through, but other vehicles will make it without difficulty. It is hard to imagine a more unusual driving experience for a conventional vehicle: The gorge ends at a narrow channel carved between sheer cliffs.

An easy and interesting 1-mile hike from the trailhead at the end of the Capitol Gorge drive takes you into this slot canyon, where on a rock wall called **Pioneer Register** you can see the names of miners, settlers, and other adventurers who passed through here starting in 1871. In fact, the labyrinthine Capitol Gorge road here was the main transport route through this region from 1884 until Highway 24 was opened in 1962. Pioneers had to remove boulders and other debris after every flash flood, and, at its best, it was a tight fit for big wagons or trucks.

Turn around and retrace the scenic drive. An unpaved road that heads off to the right (south) when the gorge spur cuts off to the left leads to a rough road, best suited for 4x4s, that eventually connects with Highway 12.

There are many excellent walks in the park and very good rock climbing in vertical cracks of hard Wingate sandstone. If you're into hiking, you're going to love this place—pick up a trail brochure and ask park staff for suggestions based on your time frame and ability. Always bring sun protection and lots of water. The rangers at the visitor center will also issue free backcountry (overnight) hiking permits along with recommendations for backcountry campsites.

The Cassidy Arch hike leads along the edge of a cliff above the road in Capitol Reef.

After a visit to Capitol Reef's rocky wilderness, the green groves and fruit orchards around the intersection of Highway 24 and the park scenic drive are a cool and welcome sight. Just after the turn of the 20th century, the Mormon community of **Fruita,** nestled in the shaded canyon formed by the Fremont River, was a lively, vibrant town of nearly 50. Though most of Fruita's residents gradually moved away after Capitol Reef's establishment as a national monument, the fields and orchards and an abundance of wildlife remain for your enjoyment. Visitors may even pick small quantities of fruit: cherries in June, apricots in July, pears in August, and apples in September. Look for U-PICK signs and be prepared to pay a small donation for any fruit you take with you (there is no charge for fruit you eat on-site). The money, collected on an honor system, goes to maintain the orchards—a very worthy cause.

The park campground, with 71 sites, water, and flush toilets (but no showers), is in the shady old Fruita area. Apart from water, bathrooms, and the orchard fruit, the park provides no other services or amenities. Nearby Torrey is the best bet for accommodations and food.

Tear yourself away from the wonders of Capitol Reef and continue east along Highway 24; there is much more to enthuse over on this drive.

Just after returning to Highway 24, note on the left the **old Fruita schoolhouse,** nicely restored and in a beautiful setting beneath towering sandstone cliffs. The one-room schoolhouse, built in 1896, remained in use until 1941. It also served the community as church and town meeting place, with the desks pushed aside for Saturday dances. Check in at the visitor center to see if this and other Fruita buildings are open to the public while you're there.

Just after the old schoolhouse, also on the left, is a petroglyph trail; beyond the petroglyph trail is the trailhead for the easy to moderate (2 miles round-trip) hike to **Hickman Natural Bridge.** This is perhaps one of the best park walks in all of Utah, with quintessential scenic views and glimpses of Fremont Culture ruins. Hickman bridge itself is a must-see. From this trail you can also see one of the large white sandstone domes that inspired the park's name. In this lightly traveled part of the world, you may have this highly recommended walk mostly to yourself.

About 5 miles east of the turnoff for the park visitor center is the well-marked **Grand Wash trailhead** on the right. From here, you can do the aforementioned hike through the Grand Wash Narrows but in reverse.

As might be expected, as soon as you leave the park boundary the landscape diminishes in interest—from incredible to just terrific. It is still beautiful, and because this is still public land, there is absolutely no commercial development immediately outside either park entrance. The most dramatic landscape features are enclosed within the park boundaries; otherwise, it is just as pristine and wild out of the park as within.

The Notom Road Scenic Backway passes by irrigated farms that lie in the shadows of the Waterpocket Fold and the Henry Mountains.

Just east of the park boundary, on the right, is the turnoff for the **Notom Road Scenic Backway.** This scenic drive, which is paved for about the first 10 miles, parallels the Waterpocket Fold and gives one of the better perspectives on its magnitude. It connects with the Burr Trail at the southern end of the national park, about 32 miles from where Notom Road Scenic Backway leaves Highway 24, to make up the 129-mile "Waterpocket District" loop. Since much of this loop is unpaved, check in at the visitor center first. Any recent rain will render it impassable, and it can be rutted and washboarded on good days. Passenger cars should have no trouble if the road is dry and has been recently graded.

To the east of the backway, the Henry Mountains loom above the high-desert badlands. Notom Road Scenic Backway reaches the **Burr Trail** in the bottom of the Waterpocket Fold, giving you a chance to climb the dramatic switchbacks that lead to the top of the fold before you set off for Boulder (see Drive 7). Ask at the visitor center for the "Loop-the-Fold" auto-tour guide; this tour takes at least half a day, with no water along the route, so plan accordingly.

About 4.5 miles east of the Capitol Reef boundary, Highway 24 enters a valley flanked by odd, soft-looking, tannish-yellow sandstone cliffs. Next comes an area of blue-gray Mancos shale, much younger in geological time than the more colorful rock of Capitol Reef. Just after you cross the Fremont River at the little gas station/cafe/campground (with showers) called **"Sleepy Hollow,"** look quickly to the right through a gap in the sandstone cliffs at the curious area of gray sand dunes. More of this gray stuff follows soon after.

The landscape has really changed by this point. The views are more expansive and the rock formations look much softer, sort of halfway between sand dunes and sandstone cliffs.

Temple Views

About 5 miles east of Sleepy Hollow, watch for the turnoff on the left for **Cathedral Valley Scenic Backway.** This 57-mile dirt track heads back to the northwest through the northern tip of Capitol Reef and into Cathedral Valley, ending at Fremont Junction on I-70. The main attractions along this desert and canyon drive are views of dramatic formations such as **Temple of the Sun** and **Temple of the Moon.** High-clearance vehicles are advised for this rather rough drive, which includes a ford of the (usually shallow) Fremont River. Short walks lead to even more awe-inspiring views; plan for at least a few hours if you make this rewarding, remote detour.

Tiny hamlets beside Highway 24 line the Fremont River Valley, along with a whimsical cluster of tepees (available for rent) at the **Luna Mesa Oasis Cafe** at **Caineville.** Just down the road, the **Mesa Farm Market** is the real oasis, selling organic fare grown on-site by truly die-hard modern pioneers who've eked a living from this valley's inhospitable soil.

Just past Caineville, look to the right where the large sandstone cliffs end and the Henry Mountains appear off to the south. East of Caineville, the landscape flattens, and the rough, empty land is reminiscent of the Dakota badlands. The good, fast road here is also a fine place to make up time after all the dawdling you probably did earlier.

Hanksville is a crossroads town in the desert wilderness of eastern Wayne County. It makes a good refueling spot and is one of the few places around here where you can find a soft bed. The town has two attractions of note: a gas station and convenience store/gift shop burrowed into a sandstone wall, and a relic of an old mill. The gas station you cannot miss; it is just south of the intersection with Highway 95.

The **Wolverton Mill** was built in 1921 by Edwin Thatcher Wolverton, a New England mining engineer who was absolutely sure he would find gold on Mount Pennell in the Henry Mountains. The mill was unique in its dual function of ore mill and sawmill, designed to both crush ore and saw timber. Wolverton never found his gold, and he abandoned his search in 1929. Today his mill stands as a monument to perseverance and blind optimism. In 1974 the BLM moved the mill from the Henrys to the BLM office in Hanksville, and volunteers completed its restoration in 1988.

Hanksville is also the northern terminus of Highway 95—the Bicentennial Highway route to Glen Canyon, Natural Bridges National Monument, and Blanding—Drive 9 in this guide. From Hanksville, it is a dramatic, if desolate, 55-mile drive north on Highway 24 to Green River on I-70. Along the way you will pass **Goblin Valley State Park,** a side trip you must take. Walking amid its bright red valley filled with sandstone hoodoos is an experience unlike any other. The state park is a paved 12-mile drive from Highway 24 and also features picnic areas, toilets, and a campground with showers ($15 per car day-use fee).

A handful of unpaved roads lead east from the Goblin Valley entrance road into the **San Rafael Swell**. Similar to the Waterpocket Fold, the San Rafael uplift is one of Utah's defining features. Its formations are easy to spot from the highways around here if you know what you're looking for. You'll see it from I-70 between Fremont Junction and Green River, which must be one of the nation's most dramatic sections of interstate. But to really get a look at its diverse geology, you have to hit the back roads. The good news is, this is major off-road recreation territory, so many gravel roads are well maintained. The Heart of Sinbad Road leads north all the way to I-70, while the flat, short Little Wild Horse Road heads southeast to the trailhead for **Little Wild Horse Canyon,** one of the state's most popular slot-canyon hikes. Don't attempt this 8-mile hike without plenty of water.

Ask about these roads at the state park or in Hanksville, and pick up one of the very helpful San Rafael Country maps produced by state and local tourism offices—download one in advance from sanrafaelcountry.com. They outline the region's most popular unpaved routes.

9

Bicentennial Highway

Hanksville to Blanding

General Description: A 133-mile high-desert drive across some of the state's most rugged canyon country.

Special Attractions: Glen Canyon crossing, views of the Henry Mountains, Natural Bridges National Monument, ancient dwellings.

Location: Southeastern Utah.

Drive Route Number & Name: Highway 95, Bicentennial Highway.

Travel Season: Year-round. Summers are very hot.

Camping: National recreation area campground at Glen Canyon, national monument campground at Natural Bridges, BLM campground at Hog Springs, commercial campgrounds at Hanksville and Blanding.

Services: Most services at Hanksville and Blanding; limited services at Hite Marina.

Nearby Attractions: Goblin Valley, Henry Mountains, Bullfrog Basin Marina, Trail of the Ancients, Moki Dugway Scenic Drive, Hovenweep National Monument, Abajo Loop Scenic Backway.

The Drive

Completed in 1976, **Utah's Bicentennial Highway** runs 133 miles from Hanksville to Blanding. South of Hanksville the highway offers fine views of the Henry Mountains to the west, then winds through rugged canyon country before crossing Lake Powell at Hite Crossing. The road surface is excellent the entire route, and traffic is generally light in this sparsely populated part of the state, though you may see trucks pulling boats to and from Lake Powell, especially around weekends. This drive can be done in half a day, with few stops and just a quick breeze through Natural Bridges. Plan on a full day if you decide to do a hike in Natural Bridges and poke around some of the Ancestral Puebloan ruins between there and Blanding.

This drive begins at **Hanksville,** which was described briefly at the end of the previous drive. Hanksville is the last stop for reasonably priced gas and supplies until you reach Blanding (gas at Hite Marina is about 15 cents per gallon more expensive), so you will probably want to fill up here and grab any snacks and water you will need for the next few hours. Besides, you should definitely check out the gas station and convenience store dug into the rock wall: a desert architectural classic. If you're in the mood for lunch or feel the need to preload calories, know that milkshakes are a Hanksville specialty; with all this desert surrounding the town, their appeal is obvious.

Bicentennial Highway

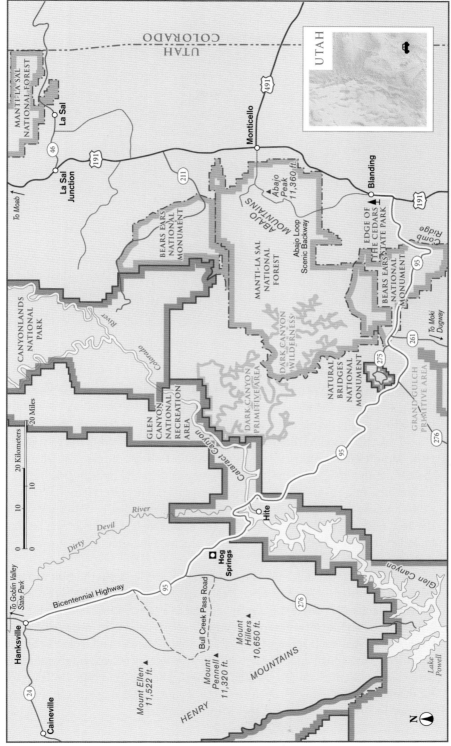

UTAH

COLORADO
UTAH

MANTI-LA SAL NATIONAL FOREST

La Sal

To Moab

La Sal Junction

46

191

211

Monticello

491

BEARS EARS NATIONAL MONUMENT

ABAJO MOUNTAINS

Abajo Peak 11,360 ft.

Abajo Loop Scenic Backway

MANTI-LA SAL NATIONAL FOREST

Blanding

191

EDGE OF THE CEDARS STATE PARK

BEARS EARS NATIONAL MONUMENT

Comb Ridge

95

CANYONLANDS NATIONAL PARK

Colorado River

DARK CANYON WILDERNESS

DARK CANYON PRIMITIVE AREA

NATURAL BRIDGES NATIONAL MONUMENT

275

261

To Moki Dugway

GRAND GULCH PRIMITIVE AREA

276

GLEN CANYON NATIONAL RECREATION AREA

Cataract Canyon

95

20 Miles

20 Kilometers

20

10

10

10

0

0

Dirty Devil River

Hite

Hog Springs

95

Glen Canyon

Lake Powell

To Goblin Valley State Park

Bicentennial Highway

95

Hanksville

24

Caineville

Bull Creek Pass Road

Mount Ellen 11,522 ft.

Mount Pennell 11,320 ft.

Mount Hillers 10,650 ft.

276

HENRY MOUNTAINS

N

Highway 95 curves along the base of red rock cliffs as it climbs out of Glen Canyon near Hite Marina.

At the eastern edge of town is the intersection of Highway 24 and Highway 95, where Highway 24 hooks north (left) and Highway 95 (signed for Hite, Ticaboo, Glen Canyon) is the right/south turn.

As you drive south from Hanksville, the Henry Mountains loom to your right. **Mount Ellen** is the first high point, **Mount Pennell** the second. This was the last mountain range in the lower 48 to be explored and named. One of the nation's few free-roaming buffalo herds makes its home in the Henrys. A handful of the animals were transplanted from Yellowstone in the early 1940s, and today the herd numbers approximately 300 to 400 head. Don't strain your eyes too hard looking for them; unless you are willing to penetrate their mountain preserve, it is doubtful you will see them.

If you do want to make the effort, the BLM has designated the **Bull Creek Pass Road** into the Henrys as a National Backcountry Byway. One access road starts in Hanksville (where it is clearly marked as a Henry Mountains access road), and there are additional access points on Highway 95 about 20 miles south of town, and farther south along Highway 276, which branches off from 95. Anyone considering this rough and very remote drive—you may not see another human being along the entire route—should first check with the BLM office in Hanksville for detailed information (it's open weekdays 8 a.m. to 4:30 p.m.). It is not recommended in anything but a stout, high-clearance vehicle.

There are three developed but remote campsites along the backway, including the evocatively named **Lonesome Beaver Campground,** and many primitive ones. As well as animal life and solitude, there's some hiking and the remains of a few mining camps; the range is still very much the province of explorers.

You will notice, as you drive south on Highway 95, the huge mesa on the right called "Little Egypt." The formation was named by early cowboys who were reminded of the Egyptian Sphinx. This part of the drive will probably remind you less of Egypt than of the high desert prairie of, say, Wyoming: mostly flat with low mesas on the horizon, sagebrush-covered land, and snowcapped mountains in the background.

At the prominent fork for Lake Powell/Ticaboo, take the left-hand branch; right will take you to Highway 276 toward **Ticaboo** and **Bullfrog Marina** (where you could continue your drive to Natural Bridges by taking the ferry to Hall's Crossing, if you had plenty of time, or join the Burr Trail). You have returned to a more characteristically southwestern landscape. Below the fork, the road winds through a gorgeous redrock canyon whose walls, though not particularly high, are magnificently carved and pockmarked. This is one of the outstanding portions of this drive. About 6 miles south of the Bullfrog fork is the well-maintained **Hog Springs** rest area. There is no drinkable water, though there are toilets and a few shaded picnic areas. A 1-mile hike leads to a spring and makes for a decent leg stretcher; also look for the petroglyphs in an alcove right off the highway just south of the picnic area.

South of Hog Springs the canyon opens up wider and the mesas on both sides (especially to the right) become much higher, with colorful cliffs rising dramatically over the valley. About 3 miles south of Hog Springs, you cross into **Glen Canyon National Recreation Area.** Within a few miles you will start to notice a brownish-green body of water on the right; at about 4 miles into the area you get your first really big vista. It is tempting to stop here for pictures, but you're better off waiting until **Hite Overlook,** 4.5 miles past the recreation area entrance, to stop for snaps. It is the best viewpoint of Glen Canyon.

The enormous body of water you see below is part of the much-widened 200-mile stretch of the Colorado River now known as **Lake Powell.** In 1956 construction began on the Glen Canyon Dam some 90 air miles to the southwest. The dam was finished in 1964 (it took three years of round-the-clock work just to pour the concrete) and began generating power two years later. By 1980 Lake Powell was full; droughts in the late 1990s and early 21st century depleted much of its water. The lake was named for the indefatigable explorer of the Colorado River Basin, Major John Wesley Powell, who named this rough stretch of the Colorado Glen Canyon.

Dam History

This rugged combination of land and water had been home to early Desert Archaic people and later Ancestral Puebloans for many centuries before Powell made his epic 1869 descent of the Colorado. The river and its deep canyon had long been an obstacle to the few travelers who passed through the region since the coming of the first white explorers and settlers. Far downstream, the returning Dominguez-Escalante party spent nearly two weeks searching for a place to cross the Colorado before finally chopping steps into the sandstone to descend to the river at what became known as the Crossing of the Fathers. In similar dramatic fashion, the Hole-in-the-Rock pioneers breached the canyon just above the junction with the San Juan River (see Drive 7).

A member of the Hole-in-the-Rock party, Charles Hall, found a more practical crossing point about 35 miles upstream from Hole-in-the-Rock, where he started a ferry between what is now Hall's Crossing and Bullfrog Basin. This was the main Colorado crossing point until Cass Hite established a general store and post office at approximately the spot below this overlook, where the river was often shallow enough to ford. A ferry service started in the 1940s, allowing cars to cross the river here for the first time. It ended, and the town of Hite was covered, with the creation of Lake Powell.

The dual purposes of the Glen Canyon Dam project were electrical energy and water management. The widening of the backed-up Colorado and its tributaries (notably the San Juan and Escalante) inundated thousands of acres of what had once been shoreline and branch canyons, drowning forever uncounted geological and archaeological treasures. But there are positive aspects of this massive transformation in the desert as well. Today more fast-food restaurants in Phoenix can sport neon lights, and the folks from surrounding areas have a great place to use Jet Skis. And, of course, we tourists have a new landscape to enthuse over.

It really is a new landscape, with nearly 2,000 miles of shoreline. And the most positive aspect of the entire should-it-ever-have-been-built controversy is the simple fact that today's Glen Canyon National Recreation Area was established in 1972 to preserve the river and nearly a million acres of adjacent desert country for public recreational use.

Because Glen Canyon is designated a national recreation area, not a park, you can camp almost anywhere. About 2.5 miles beyond the descent from Hite Overlook, there are all sorts of undeveloped campsites on the right, above the water.

About 10 miles from the overlook is the turnoff on the right (just after the second bridge) for **Hite Marina.** At Hite you will find a campground, gas station, and seasonal convenience store. This used to be a popular boat-launching site, but reservoir levels have been too low for years. Camping in undeveloped areas is free but, like the rest of the lake, completely treeless with no shade, no drinking water, and no picnic tables.

As popular as Glen Canyon is with boaters, it is remarkably undeveloped, partly because this is all public land. The landscape may be rather barren, but at least it's naturally barren, unspoiled by shoreline development (hmmmmm . . . maybe what they really need is a water slide here?).

A little more than 6.5 miles beyond the Hite Marina turnoff, you leave the recreation area. Just 24 miles from Hite you will pass the usually closed cafe/gas station/motel at the non-town of **Fry Canyon**—don't blink! Canyoneers know that the Fry Canyon area is also great for exploring slot canyons. Be sure to do your research before you attempt any of them.

Past Fry Canyon the landscape gets a little greener with a sparse covering of juniper and pinyon, but there is still not much chance for a shaded picnic site until you reach Natural Bridges. Twelve miles past Fry Canyon, at the turnoff on the right (Highway 276) for Hall's Crossing, continue straight ahead for Blanding and Mexican Hat.

Natural Bridges

As you start to descend toward **Natural Bridges National Monument,** the groundcover becomes more luxuriant and the trees taller. You cannot see the chaotic landscape of Natural Bridges from the highway, tucked away as it is off to the north. The entrance to the monument, with visitor center and scenic drive, is approximately 44 miles from Hite Marina, on the left. Then it's a 4-mile drive in.

There is ample evidence that ancient people occupied this complex system of canyons from about 500 BC until around AD 1270. The earliest inhabitants probably lived in pit houses on the mesa tops, while the later Ancestral Puebloans built cliff dwellings that can still be seen today. They likely farmed up on the broad mesas, not in the narrow canyons. Cass Hite explored the region in 1883 while on a gold-prospecting sortie from his camp on the Colorado. A 1904 National Geographic expedition first brought the area to the public's attention. Four years later, Theodore Roosevelt made this the first national monument in Utah.

Given its remote location, it's no wonder the park has some of the world's least light-polluted night skies. The **International Dark-Sky Association** named Natural Bridges the world's first "International Dark Sky Park." Accordingly, park rangers not only give interpretive discussions on astronomy but also changed out the park's light fixtures to reduce their own light pollution. The visitor center is also entirely solar-powered.

There are few facilities at Natural Bridges and no services at all; the fee to enter is $15 per vehicle. At the visitor center (open 8 a.m. to 5 p.m. daily; closed

A short trail in Natural Bridges National Monument leads right to the underside of Owachomo Bridge.

Tues and Wed mid-Oct through Mar), you will find nice interpretive displays to introduce the area and describe the attractions along **Bridge View Drive.** There's no water at the attractive but spartan 13-site campground here, but campers can fetch up to five gallons per day from the visitor center. It has the only drinking water within the monument, so fill your water bottles here. It is also requested that you leave trailers here rather than pull them along the Bridge View Drive.

Arches and bridges, as geological formations, differ chiefly in the way they were formed. Natural bridges are the result of erosive action by running water, while arches are formed by gravitational collapse and erosion from wind and freeze/thaw action. These bridges are relatively new and will soon (in geological time) collapse. The largest natural bridges are believed to be only about 5,000 years old.

Bridge View Drive is sensibly organized as a one-way loop, so you can rubberneck all you want and not worry about head-on collisions—not that you can see much from the road. The paved 9-mile drive leads to overlooks and trailheads above the three bridges that are the park's chief attractions. While all of the bridges can be viewed from the easily accessible overlooks, trails—some short and easy, some longer and more challenging—provide more intimate contact. The easiest is a moderate half-mile jaunt to the last bridge, Owachomo. Whatever else you do, leave a little time at the end of the drive and walk the trail to stand under its massive span.

Natural Bridges makes a very nice 2- to 4-hour diversion, depending on how much you like to hike. The only real problem here is the lack of suitable picnic sites. The sole designated picnic area has but two tables atop the windswept mesa.

Now back to Highway 95 continuing east. About a mile or so past the Natural Bridges turnoff is the intersection on the right with Highway 261. This is the much-recommended **Moki Dugway Scenic Backway,** which presents something of a logistical dilemma for travelers (and for driving-guide writers). It is a recurring problem in Utah whenever you reach a crossroads: too many interesting things to see down too many roads running in too many different directions. So some choices need to be made.

Driving Options

At the lower end of the drive down Highway 261 is the very dramatic (read: "steep, scary, unpaved, and with no guardrail") 1,000-foot switchback descent of the Moki Dugway. The views from the **Dugway Overlook** and nearby **Muley Point** are among the finest in southern Utah, if not the world, and the view of the meandering San Juan River from **Goosenecks State Park** in the valley below them is unique. But once you have driven as far as Goosenecks, you probably will not want to retrace your route back up to finish the Highway 95 drive to Blanding. This is especially true if you are driving an RV, because you will not want to re-ascend the gravel 10 percent grade of the Moki Dugway. I wouldn't recommend it at all for anyone pulling a trailer. In fact, descending the Moki Dugway in a large vehicle will test your nerve and driving skills—perhaps more than your passengers will appreciate.

Goosenecks can be reached easily as a side trip from Drive 10, but reaching the Dugway/Muley Point overlooks from the south requires ascending the Dugway. Another alternative would be to terminate this drive here, do the Moki Dugway drive, and join Drive 10 at Mexican Hat. A final (longest) option would be to drive down to the overlooks, return north to Highway 95, then visit Goosenecks from Drive 10. This would avoid the short, steep, unpaved descent entirely, though it would mean driving 24 miles mostly for the overlook views—they are worth it. This last option is probably the best for drivers of large vehicles.

If you do take this highly recommended side trip, by all means stop in at the **Kane Gulch Ranger Station,** on Highway 261 about 3 miles south of the Moki turnoff, for information on the fascinating wilderness through which you will drive. The **Grand Gulch Wilderness Study Area** and southerly sections of the **Bears Ears National Monument,** accessed by dirt roads and trails surrounding this station, are some of the richest Native American artifact areas in all of south-eastern Utah, if not the country.

This entire Cedar Mesa plateau is scattered with important sites. President Obama established Bears Ears in 2016, after much discussion with local Native American groups. Now, those groups are part of the Bears Ears Commission, which still advises the BLM and Forest Service, which jointly manage the area. Monument boundaries were redrawn in 2017 to create two far smaller sections: Shash Jaa, to the west of here, and Indian Creek, just east of Canyonlands National Park. Both contain innumerable treasures sacred to local tribes. The monument's name comes from two adjacent matching buttes just east of Natural Bridges and directly north from the turnoff to 261.

The ranger station is open April through September; day-use fees ($2 per person) are required to hike to the best-known archeological sites, the closest of which are 4 miles from the station area. Backcountry permits ($5-$8, depending on season) are needed for overnight trips. Some can be reserved at recreation.gov, while some are held back for walk-in visitors. Do not venture far in this remote area without checking in with rangers, and be fully prepared for strenuous hiking in desert conditions.

The turnoff on the right for the **Muley Point** overlook is about 15 miles south of the ranger station on Highway 261. The pavement ends and the 5-mile maintained gravel spur begins to descend, but most vehicles, with the exception of larger RVs, should have no difficulties reaching Muley Point. Here, on the very tip of Cedar Mesa, are mind-bogglingly beautiful views of Monument Valley's redrock spires rising from the vast desert floor.

So, decisions, decisions . . . If you're heading back up Highway 261 and driving to the eastern end of Highway 95 and Blanding, you will pass a succession of well-preserved archaeological sites, part of a large loop known as "the Trail of the Ancients" that circumnavigates much of southeastern Utah. Many of these sites are now within the Bears Ears monument, a designation one can only hope will help preserve them. East of Natural Bridges the landscape opens up, and way off to the east you may notice the snowcapped peaks of the San Juan Mountains in neighboring Colorado.

At 10 miles from the Natural Bridges turnoff is a nice short stop at the Ances-tral Puebloan ruins at **Mule Canyon.** Just 100 yards from the road, they can be seen in 10 minutes. The ruins include a partly restored kiva, a tower, and a small block of rooms. Just beyond this site is **Cave Towers viewpoint.** Seven Anasazi stone towers perch on the canyon rim, three of which are clearly visible here. Just 10 miles east of Mule Canyon is **Butler Wash Indian Ruins,** another nice archaeological attraction, this time involving an easy 1-mile trail walk leading to an overlook of several ancient dwellings.

Highway 95 runs past Comb Ridge west of Blanding.

The signage for these turnoffs seems to disappear (both the ruins and signage are susceptible to vandalism in this part of the world), so if these ruins interest you, bring a map that notes where they are or ask about them at Natural Bridges or the Kane Gulch Ranger Station.

The intersection with US 191 is a little more than 30 miles east of Natural Bridges. North goes to Blanding, Monticello, and escape routes to the interstates; south leads to Drive 10 (although you may want to drive up to Blanding first for fuel and provisions). On its way, the road cuts through the Comb Ridge uplift in impressive fashion. Unfortunately, there are no pull-outs near this marvel of excavation, so you can't stop and get a closer look.

One more important archaeological site is worth a visit on the way north to Blanding. About 2 miles north of the Highway 95/US 191 intersection, watch for **Blue Mountain Trading Post.** A few blocks past the trading post is a paved road on the left. The road is unsigned, but the street is called Old Ruin Road. The overlook for fairly extensive ruins is just 2 miles down this road.

The town of **Blanding,** originally settled by the Hole-in-the-Rock pioneers, has a distinct aura of "somewhere-elseness." It is a fairly substantial community of about 4,000 residents but a long way from any urban center. Places like Blanding and nearby Monticello have to be self-sufficient, commercially and culturally. If you're planning to stay in this area, note that Blanding is Utah's only dry town. For some reason (by law?) every business in town, including gas stations and grocery stores, closes by 9 p.m. This makes Blanding's name very apt but diminishes its appeal as a destination. Blanding does have an attractive and comprehensive visitor center and pioneer museum in the middle of town, right off the highway. It's open 8 a.m. to 8 p.m. Mar through Oct, and until 4 p.m. otherwise.

Museums to Visit

The chief attraction in Blanding is the very fine **Edge of the Cedars State Park.** Actually, this is more a museum than a park, with outstanding exhibits describing the various inhabitants of the region: from prehistoric Ancestral Puebloans through the later Navajo and Ute Indians to the more recent Euro-American settlers. The museum houses one of the finest collections of Native pottery in the entire Southwest. Behind the museum is an interpretive path leading through an actual excavation, some of which is open for exploration. Open 9 a.m. to 5 p.m. Mon to Sat (until 4 p.m. on Sun) and costing $5 per person, Edge of the Cedars is on the northwest edge of town; just follow the many signs.

On the south side of town is a dinosaur museum with life-size models, fossils, skeletons (open Apr 15 through Oct 15). Nearby, at the end of 500 South, is a nice free outdoor exhibit called the **"Nations of the Four Corners Cultural Center."** This attraction features a self-guided walking tour that leads to a Navajo hogan, a Ute tepee, a Mexican hacienda, and a settler's log cabin.

If you're headed north from Blanding, the drive to Monticello is scenic though not spectacular. Just south of Monticello you begin to catch glimpses of the snowcapped La Sals to the northeast. If you have about 3 hours to spare and a vehicle suitable for dirt-road driving, a more interesting alternative to US 191 is the **Abajo Loop Scenic Backway.** This 22-mile mountain drive loops up through the forested Abajo Mountains north of Blanding, climbs to nearly 11,000 feet, then descends to Monticello. The road is single-lane gravel and is impassable when wet. The mountain scenery and the views of the southern part of Canyonlands National Park are superb. Inquire in Blanding about road conditions to determine whether your vehicle is up to the task.

Bluff and Monument Valley

Blanding to the Navajo Nation

General Description: A 45-mile drive through the desert grandeur of southern San Juan County and the Navajo Nation, highlighted by views of desert spires and mesas.

Special Attractions: Mexican Hat Rock, views of Monument Valley, Navajo crafts and culture, float trips on the San Juan River.

Location: The extreme southeast corner of Utah. The second half of the drive is on the huge Navajo Reservation.

Drive Route Number & Name: US 163/ Bluff Scenic Byway.

Travel Season: Year-round.

Camping: Limited choices. One BLM camp-ground at Sand Island; one state park campground at Goosenecks; commercial campgrounds at Bluff, Mexican Hat, and Monument Valley.

Services: All services at Blanding; most services at Bluff and Mexican Hat; limited services at Monument Valley.

Nearby Attractions: Hovenweep National Monument, Four Corners, Valley of the Gods, Muley Point, Goosenecks.

The Drive

This is beauty on a grand scale. While the landscapes to the north and east are characterized by dramatic ancient bucklings of the earth and by intricate, maze-like canyons carved by the persistent action of rushing waters, the country on this drive is more spacious and more serene in its magnificence. Rather than narrow canyons and steep, confining barrier reefs, US 163 traverses land that is broad, open, and windswept. It is very hot at the height of summer in this corner of the state. Otherwise, no real seasonal distinctions can be made, and driving poses no impediments for any sort of vehicle.

While this scenic drive is congruent with the state's US 163 Scenic Byway, the rugged country between Blanding and Bluff is not without interest. If you've just finished the Highway 95 drive (Drive 9) and don't want to make the detour north on US 191 to Blanding, there is gas at White Mesa, just south of the Highway 95/ US 191 intersection, and at **Bluff,** 22 miles south.

Just south of the Highway 95/US 191 intersection, on the left, is a monument to **Chief Posey.** The Ute Indians of White Mesa and Allen Canyon were the last free-roaming Native American band in the country. Their frequent conflicts with white ranchers culminated in the Posey Wars of 1915 and 1923, some of the last open gunfights between whites and Native Americans in America. As his people

Bluff and Monument Valley

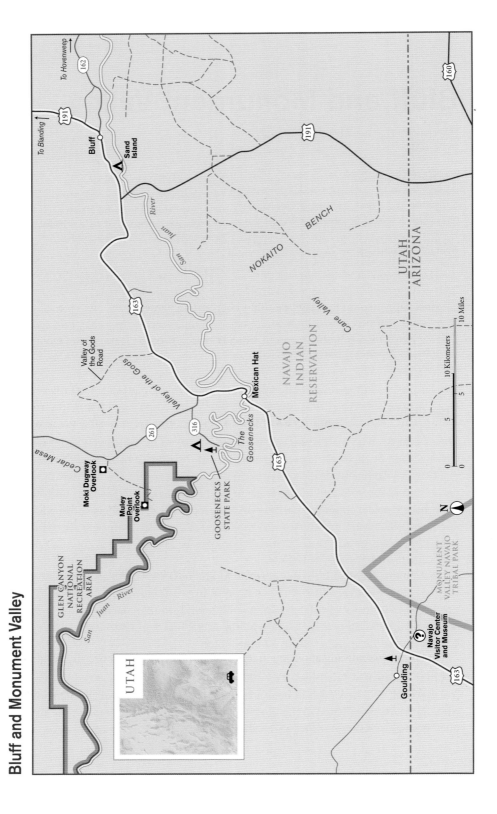

fled into the mountains, Posey was shot but managed to escape into a remote canyon, where he died from his wounds.

Deserted Ruins

Eleven miles south of the Highway 95 intersection is the well-marked turnoff on the left for Highway 262 and **Hovenweep National Monument.** Hovenweep is the site of the best Ancestral Puebloan ruins in Utah, yet it is one of the state's least visited national monuments. It makes a highly recommended side trip for anyone interested in the cultural history of the Southwest.

Unlike the cliff dwellings at Mesa Verde and Canyon de Chelly, these stone structures, built sometime around AD 1200, are organized into six mesa-top villages. The name is Ute for "deserted valley," which this definitely was by the time the Utes happened on it; it still seems an appropriate name today. The monument, with visitor center and campground, is 24 miles east via mostly paved road. Using a paper map is highly recommended in this part of the state, where many roads criscross the route to Hovenweep and cell phone coverage is generally nonexistent.

The drive to the national monument crosses a rolling plateau top that is unremarkable except for views of canyon drop-offs and far away mountains. The visitor center and the **Square Tower Group** of structures are accessible via paved road, while other sites are only reachable by short gravel roads in various conditions. Even if you only see the Square Tower Group, though, you'll be intrigued by the tower builders' masonry skills.

The visitor center is open daily from 9 a.m. to 5 p.m., except for Thanksgiving, Christmas Day, and New Year's Day. It is closed on Tues and Wed during the winter. There is no entrance fee. A small but pleasant campground (no hookups or showers) has 31 sites available on a first-come, first-served basis.

If the **Four Corners Monument**—where Utah, Colorado, Arizona, and New Mexico meet—is on your lifetime agenda, it's a relatively easy, if not short, jaunt south of here. Take paved roads to the intersection with Highway 162, which eventually leads to US 160 in Colorado (ask at the Hovenweep or Blanding visitor center for directions). There is no easy way to reach the Four Corners without leaving Utah.

If you are wondering about the frequency of the word "recapture" in this area (Recapture Pocket, Recapture Creek, Recapture Reservoir), it may relate to the name "Montezuma" (for a creek, a town, and a trading post). An apocryphal local legend says Montezuma, the last Aztec ruler of Mexico, escaped his Spanish captors, fled north, and was supposedly "recaptured" here.

As you continue south on US 191 (also US 163 through here), the scenery really starts to get good just north of the village of Bluff. This part of Utah was settled late, when hardy pioneers from Escalante came via the famous Hole-in-the-Rock Trail in 1880 and established homesteads. From the start, ranching prevailed over farming in this land of unpredictable water. After eight years of increasingly difficult times, several families saw the light of reason and moved north, establishing a more practical agricultural community at the current site of Monticello.

Today Bluff is a peaceful place whose biggest attraction is San Juan River excursions. Bluff has a nice little historic loop, featuring preserved or reconstructed pioneer buildings, on the right just as you enter town. Note especially the Bluff library, a fine old stone building. A local history association publishes an excellent tour brochure describing historical houses and other sites in Bluff; download a PDF version from bluffutah.org/bluff-history-tour. Note the **Twin Rocks Cafe,** incredibly situated just underneath a couple of rock spires. The tour brochure is usually available there.

The moon rises over the Square Tower Group ruins at Hovenweep National Monument.

The Friends of Cedar Mesa volunteer and advocacy group runs a visitor center for the Bears Ears National Monument on Main Street; the monument's southern section lies north and west of here. At nearby **Sand Island Recreation Area,** 2 miles past Bluff, an excellent petroglyph panel features five representations of Kokopelli, the humpbacked flute-player. Watch carefully for the Sand Island Road, on the left, just before the major turn toward Mexican Water. The small, basic (no drinking water) campground here doesn't take reservations and fills up quickly.

About 3 miles west of Bluff, US 191 makes a sharp left turn and heads south to Mexican Water, Arizona. Continue straight on US 163.

The highway crosses Comb Wash, revealing the dramatic cliffs of **Comb Ridge,** a huge redrock escarpment running north–south. This eroded monocline begins just south of the Abajo Mountains (west of Blanding) and runs 80 miles south to Kayenta, Arizona. After driving through the gap in this striking formation, it is worth stopping to look back and study the impressive natural barrier. Just past Comb Ridge, you climb out of the ravine and begin to see the outline of Monument Valley's dramatic formations way off in the distance.

Divine Valley

It's about 16 miles from Bluff to the eastern entrance, on the right, of **Valley of the Gods,** a highly recommended side trip. Valley of the Gods is like a miniature version of Monument Valley without all the people. Its mesas and spires are formed of the same Cedar Mesa sandstone as the somewhat larger formations at Monument Valley. The 17-mile loop drive on (mostly good) dirt road is suitable for all but the most low-slung passenger vehicles in good weather. Definitely consider driving this beautiful, lonely loop—though not in a large RV and not dragging a trailer. Stay away after heavy rains.

Valley of the Gods is also a very good place to camp if you are entirely self-sufficient. There are no established campgrounds and no facilities, but there are plenty of places to camp in the wild. It is incredibly quiet, and watching the moon rise here is a once-in-a-lifetime experience.

The loop finishes on paved Highway 261 just south of the descent from the Moki Dugway and north of the turnoff for Goosenecks State Park. Half a mile before reaching Highway 261, you will pass the only man-made structure in the entire valley: the **Valley of the Gods Bed-and-Breakfast** ranch, which might be an excellent base for exploring this wild region (it's very small, so reserving in advance is a good idea).

To see the impressive **Muley Point** overlook's expansive views (see description under Drive 9), turn right and immediately climb the 1,000-foot graded

The Moki Dugway's gravel switchbacks make for white-knuckle driving.

gravel road up the **Moki Dugway.** If you haven't taken the Valley of the Gods option, turn right and head north on Highway 261 for about 9 miles to get here. Just at the crest and right before the pavement resumes, look for the turnoff to the left for the 5-mile gravel road to the dugway overlook. Trailers and large RVs will find the long climb up the cliff face nerve-racking to impossible, but the steep switchbacks and unbeatable scenery make this one of the most thrilling drives in the state.

The turnoff for **Goosenecks State Park** is about 8 miles south of the Moki Dugway on the right (west). It would be a shame to miss this fascinating attraction ($5 entrance fee). The overlook at the park will reward you with one of the most impressive views of entrenched river meanders in all of North America. The San Juan River snakes for more than 5 miles here in its deeply cut canyon to cover just 1 mile as the crow flies. There is a nice picnic area with a few primitive campsites ($10 per night) along the cliff's edge but no water. Return to Highway 163.

Navajo Land

The namesake formation for the town of **Mexican Hat** is actually about 1.5 miles north of town on the left, well-marked and with good dirt roads leading right to it. Local legend tells of the love of a young Mexican vaquero for a Native American maiden who, alas, was already married to an evil old medicine man. When the medicine man learned of the affair, he turned the vaquero to stone. If the rock doesn't seem to look much like a sombrero to you, it might help the illusion to consider it to be upside down, suggesting the medicine man first turned his rival on his head. Behind the sombrero is an interesting geologic formation called the Navajo Rug, a wavy pattern in the cliff strata.

The little town of Mexican Hat has depended largely on several minor oil and mining booms; today it benefits from the fair stream of tourists to this remote corner of Utah. It's home to several land and river tour companies and makes a good base for exploring the surrounding wilderness areas, though lodging is scarce.

From Mexican Hat, cross the San Juan River and, as the sign says, you are entering Navajo land. The Utah section of the 25,000-acre **Navajo Nation** is home to a small portion of the Navajo Tribe's nearly 360,000 members. While the Navajo have long been considered one of the most peaceful of the Native American nations, during the middle part of the 19th century they were a powerful people who fought the invading white Anglo-Americans as hard as any other indigenous group in defense of their land.

In 1864, after a long period of hostility between the Navajo and white settlers, the Navajo were forcibly evicted from their home in the Four Corners region and made to march east across New Mexico. When these attempts at forced relocation ultimately failed, the Navajo were allowed to return to their traditional home.

Today the Navajo are a friendly, hospitable people, proud of their desert home, rich culture, and beautiful crafts. The Navajo Nation depends greatly on tourism, and they are happy to share their land and demonstrate their way of life. Still, the perpetual wave of tourism must at times be annoying; perhaps some feel somewhat uncomfortable with the idea that the homeland for which they struggled so hard remains subject to constant invasion, albeit of a more friendly sort.

As soon as you climb out of the San Juan gorge, the views of **Monument Valley** spread out before you, turning your windshield into an oversize, moving postcard. The next 25 miles are among the most attractive highway stretches in the entire country, memorialized in many films over the years.

After 21 miles you reach the well-marked turnoff on the left for the tribal visitor center at Monument Valley. This intersection is like an open-air shopping mall for souvenirs—many, except for the glorious handmade rugs, made in China or Mexico—and Native American art and food. From here it is 4 miles to the **Monument Valley Navajo Tribal Park.** The Monument Valley visitor center and scenic drive are actually on the Arizona side of a dividing line that is only nominal on the reservation. Good literature on the park and the drives within it is available at the visitor center. There is a small park entrance fee ($20 per vehicle); it is definitely worth a visit. The visitor center parking lot teems with local jeep tour companies, eager to whisk you off on guided tours of varying duration and difficulty. The valley's more out-of-the-way spots can only be reached with a guide.

From Monument Valley, your options are to return (via US 163) to Bluff and US 191 northward or to continue south to the Arizona town of Kayenta at the intersection with US 160 (from there, you could return to Utah via Highway 89). The Arizona portion of this drive, along with a detailed description of the Monument Valley scenic drive, are outlined in Stewart Green's *Scenic Driving Arizona*, also from Globe Pequot Press.

Indian Creek Scenic Byway

Monticello to Needles District, Canyonlands

General Description: A 50-mile desert canyon drive with a variety of geologic, scenic, and historic attractions.

Special Attractions: Newspaper Rock petroglyphs, Needles District of Canyonlands National Park, hiking, rock climbing.

Location: Southeastern Utah.

Drive Route Number & Name: US 191/ Highway 211, Indian Creek Scenic Byway.

Travel Season: Year-round.

Camping: One state park campground, three national park campgrounds, two Forest Service campgrounds west of Monticello and three others along the Needles Overlook road, commercial campgrounds at Monticello and Needles Outpost.

Services: All services in Monticello; basic services at Needles Outpost; no services north on US 191 until La Sal Junction.

Nearby Attractions: Abajo Mountains, Abajo Loop Scenic Backway, Needles and Anticline overlooks.

The Drive

The official Indian Creek State Byway is limited to Highway 211 between US 191 and the Needles entrance to Canyonlands National Park. But the entire corridor of US 191, along with the fantastic geological jumble to the west, deserve exploration. This drive begins in Monticello, focuses on the very attractive and interesting drive east along Highway 211, and ends with a recommendation for continuing north to Moab.

Monticello (pronounced "Mont-e-SEL-lo," even though it was named for Thomas Jefferson's famous estate) seems somehow out of place here in remote southeastern Utah. It has an almost midwestern look, like one of those marginally prosperous farm towns in downstate Illinois. The lawns are green and nicely trimmed, and the many nice old houses have an almost genteel look about them. Partly because Monticello is the site of a regional LDS temple, it has more restaurants and other amenities than Blanding.

Various entities operate a joint welcome center at Main Street (US 191) and 200 South, open weekdays 8 a.m. to 6 p.m., weekends and holidays 10 a.m. to 6 p.m. The knowledgeable folks there provide detailed information on whatever you need to know about the region, including road conditions. While there is a park visitor center at the Needles entrance to Canyonlands, picking up your Canyonlands literature here will allow you to plan your visit in advance.

Several nice scenic drives head up into the **Abajo Mountains** to the west of town. The **Blue Mountain Loop/Harts Draw Road** is an attractive 20-mile drive

Indian Creek Scenic Byway

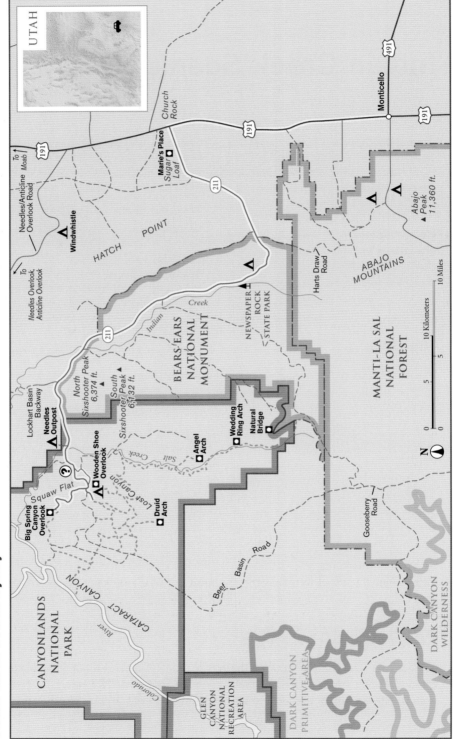

The Harts Draw loop climbs into the Abajo Mountains, making for a cool break from the desert as well as nice views of the farmlands around Monticello.

on good paved road that starts as Monticello's 200 South Street but climbs after it leaves town, entering the forest and giving a respite from the heat of the valley. It loops 9 miles up the mountain's flank and turns into Hart's Draw Road (stay to the right, or the pavement ends) then descends to meet Highway 211 just east of Newspaper Rock State Park (described below). About 5 miles west of Monticello on this drive are two national forest campgrounds that might prove handy.

There aren't many pull-outs; take advantage of those that exist to take in the scenery, especially on the road's north end. There, views looking down into Canyonlands, with the La Sals rising in the background, are glorious. The Harts Draw-Canyonlands Overlook is particularly breathtaking.

The entire stretch of US 191 from Monticello to La Sal Junction offers increasingly fine views to the northeast (ahead and to the right) of the La Sal Mountains. As you drive north through attractive ranch and farm country, the distant snowcapped San Juan Mountains rise off to the east in western Colorado. The early Spanish Trail ran approximately parallel to US 191.

About 7 miles north of the Monticello town limit, the road descends and you get your first glimpse ahead of the very prominent roundish tan rock called **Church Rock,** your landmark for the left turn on Highway 211. Church Rock is an isolated chunk of harder Entrada sandstone material, around which softer mudstone layers have eroded. The most remarkable aspect of this rock is that it is

Church Rock is a well-known landmark near the turnoff for Canyonlands National Park.

partially hollow. According to local legend, settlers used Church Rock for prayer services (the truth—a rancher using it for storage—is not as interesting). Today it sits on private land. A road leads up to the cave entrance, suggesting that perhaps the owners may one day turn this into one of the world's more interesting road-side hamburger stands.

Take the left turn here onto Highway 211, signed for Canyonlands National Park and Newspaper Rock. This is the start of the **Indian Creek Scenic Byway.** The byway travels southeast across beautiful high desert and ranch land for 12 miles before descending into the wooded canyon of Indian Creek.

Marie's Place

A little more than 3 miles along Highway 211, you may spot a collection of long-abandoned ranch buildings behind a weathered sign reading MARIE'S PLACE. This was the site of Marie Ogden's Theosophist colony, one of several religious cults of the 1930s calling themselves the **Home of Truth.** Marie, a widow originally from New Jersey, and her followers arrived here in 1933 from Boise, where she had been lecturing on the occult. This precise spot was chosen for the site of the colony based upon a revelation she had received that this was the true axis of the world and the appointed place to establish "the Inner Portal," the only place on Earth that would survive the rapidly approaching end of the world.

Marie received periodic divine communications during spirit-guided typing sessions. Her rough-hewn colony was essentially monastic and communal, renouncing all material wealth, contemplating the apocalypse, and waiting intently for the next divine message from Mrs. Ogden's theo-telegraphic typing machine.

Locals seemed not to give the Home of Truth folks much mind, even when Mrs. Ogden purchased the county newspaper and began to publish her divine wire service reports.

In 1935 a regional scandal erupted when a member of the colony died and Mrs. Ogden refused to give up the body for burial, claiming the deceased was, in fact, simply in suspended animation pending return in a higher, more sanctified state. She even reported in the paper various communications she had received from her dormant disciple. This went on for about two years, despite official attempts at claiming the corpse, which witnesses said had been mummified in the dry desert air. Disgraced by the affair, the colony dwindled to Marie and just a handful of the faithful who lived on here for several decades. Marie moved to a nursing home in the mid-1970s and died shortly thereafter.

Now only these ruins remain here, although her papers are housed at the Frontier Museum in Monticello.

Rock Art

The road meets Indian Creek at **Newspaper Rock State Park,** one of the better roadside rock-art viewing sites in Utah. A 50-foot-high sandstone face is covered with a variety of fine petroglyphs from several periods. Most of the several hundred figures appear to be Ancestral Pueblo, but there are also later examples of Ute artwork, including one prominent figure of a hunter on horseback. There is also a small basic campground (no drinking water). Take a few minutes to try to decipher the stories told here through pictures that appear to be hunters and their prey, other animals, landscapes, and shapes that are open to interpretation.

From here the byway follows Indian Creek through a gorge lined with white sandstone walls, which then opens up a bit wider on the left. At this point the character of the rock on the right changes to a towering red palisade of sheer Wingate sandstone. This is one of Utah's premier sandstone rock climbing areas, site of the famous **Supercrack.** All along the buttresses on the right are long vertical cracks, and you may see climbers at play.

It is a little less than 20 miles from Newspaper Rock to the Needles entrance of Canyonlands National Park, through part of Bear Ears National Monument. Along Indian Creek, farmland and ranchland is surrounded by redrock cliffs—a striking setting for agriculture. About 1.5 miles beyond the park boundary is the well-marked turn on the right for **Needles Outpost.** This is a low-key commercial

The valley along Indian Creek, now part of Bears Ears National Monument, is surrounded by beautiful cliffs.

facility with a small store, cafe, gas—though you'll pay about $1 more per gallon than in Monticello—and a campground with hot showers. The proprietors will cook you the only hot meal available for miles. The Outpost is closed from Dec 1 until Mar 1.

Canyonlands National Park is a very large, very complex place. At 337,570 acres, this is Utah's largest national park, its newest (1964), and its wildest. Because of the remoteness of this corner of Utah, Canyonlands sees far fewer visitors than the parks along the more popular tourist corridors to the west. This is where people go to truly get away from it all.

Around 300 million years ago a depression formed where this canyon system lies. At about the same time, the highlands of the Uncompahgre Uplift were created to the north and east. Over millions of years, a thick layer of salt was deposited on the bed of an ancient sea that covered what is now Canyonlands, and sediment flowed down onto this bed from the wet highlands. The sea drained away and sand dunes covered the entire area for millions of years. The process was repeated more than two dozen times. The different layers of hardened strata rested on an unstable bed of salt that buckled and flowed, causing cracks in the surface that widened into chasms, which later became the course of least resistance for the streams and rivers that further etched the earth's surface.

The Eye of the Needles

All this abuse of terra firma resulted in the chaotic landscape presented so graphically in the **Needles District of Canyonlands.** The "needles" are actually rock pinnacles, often red-and-white striped as indication of the repeated layering of different strata. The Needles District differs from the other main section of the park, Island in the Sky (see Drive 12), in the same way that Capitol Reef differs from Bryce (or the Grand Canyon). In the Needles, as in Capitol Reef, you are down in the midst of intricate canyons and sheer formations; at Island in the Sky you are essentially up on the rim looking out across broad vistas below.

Many dirt roads of varying difficulty lead off the main paths, making the Needles a better place to drive around than Island in the Sky and definitely better suited to walking tours. The most remote part of Canyonlands for both driving and walking is the third section of the park, called the **Maze District,** but that area of limited access and difficult roads is strictly for hard-core canyon junkies. The Needles offers a good compromise of relatively navigable roads and trails and a real sense of wilderness.

Do not expect much in the way of visitor services or amenities. About 4 miles past Needles Outpost you reach the Needles District visitor center (open 8 a.m. to 5 p.m. early Mar through late Nov, though bathrooms are open and water is available year-round), where you can pick up any material you may have missed at the information office in Monticello. The center has a nice, small interpretive museum. A few miles beyond the visitor center is **The Needles Campground,** in a pretty setting but without hookups or showers. The fee for a campground spot is $20 per night. It's worth noting that the $30 park entrance fee is good for seven days of unrestricted entry and is also honored at Island in the Sky; hang onto the receipt if you are continuing north to Moab.

The park here has only 10 miles of paved roads and many miles of dirt tracks of varying roughness (it's worth noting that tow fees for stuck vehicles run at least $1,000 per incident). The longest branch of the paved road leads to **Big Spring Canyon Overlook.** Along the way are several stops at man-made or geological points of interest. The best thing to do in the Needles is get out of the car and walk. Short interpretive walks, ranging from a third of a mile to 2.4 miles, and longer hikes of all degrees of difficulty add up to of 55 miles of developed trails in this area. Consult with the rangers at the visitor center to determine the most appropriate trails for your fitness level and itinerary.

Two premier hikes (both 11 miles round-trip) are the outing to **Confluence Overlook,** with the confluence of the Colorado and Green Rivers 1,000 feet below, and the excursion to **Druid Arch** and **Chesler Park,** which passes through grassy

Many dirt roads serve as jumping-off points for further exploration into the Needles District of Canyonlands.

meadows surrounded by tremendous stone formations—some of the finest scenery in the park.

From the Needles it is possible to return to US 191 at Blanding (south of Monticello) via a series of very rough roads to the south or to drive directly north to Moab on the **Lockhart Basin Scenic Backway,** a rough 57-mile jaunt that departs Highway 211 to the north about 4 miles east of Needles Outpost. Both require good weather, a stout four-wheel-drive vehicle, and plenty of time. Check at the outpost or visitor center for specific directions and road conditions.

The less adventurous will have to retrace the route back to US 191.

The drive north along US 191 to Moab is continuously scenic and deserves some mention. Six miles north of Highway 211 is the turnoff on the left to **Canyon Rims Recreation Area** and **Anticline and Needles Overlooks.** This drive, called the **Needles/Anticline Overlook Road Scenic Backway,** is a highly recommended side trip. From Needles Overlook you have the best view of the Needles area and get perhaps the best idea of just how big Canyonlands is. These are by far the grandest views of the rugged canyon country to the east of the Colorado River. It is 21 miles on good paved road to Needles Overlook and another 17 on good, mostly level gravel to Anticline Overlook. At Anticline Overlook you look directly across to Dead Horse Point about 6 miles to the north (and just over 100 miles by road!). You also get a unique view of Arches National Park.

There are two BLM campgrounds in the Canyon Rims Recreation Area: **Wind Whistle Campground** (seasonal drinking water) is about 7 miles west of US 191, and **Hatch Point Campground** (no drinking water) is about 7.5 miles along the gravel road to Anticline Overlook. They're great places to escape any national park crowds without risking your life (or your car's).

Just south of La Sal Junction on US 191 you get a really good visual lesson on the arches for which this part of Utah is so famous. Be sure to stop at the **Wilson Arch Viewpoint** for a look at an actual arch—without even having to leave the car. A very informative BLM sign gives a clear and succinct explanation of the formation of sandstone arches.

Don't miss **Hole N' the Rock** (the punctuation is theirs), just past La Sal Junction. In general, it's unfortunate what so often happens to roadside landscape left in private hands; in this case the landowners were so over-the-top in what they did with their own private chunk of redrock that it evolved into an inspired masterpiece of roadside ultra-kitsch. Over a 12-year period, Albert Christiansen excavated 50,000 cubic feet of sandstone to create a 5,000-square-foot cave dwelling and souvenir shop, consisting of 14 rooms with huge stone pillars. Hole N' the Rock is open daily from 9 a.m. to 5 p.m., with continuous guided tours.

It is about 15 miles from here to Moab, which has all services and is described in more detail in the next drive.

Round About Moab

Shafer Canyon, Dead Horse Point & Arches

General Description: Indescribable scenic beauty and fascinating geology on a somewhat disjointed three-part drive.

Special Attractions: Terrific sandstone formations, views of Canyonlands and the snowcapped La Sal Mountains, dinosaur tracks, petroglyphs, rock climbing, thrillingly steep driving for adventurers.

Location: Southeastern Utah.

Drive Route Numbers & Names: Highway 279/313, US 191, Potash Scenic Byway (Shafer Trail Scenic Drive).

Travel Season: Year-round.

Camping: National park campgrounds in Canyonlands and Arches, state park campground at Dead Horse Point, commercial campgrounds in and around Moab, BLM and undeveloped camping along Colorado River/Highway 128.

Services: All services in Moab.

Nearby Attractions: Colorado River; Canyonlands National Park; four-wheel-driving, hiking, and biking.

The Drive

This is a special place, and it's no wonder its geographic features lure visitors from all over the world. But the country around Moab presents logistical problems for drivers. There is just too much to see in too many directions; except for the La Sal Mountain Loop (described as a side trip to Drive 13), there are no neat, concise loops that take in all of the attractions in any systematic fashion.

Moab itself is a veritable campaign headquarters for half- or full-day outings in every direction. Your driving strategies here will likely depend on the type of vehicle you're driving, where you plan to overnight, and how much time you'll spend hiking, picnicking, or gazing at the landscape. This drive, therefore, is less a continuous excursion than a series of three distinct drives that might easily be combined as a daylong (*very* long) project or extended over several days. The bottom line is that the roadside scenery around Moab is as spectacular as it gets anywhere in Utah, so just strap yourself in and hit the road.

The roads described here are appropriate for all vehicles, with the sole exception of the latter part of the Shafer Trail Scenic Drive, which is unpaved, narrow, and rough. This climb from the canyon floor to the rim at Island in the Sky is steep, thrilling, demanding, and not suitable for many vehicles. Drivers with the nerve and appropriate rig can use this steep ascent route and complete a more-or-less continuous loop, adding spur drives to Dead Horse Point and into Arches. If you do not make that climb, you will have to retrace your route back to US 191, then use the more conventional approaches to Arches, Island in the Sky, and

Round About Moab

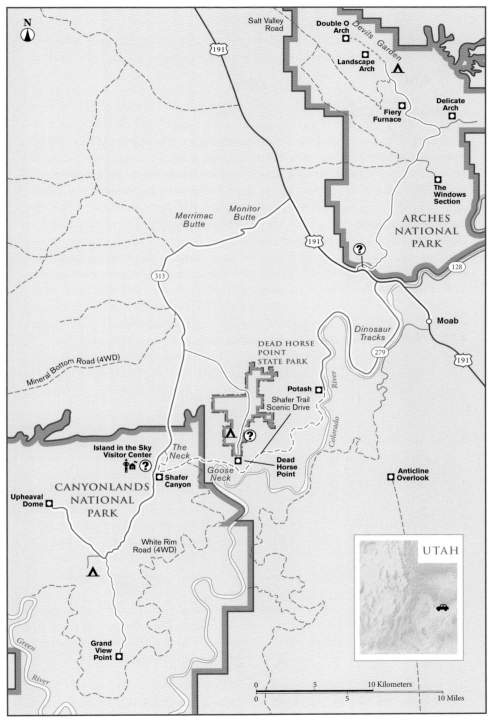

N

Salt Valley Road

Double O Arch

Devils Garden

Landscape Arch

Fiery Furnace

Delicate Arch

The Windows Section

ARCHES NATIONAL PARK

191

128

Merrimac Butte

Monitor Butte

313

Moab

Dinosaur Tracks

DEAD HORSE POINT STATE PARK

279

191

Mineral Bottom Road (4WD)

Potash

Shafer Trail Scenic Drive

River

Colorado

Island in the Sky Visitor Center

The Neck

Goose Neck

Dead Horse Point

Anticline Overlook

Upheaval Dome

CANYONLANDS NATIONAL PARK

Shafer Canyon

White Rim Road (4WD)

UTAH

Green

River

Grand View Point

0   5   10 Kilometers

0   5   10 Miles

Dead Horse Point. The visitor center in downtown Moab should have fairly good information on road conditions on the Shafer Trail, which can vary from rough to bone-crunching.

Canyon Capital

What Banff is to the Rocky Mountains, **Moab** is to canyon country. This is the capital city of Utah's sandstone wilderness, a focal point for desert and river adventure, a mecca for slickrock tourism. People come to Moab from all over the world to hike, bike, and raft, and to drive the fantastic desert landscape. They come for less strenuous pursuits as well: to visit nearby Arches and Canyonlands National Parks and for the view from Dead Horse Point. The town offers all services, including a fair number of decent restaurants and more opportunities to drink good beer than anywhere else in southern Utah. Although it's constantly adding hotel rooms, book early for weekend stays during high season (spring and fall)—this is where northern Utah comes to play.

Grand County was named for the Grand River, the original name of the Colorado. The first Europeans to enter the area were Spanish explorers who discovered a Colorado River crossing at the approximate site of today's highway bridge at Moab. Until pioneers established crossings at Lee's Ferry, Hall's Crossing, and Hite's Crossing, this was the closest place for traffic from the old Spanish settlements of New Mexico to breach the barrier of the Colorado River and its imposing canyons.

Mormon pioneers arrived at Moab early (1855), where they established the Elk Mountain Mission but were quickly driven out by Native Americans. It wasn't until the end of the 1870s that the Mormons sank permanent roots here. They named their new settlement for a remote desert land referred to in the Bible as "the land beyond Jordan." A ferry operated here from 1885 until 1912, when the first bridge was built. For most of this century, Moab toddled along as a quiet ranching center, until a uranium boom in the 1950s caused the population to soar—there were more residents in 1960 than the 5,200 who live here today.

As in other western mining boom towns that ran dry, tourism came in to fill the economic void, and catering to visitors is the primary source of livelihood for Moab today. Arches and Canyonlands are the headliners on the tourism bill, but outdoor recreation is increasingly more important. Over the past 30 years Moab has established itself as one of the most significant regional centers for river running and the explosively popular sport of mountain biking. One interesting

A short roadside trail off Highway 279 leads to dinosaur tracks preserved in rock.

legacy of the region's mining activity is the number of rough roads "leading off to nowhere," which is precisely where cyclists and four-wheel-drive enthusiasts want to go. Moab's excellent information center, at Center and Main Streets in the heart of town, has all the literature you need for your stay.

Moab has been a filmmaking center since John Ford filmed his version of the Hole-in-the-Rock pioneer journey (see description under Drive 7), *Wagon Master*, in 1949. In more recent years, Moab locations appeared in such films as *Indiana Jones and the Last Crusade, Thelma and Louise, Geronimo, City Slickers II*, and *127 Hours*. A "movie location auto tour" brochure is available from the Moab visitor center.

You can do the three segments of this drive (Arches, Canyonlands, and Potash Road to the Shafer Trail) in any order. Note: If you hope to stay at an Arches or Canyonlands campsite anytime except in winter, reserve as far in advance as possible. Your chances for finding a walk-in national park site are slim. Other campgrounds and undeveloped sites are plentiful; check the Moab tourism website (discovermoab.com) for details.

Our first segment is a state-designated scenic drive called the **Potash Scenic Byway.** Head north out of Moab on US 191 and resist the temptation to go directly to Arches. Instead, take the first left turn (Highway 279), signed for Potash.

The Potash road follows the contour of the Colorado River. At mile 3.2 is a sign for **Native American ruins,** referring to a difficult-to-discern granary in the cliffs. Along the road are several attractive campgrounds maintained by the BLM. As with national park campgrounds, spaces are available on a first-come, first-served basis.

It is doubtful you will find another drive with as much vertical redrock rising so abruptly from right beside the road. This is a very popular roadside rock climbing site; starting about 4 miles in, the scenery combines rock-climbing classes and Indian petroglyphs for a mile or so. With cliffs rising immediately on the right and the more-green-than-red Colorado River on the left, this is a most picturesque drive.

At mile 5.5 is a nice undeveloped camping area, then a sign for dinosaur tracks, which you can see from the road if you know where to look. Get a better look, plus explanatory panels, from the parking area. Hike uphill a bit for even better views of this unusual feature.

If you're a fan of hikes, red-orange slickrock, and natural features, the 3-mile (round-trip) Corona Arch trail, about 10 miles in, feels much like those in Arches National Park—without most of the people. Turn around after your first view of

Petroglyphs are visible from the Potash road.

140-foot-wide Corona Arch if you don't like heights. Otherwise, you can walk right under it.

As you may have guessed, **Potash** is a chemical extraction operation and *not* a town. Utah is a leading producer of phosphates, used primarily for fertilizer. The canyon is less hemmed in, and there are fine, broad vistas of the La Sal Mountains to the east. Many things change here. The pavement grows narrower and rougher, then ends 1.5 miles past Potash, right where the road begins to climb out of the Colorado River Canyon. This is the start of the extensive **White Rim Trail,** a favorite of both machine- and muscle-powered off-road enthusiasts; the **Shafer Trail Scenic Drive** is one branch of it. Don't even attempt to drive the very remote 100-mile White Rim Trail until after a long talk with rangers and lots of preparation.

Look on your left to see where some of the commercial float companies put in for the popular trips through Cataract Canyon. This is the end of the officially designated Potash Scenic Byway and the practical limit of travel for most vehicles. Robust, high-clearance rigs can continue—with care—into Canyonlands National Park, all the way to the thrilling switchback climb to **Island in the Sky**. Otherwise, turn around and retrace this drive to US 191. Do continue as far as you feel comfortable, since the scenery gets better and better the farther you go. If you have nerves of steel but not a 4x4, you can drive down the switchbacks and back up again from Island in the Sky without tackling the often-hairy Jeep road between; ask about the descent at the visitor center up top before you try it.

Beyond Potash the road winds up through a tortured landscape, a rough and inhospitable place. You will drive right beside a couple of huge evaporation ponds, an imposition of industry on this wilderness that are visually striking in their own way. The Potash folks have done a good job of marking the side roads that they do not want you on.

There are a couple of short, steep intervals, then at about 2.5 miles beyond the pavement's end you come upon a fascinating expanse of level redrock. You might want to get out of the vehicle and explore this on foot a bit. At mile 8.5 you come up on top of one of those great, broad, grass-covered mesas overlooking the Colorado River. The views here are breathtaking, and you will probably have them mostly to yourself. This fascinating drive makes a good overnight trip for self-sufficient campers; past the chemical operation at Potash you can camp anywhere short of the national park.

The Shafer Trail backway forks here at the first big river vista. Take the more prominent fork to the right. If you look up and to the right at the big, dark, blocky formation about 1,000 feet above, you can actually see the observation deck at Dead Horse Point. At mile 9.5 there is about 100 feet of nerve-wracking road (with a big drop on the left—oooooooeeee, scary!).

Thrilling Ascent

Just past mile 11 you enter **Canyonlands National Park** (via this very back way, there's no entry station). At just under mile 13 is a major T. A left turn here will take you down an eternity of rough roads and wild canyon country. If you're prepared for a real driving adventure and are operating a high-clearance vehicle, take the right turn, well-marked for Island in the Sky and Visitors Center. You will need low gears and plenty of nerve for the next 3 miles or so of white-knuckle switchbacks, as the road (an engineering wonder) climbs out of the canyon. This road was pioneered by ranchers Frank and John Shafer—whose cattle must have been fearless critters—and later improved by uranium prospectors.

If you saw the road-trip buddy film *Thelma and Louise*, you may recognize this as the location of the final dramatic chase scene (although it is represented in the movie as the Grand Canyon). If you're into scary, steep "thrill driving," you'll love this one. There are no guardrails, and it is definitely better driving up it than down. Thinking, again, of that final dramatic scene from *Thelma and Louise*, the thought of "life imitating art" makes the descent nerve-wracking. If you do make the climb up to Island in the Sky, you can return to Moab via Dead Horse State Park and Arches National Park, making this a long, but very eventful, loop. With this option, your route is obvious from the canyon rim.

If you choose not to make the climb up to the Canyonlands visitor center, you must retrace your route to US 191 and do the conventional approaches to Island in the Sky and **Dead Horse State Park.** There are potentially serious consequences to misjudging your vehicle's ability to tackle the Shafer Trail: This is one place where discretion really should be the better part of valor.

Three Destinations

For those returning to US 191, your only real decision is in which order to visit Arches, Island in the Sky, and Dead Horse Point, or whether you will even try to visit them all in one (very long) day. I recommend the order stated, because the day's end from Dead Horse Point is especially nice. If you're spending multiple days (which I recommend) and want to hike to iconic **Delicate Arch**, do that one later in the day as well.

Return to US 191 and turn left (north). The turnoff for **Arches National Park** is on the right, just under a mile up the road. The entry fee for Arches is $30 per vehicle, payable just before you reach the nice visitor center, open 7:30 a.m. to 5 p.m. Arches is a wonderland and the sort of place that brings out the amateur geologist or landscape photographer in even the most citified of us. It was established as a national monument in 1929 and upgraded to national park status in

1971. Arches offers more bang for your sightseeing buck than just about any other park. The park contains more than 1,500 recognized natural arches, ranging in size from just a few feet to the 306-foot span of mammoth **Landscape Arch.**

As always, stop first at the visitor center, just inside the entrance, for an orientation and for information on drives and hikes within the park. There is a very nice self-guiding booklet for the park road drive. The road was very well designed to bring visitors close to park attractions, so it is easy to have a memorable experience in just a few hours of touring. However, you can spend days here.

These fabulous geological oddities are thought to result from the movement of unstable strata deep beneath the earth's crust, then subsequent erosion by wind and water along with the weakening effect of freezing and thawing cycles on delicate sandstone formations. Beneath the earth's surface here lies a thick salt bed, the residue of a vast sea that covered the land hundreds of millions of years ago. Geologic deposits as much as a mile deep built up over this thick bed of salt, and the sea gradually disappeared. The unstable salt layers buckled and shifted beneath the weight of the hardened upper layers, creating faults and domes on the surface. As the surface was eroded by wind and water, delicate fins, spires, and balanced rocks—and, of course, arches—of harder stone were exposed and sculpted. These formations were further acted upon by wind, water, and extremes of temperature, leaving us this incredible geological treasure. (That's the reasonable theory, but if your kids think these formations were left by gigantic prehistoric space invaders playing in a big terrestrial sandbox, they just might be right.)

Most of the formations are accessible via short trails. **Delicate Arch,** used to symbolize Utah everywhere (including on some of Utah's license plates), is a moderately steep but very worthwhile 1.5-mile (each way) hike.

Unbeatable Vistas

Now for our next park. The well-marked turnoff for Canyonlands and Dead Horse Point is on the left at Highway 313, 6 miles north of the Arches turnoff. After the wonders of Arches, this landscape may seem perfectly prosaic compared to the parks' more dramatic landscapes. A few miles along Highway 313, note on the right **Monitor and Merrimac Buttes,** looking like their namesake Civil War ships. At mile 15 is a prominent fork: left 4 miles to Dead Horse State Park, straight 4.5 miles to Canyonlands/Island in the Sky. Let's head first to Island in the Sky (though it really is "take your pick" on this choice).

Island in the Sky, the name given to the elevated northern section of Canyonlands National Park, is almost precisely that: an isolated piece of land far above

The hike to iconic Delicate Arch is especially popular at sunset.

the deep canyons of the Green and Colorado Rivers. And it certainly does have the airy and Olympian aura of a floating island, detached from the earth below. This narrow "peninsula in the sky" was, in fact, carved by the two great rivers as they flowed ever closer to their confluence at Cataract Canyon.

From the Plateau, expansive vistas give top-down views of Canyon Country, including Canyonlands' other two sections. The views from this height are spectacular in all directions, and several strategically placed overlooks offer fine panoramas and short, easy trails with interpretive signs describing the intricate maze of canyons below.

Canyonlands, which became a national park in 1964, is a wild and wonderfully undeveloped place. Even the nature of the visitor facilities at Island in the Sky reflects this minimalist approach. Unlike, say, Bryce and Zion, Canyonlands does not offer much in the way of creature comforts. There is a water fountain at the visitor center (along with helpful rangers and plenty of useful literature on hiking and geology) March to December, but that is about it for frills. The small **Island in the Sky Campground** has no water either, so come prepared. The cost to enter is $30 per vehicle, good for 7 days—so keep your receipt if you're planning to do the Needles section (Drive 11) after this.

The terrain between Island in the Sky and Dead Horse Point is BLM-administered public land. If all other camping options have been exhausted, those prepared for self-sufficient (and minimum-impact) camping might find decent primitive sites along dirt roads to the west of Highway 313 between Island in the Sky and the Dead Horse Point turnoff. Keep in mind that camping on public land at undesignated sites requires special diligence to maintain the pristine nature of the land. Use existing fire rings or do without your evening campfire, and remember that campfires are often prohibited by late summer.

The road splits in the park, leading to the many roadside viewpoints as well as a great variety of hiking trails, some of which descend into the valley below. If you can, get out of the car and do some of these hikes—perhaps even more rewarding here than in other parks. The Shafer Trail climb reaches the rim right near the visitor center; whether you'd like to attempt it or not, you might want to look over the edge for a minute and marvel.

Dead Horse Point is administered as a state park and has slightly more elaborate facilities than its spartan neighbor, Canyonlands. The park maintains a visitor center, two campgrounds (including yurts!), and a museum that are open year-round, plus a seasonal coffee shop; the cost to enter is $20 per vehicle. The campground here has electrical hookups and water, and, unlike the first-come,

The Park Avenue trail, just off the road in Arches, is one of many easily accessible walks with stunning views.

The panorama from Dead Horse Point is especially popular at sunset.

first-served national park campgrounds, you can use your credit card to reserve a site (go to reserveamerica.com or call 800-322-3770).

The name supposedly comes from an unfortunate incident that occurred back when local cowboys used this point as a natural corral to round up and break the many wild horses inhabiting the region. According to the most popular story, a band of undesirable horses was left behind on the mesa, the assumption being they would find their way off the mesa to freedom. They didn't, and they died there of thirst.

Dead Horse Point is, like Island in the Sky, an isolated promontory of stone jutting out over the deep gorge of the Colorado River. The overlook provides some of the most famous views in the region, especially of the Colorado River 2,000 feet below. Sunset is an especially good time for photography or just gazing at the surrounding redrock, which seems to glow in the slanted light. Between the overlook and the river, you can see clearly the Shafer Trail road, giving a nice sense of cohesion and closure to this admittedly disjointed drive.

Colorado River Scenic Byway

Moab to I-70

General Description: A 44-mile run through a redrock canyon carved by the Colorado River, then across the desert to the major east–west travel corridor of central Utah, possibly combined with a 60-mile jaunt into the mountains.

Special Attractions: Colorado River, Professor Valley, Fisher Towers, views of the La Sal Mountains.

Location: Southeastern Utah.

Drive Route Number & Name: Highway 128, Colorado River Scenic Byway.

Travel Season: Year-round.

Camping: Five BLM campgrounds and two BLM semi-developed camp clusters along the Scenic Byway; undeveloped Forest Service campgrounds along the La Sal Loop; commercial and public campgrounds in and around Moab and Green River.

Services: All services in Moab and Green River; no services along the route.

Nearby Attractions: Negro Bill Canyon hike, La Sal Mountain Scenic Backway, Sego Canyon Rock Art Site.

The Drive

What distinguishes this drive from other canyon drives in southern Utah is that while this drive does follow a narrow canyon with steep sandstone walls, it also follows the Colorado River—a fairly substantial body of water. This is one of the very few places in the state where you can actually drive beside one of the major rivers that cut the dramatic gorges for which this part of the country is famous. In fact, Highway 128 is the only road that runs along a significant stretch of either the Colorado or the Green River. This is a favorite area for bicyclists and river floaters, and you are likely to see both on this drive. The rafters are fun to watch; the cyclists require your attention.

This is a relatively short drive; at 44 miles it makes a nice afternoon excursion from Moab. Though it's short, note that you will not find services along this drive until Crescent Junction or Grand Junction (depending on your direction) if you are not returning via this route to Moab. So be sure to gas up in Moab and bring as much food and drink as you will need for the drive and maybe a short hike. (Moab, the tourist center of Utah's eastern canyon country, was briefly described at the start of Drive 12.) The attractive Lions Park, right at the junction of Highways 191 and 128, is a great place to fill up water bottles and hit a bathroom one last time.

This drive makes an attractive connecting route from the canyon country of southeastern Utah to I-70 and points beyond. To avoid simply going out and back on this drive, you might loop back to the west on the interstate and then return to

Colorado River Scenic Byway

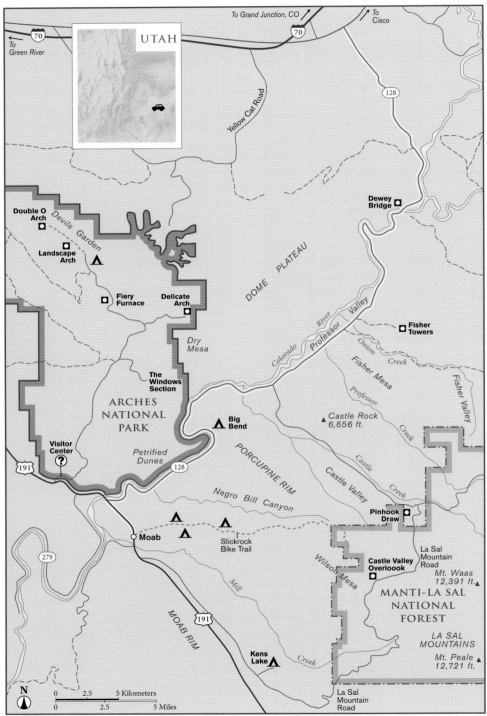

Castle Valley's namesake mesas rise in the distance.

Moab, 31 miles south of the Crescent Junction exit via US 191. A more attractive option, which incorporates very different territory than you'll see along the river, is to combine this drive with the beautiful La Sal Mountain Loop by tackling the mountain loop either first or on your return to Moab.

Leave Moab on US 191 north, as if headed to Arches. Just before the Colorado River (a mile or so out of Moab) is the turnoff on the right for Highway 128, which soon follows the Colorado River. A little more than 3 miles from the start of Highway 128, you will reach the pull-out on the right for **Grandstaff Canyon.** Named for the early settler William Grandstaff, an African American cowboy who kept cattle in the canyon in the late 1800s, this is one of the most popular short trails in the Moab area. This moderate trail is just under 2 miles each way and ends at **Morning Glory Natural Bridge.** At 243 feet, this is the sixth-longest natural bridge in the nation. It's especially attractive in early-morning light.

Starting about 3 miles beyond Negro Bill Canyon are multiple BLM campgrounds, including **Hal Canyon, Oak Grove,** and **Big Bend**. In addition, there are two camp clusters (**Drinks Canyon** and **Upper Big Bend**) on either side of the developed campgrounds. At about mile 15 from the start of Highway 128, the canyon opens up at **Professor Valley,** where you pass some ranches and farms. This area is famous as the site of such films as *Rio Grande, Ten Who Dared, Wagon Master, Cheyenne Autumn, Against a Crooked Sky, Choke Canyon,* and the latest *Lone Ranger.*

Approximately 16 miles from Moab is the turnoff on the right for **Castle Valley** and the **La Sal Mountain Scenic Backway.** This very attractive, 60-mile desert/alpine loop is fully paved and comes out on US 191 6 miles south of Moab. This makes a nice afternoon excursion from Moab, returning you to town for the night. The drive takes from 2 to 4 hours to complete and is drivable in most passenger vehicles. A couple of steep and narrow switchbacks make it impractical for larger RVs and trailers, and much of the route is impassable when snow covered.

The loop starts in the desert, rises into a mix of desert and alpine, and enters lush forest at high elevation, making it a nice break from the heat of the valley. Attractions along the drive include terrific views of the La Sals, the Abajo Mountains, Castle Valley, Arches, and Canyonlands. The drive also passes mostly undeveloped Forest Service campgrounds (at the end of rough, unpaved branch roads), a couple of Forest Service fireguard stations, many hiking trails, and the famously demanding **Porcupine Rim** mountain-bike trail/jeep road.

One of the bloodiest confrontations between white settlers and Native Americans in Utah history took place at **Pinhook Draw** on the northwest edge of the La Sals. A band of Paiutes ambushed a posse that was after them for the murder of two ranchers. Nine members of the posse and an unknown number of Indians died in the ensuing fight. A monument to the battle has been erected alongside the road to remember those who died that day.

If this loop appeals to you, you can drive it from the south (from US 191, follow signs for Kens Lake and the La Sal Loop), then pick up this drive here. Otherwise, follow Highway 128 until your interest wanes and return for the La Sal Loop.

Road to Towers

Castle Valley is the site of Castle Creek, one of Utah's few wineries (Spanish Valley Vineyards is just south of Moab). Subdivided mostly into 5-acre lots, the valley is also popular for modern homesteaders. Past the next mesa is Professor Valley, where the view ahead is dominated by **Fisher Towers,** striking bright red rock columns rising some 1,500 feet from the surrounding desert. To visit Fisher Towers, do not take the second dirt road on your right (well-marked for Fisher Valley Ranch/Taylor Livestock). That is a really nice, fun drive on good dirt road (for any vehicle but RVs/trailers) along Onion Creek, with excellent scenery, but it is not the road to Fisher Towers.

The well-marked proper turnoff for Fisher Towers is about 0.75 mile past Fisher Valley Ranch Road. It is about a mile on good dirt road to the parking area, information board, and primitive campground at the trailhead. The Fisher Towers Trail is a somewhat-grueling 2.2 miles but definitely worth the hike if it is not too hot. There is no water and there are lots of ups and downs, but the views of

Fisher Towers' bright red spires are especially impressive in evening light.

the towers change as you contour around their base from north to south. The rock almost seems to glow at sunset.

From here, if you look straight back from where you've come (southwest), there is an excellent view of **Castle Rock** (also known as Castleton Spires/Castleton Rock), where a famous Chevy commercial was filmed in the 1960s. Castleton is the largest spire; to the right is a large blocky formation called the Rectory, then two smaller spires called the Nuns, and a final spire called the Priest. Look to the northeast to see nice views of the cliff-flanked Colorado River off in the distance.

Five miles or so past Fisher Towers, as the highway rises up toward a gap, look back for really terrific views of Fisher Towers with a backdrop of the La Sal Mountains and the Colorado River in the foreground. This view encapsulates all that is best about Utah roadside scenery: desert spires, snowcapped peaks, and a rugged, river-worn desert gorge.

A few miles past this viewpoint is **Hittle Bottom Recreation Site,** the put-in for most of the commercial float trip companies out of Moab. Approximately 29 miles from Moab you cross the Colorado at **Dewey Bridge.** A seven-site BLM campground is located here. The original Dewey Bridge was built in 1916 and was the only crossing until 1986, when the new bridge was finished. Sadly, the old wood-slat bridge—the longest suspension bridge in Utah, it was listed on the national Historic Register—was burned down in 2008 by a kid playing with matches, and only the towers and cables remain.

Beyond Dewey Bridge the scenery decreases in interest. At this point you may decide to return to Moab (perhaps via the La Sal Mountain Loop), unless you intend to access the interstate. Past Dewey Bridge the road follows the river for a few miles, then strikes out across the desert. Once out of the confines of the river valley, you can see how much the land depends on the river: The next 5 miles are very much scrub desert.

Turn left at the end of Highway 128 and it is just under 3 miles to the interstate entrance.

Interstate Attractions

If you are heading west on the interstate, consider stopping off in **Green River** to see the very fine **John Wesley Powell River History Museum,** one of the better places to learn the story of exploration and travel on the Green River and about one of Utah's most important explorers. The museum is open daily from 9 a.m. to 7 p.m., with shorter hours in winter; admission $6. Green River itself feels a bit rundown but is friendly and a possible place to stay if Moab is booked solid (which happens). If you do stay in Green River, whether it's for a night or just for lunch, make the short jaunt along the Green River to **Swaseys Beach,** a sandy riverfront park that makes a nice evening picnic spot.

The pictographs in Sego Canyon are easily accessible.

Ray's Tavern is a landmark in Green River for everyone from river rafters to bikers to farmers.

Another worthwhile stop just off the interstate is the **Sego Canyon Rock Art Site,** one of Utah's most accessible major rock art panels. The beautiful and remarkable panels contain both painted pictographs and incised petroglyphs, some dating back as far as 500 BC. There is also Fremont Culture art from around AD 1000 and Ute Indian art from the past century and a half.

To reach them, exit the interstate at Thompson, drive through town, and where the road curves proceed straight ahead on the narrow but paved road until you arrive at two dusty washes about 4.2 miles from the I-70 turnoff. The panels are near a rudimentary corral a little way past the Sego ghost town's crumbling buildings. More recent arrivals have, unfortunately, also succomed to the desire to say "I was here" in stone, but this site won't be open long if it's vandalized. Please do not touch the panels.

A Fishing Oasis in the Heart of the Desert

Fish Lake to Loa

General Description: A 40-mile alpine and high-desert drive commencing with the Fishlake Scenic Byway.

Special Attractions: Beautiful Fish Lake, with abundant opportunities for fishing and boating.

Location: Central Utah, in the Fishlake National Forest.

Drive Route Numbers & Names: Highways 25 and 72, Fishlake Scenic Byway.

Travel Season: Year-round, though heavy snow may be a problem between Fish Lake and Highway 72.

Camping: Numerous national forest campgrounds along Fish Lake, primitive campsites at Mill Meadows Reservoir.

Services: Most services in Loa, all services in Richfield; basic services at Fish Lake.

Nearby Attractions: Grass Valley/Otter Creek, Cove Mountain Road Scenic Backway, Thousand Lake Mountain Road Scenic Backway, Loa to Hanksville Scenic Byway.

The Drive

This drive through lush mountain scenery and high sagebrush flats is highlighted by a visit to a very pretty alpine lake. When the eminent soldier-geologist Clarence Dutton first saw Fish Lake he was prompted to write: "No resort more beautiful than this lake can be found in southern Utah. Its grassy banks clad with groves of spruce and aspen; the splendid vista down between its mountain walls with the massive fronts of mounts Marvine and Hilgard in the distance; the crystal-clear expanse of the lake itself, combine to form a scene of beauty rarely equaled in the West."

It was like that in 1875 and remains so to this day. There are a few more folks visiting the lake resorts now than in Dutton's day, but the beauty of the lake and

Signs on local restaurants remind visitors that this is serious pie country.

Fish Lake to Loa

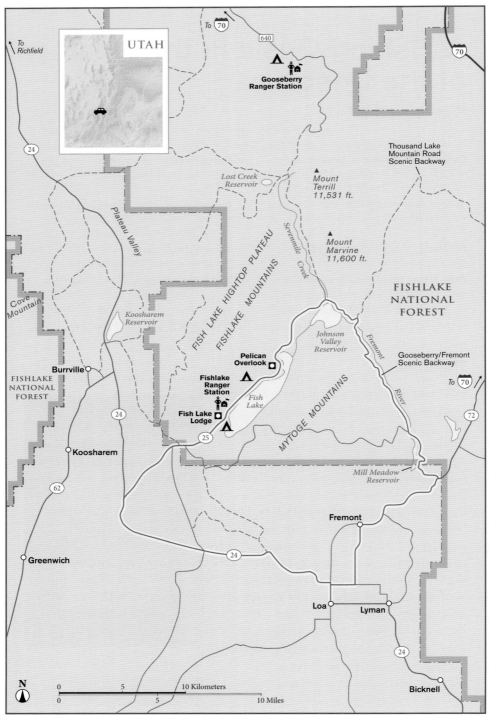

To 70

640

UTAH

To Richfield

Gooseberry Ranger Station

Thousand Lake Mountain Road Scenic Backway

70

24

Lost Creek Reservoir

Mount Terrill 11,531 ft.

Plateau Valley

Sevenmile Creek

Mount Marvine 11,600 ft.

FISHLAKE NATIONAL FOREST

Cove Mountain

Koosharem Reservoir

FISH LAKE HIGHTOP PLATEAU

FISHLAKE MOUNTAINS

Johnson Valley Reservoir

Fremont

Gooseberry/Fremont Scenic Backway

Pelican Overlook

Burrville

FISHLAKE NATIONAL FOREST

Fishlake Ranger Station

Fish Lake Lodge

Fish Lake

MYTOGE MOUNTAINS

River

To 70

72

24

25

Koosharem

Mill Meadow Reservoir

62

Fremont

Greenwich

24

Loa

Lyman

24

N

0   5   10 Kilometers
0   5   10 Miles

Bicknell

surrounding mountains and the clear air have been preserved for the public's pleasure.

This drive is described as a 40-mile loop continuing to Loa. The main roads are paved, well maintained, and suitable for all vehicles. Traffic is light to moderate except for weekends in the immediate area of the lake resorts. Winter driving may be slowed by icy conditions, especially beyond the Fish Lake basin, but the inconvenience is compensated by the beauty of the area in snow. Several unpaved scenic backways branch from this drive, providing a fine variety of alpine driving experiences.

A Pleasant Approach

The **Fishlake Scenic Byway** begins at the intersection of Highways 24 and 25, just north of Loa. Most travelers will reach this intersection via Richfield on I-70 or from US 89 in the Sevier River Valley. Either is a pleasant drive and deserves mention.

Highway 119 east from Richfield is a scenic route, starting out through pretty farmland then climbing into wild, open, undeveloped desert hills. It is 9 miles to the intersection with Highway 24. Angle to the right, signed for Fish Lake, Loa, and Capitol Reef. Highway 24 is very scenic, through mostly undeveloped public land—high-desert prairie covered with pinyon, juniper, and sagebrush. A few miles farther you reach the northern end of Koosharem Reservoir.

From the south, take the turnoff from 89 near Junction onto Highway 62, which leads through lovely Kingston Canyon, sort of a less dramatic and more verdant (and less busy) mini–Capitol Reef. Follow 62 north, past the Otter Creek Reservoir, to the junction with Highway 24. If you drive through either of these valleys in the right sort of evening light, it just might strike you as bucolic perfection.

From eastbound Highway 24, take the well-marked turnoff on the left for Highway 25, the proper start of the Fishlake Scenic Byway.

The Fishlake byway, somewhat narrow but paved and well maintained, continues climbing and enters **Fishlake National Forest** 4 miles from the start of Highway 25. By this point you have completed most of the initial altitude gain on this drive. From here the road actually descends slightly to Fish Lake at mile 7. Dense stands of aspens make this drive especially attractive in the fall. At this elevation even summer nights are brisk, and the days are cool and pleasant.

Lakeside Delights

Fish Lake, Utah's largest natural mountain lake, lies in a down-faulted valley (technically known as a graben) at an elevation of 8,843 feet. The 5.5-mile-long lake is one of the most popular fishing resorts in the state, attracting as many as 7,000 visitors on summer weekends. It is well known for trophy lake trout that often exceed 20 pounds. Across the lake, the long ridge of Mytoge Mountain forms the eastern limit of the Fish Lake basin. To the north, Mounts Marvine and Hilgard, both well over 11,000 feet, remain snowcapped for most of the summer.

On the hills just southwest of the lake, 106 acres' worth of genetically conjoined quaking aspen make up Pando (Latin for "I spread"), which collectively constitutes one of the largest and heaviest organisms on earth. Its root system is estimated to be 80,000 years old. Take a moment to marvel at this ancient giant.

The lake shore is dotted with a handful of commercial resorts, RV parks, and campgrounds, as well as numerous trailheads, picnic areas, and boat launches. At just under mile 8, note the large board locating the several campgrounds within the **Fish Lake Recreation Area.** Though camping is abundant, count on the campgrounds filling up quickly on summer weekends. There's a full-scale cabin-and-RV resort development here, but it is on a low-key and fairly unobtrusive scale. Here you will find a gas station, general store, marina, and even a laundry.

At about mile 8.5 is the truly outstanding **Fish Lake Lodge.** The current lodge (the third on this site) was built between 1928 and 1932 and still retains a distinct rustic charm. In many ways the lodge is reminiscent of some of the classic Adirondack or White Mountain resorts built around the same period—like something right out of a 1930s movie. The dining room is rustic perfection and is open to the public for all meals. There are also 25 wooden cabins for rent here.

The lodge is also the best place to pick up information, including detailed maps outlining the numerous area hikes and biking trails. A useful self-guided auto tour brochure will help explain the geology of the Fish Lake basin.

About 2 miles beyond the lodge, past **Bowery Haven Resort** with its cafe, RV park, and cabins, you leave most of the hubbub of the Fish Lake resort development behind. Even as laid-back as the development is, it's nice to be past the cabins, marinas, and paved bicycle paths. Here you can see the unspoiled northern end of the lake as you drive through gorgeous meadowland and sagebrush flats. The marsh and meadowland is perhaps the most beautiful aspect of this entire basin and a real delight for bird-watchers. Keep your eyes open for moose.

In another few miles you reach the lake's northern limit and leave the recreation area. Two miles farther is Frying Pan Campground, and 1 mile beyond, you

Fish Lake Lodge has an old-fashioned feel reminiscent of classical national park buildings.

descend to 1-square-mile Johnson Valley Reservoir, the source of the Fremont River.

Side Trips

Just at the northern edge of **Johnson Valley Reservoir,** on the left, is the southern end of the **Sevenmile-Gooseberry Road.** This lovely route runs from here to the Salina area on I-70 to the north. Here, your choice depends on whether you're headed generally north or south. To the north, the Sevenmile-Gooseberry Road (County Road 640) is a combination of good graded dirt and pavement. The state has long been in the process of paving it, which will give recreationalists of all kinds easy access to Fish Lake from the north. The road is fine for most passenger vehicles, but it's best to check on current conditions at Fish Lake.

Another excellent option for heading north from this drive is the fully paved **Highway 72**, a left turn another few miles along. These backways access some of the region's finest forest and meadow scenery and are locally renowned as spectacular fall drives. Blankets of wildflowers appear below the surrounding mountain peaks in summer.

Stay to the right at Johnson Valley Reservoir to go south toward Fremont. A mile or so beyond the high point above the reservoir, Highway 25 crosses the

Route 72 heads north toward I-70 through pristine, well-watered valleys.

Fremont River at Zedds Meadow. The road rises quickly and steeply for about 1 mile, then begins a long descent into the valley on the other side. The landscape is drier on the far side, with fewer trees and more open views. The views to the south are especially fine. The more you descend, the more this begins to look like desert. There are no pine trees here. A few aspen are up high, but trees at the lower elevations are mostly pinyon and juniper.

The river bottom is lush and dense with cottonwood and box elder. The road crosses the Fremont River again, where the now greatly expanded stream announces the small earthwork dam, **Mill Meadow Dam,** just downstream. There are lovely spots to camp along the little reservoir here. It is 3 miles farther to the intersection with Highway 72, where you can turn right to reach Loa or left to drive 27 very scenic miles north on Highway 72 and join I-70 at Fremont Junction. This is a little-traveled but convenient link to I-70, with desert and mountain views along the way often supplemented by wildlife sightings, and an easy way to connect with Drive 18 to the north.

About 4 miles north on Highway 72 is the start of another attractive side trip: **Thousand Lake Mountain Road Scenic Backway.** This 35-mile backway loop runs over the northern flank of Thousand Lakes Mountain, then descends to connect with the Cathedral Valley loop through the northern tip of Capitol Reef National Park. The scenery along this backway is an impressive combination of high alpine and high desert. The road is rough, can be very dusty, and is impassable when wet. High-clearance vehicles are required.

Headed south toward Loa, Highway 72 is as scenic as Highway 25 began. From here you can see south into Canyonlands. The land here is a mix of BLM and private, though it is hard to distinguish one from the other. It's all mostly pasturage and rugged desert hills. About 2 miles from the Highway 25/Highway 72 intersection you come into the irrigated valley at the community of **Fremont,** an eclectic mixture of new ranch homes and old ranches, trailer homes, and log cabins spread out for about 3 miles along the valley. There are no services. From Fremont to Loa it is 9 miles of ranchland and farmland.

Settled in the 1870s, **Loa** was named for Mauna Loa volcano by a fellow who had served a Mormon mission in Hawaii during the 1850s. The Wayne Stake Tabernacle is a classic LDS community church.

In order to complete this drive as a circle, head west on Highway 24 for 12 miles, back to the Fish Lake turnoff. The last leg of your drive traverses undeveloped BLM land, mostly sagebrush-covered desert hills. A possible option for a scenic return to Richfield might include a side trip along unpaved **Cove Mountain Road** (FS Road 068)**,** a popular drive during fall colors. The backway runs from Koosharem, a bit south of here on Highway 62, north to Glenwood, 10 miles east of Richfield, offering beautiful views of the Koosharem and Sevier Valleys. The backway is suitable for most passenger vehicles when dry.

Other options from Loa include striking east on Highway 24, which is described in Drive 8.

Beaver Canyon & the Sevier River Valley

Beaver to the Sevier Valley

General Description: A 17-mile mountain and canyon drive between the town of Beaver and Eagle Point Resort that continues, unpaved, over the Tushar Mountains and down into the attractive Sevier River Valley corridor.

Special Attractions: Historic Beaver, high mountain scenery, Fishlake National Forest, Puffer Lake, scenic/historic Sevier River Valley, hiking, fishing, camping.

Location: Central Utah, in the western section of Fishlake National Forest.

Drive Route Numbers & Names: Highway 153/Beaver Canyon Scenic Byway, Kimberly/Big John Scenic Backway, US 89.

Travel Season: Year-round as far as Eagle Point except for some vehicles in snowy conditions. Highway 153 beyond the resort is closed in winter and impassable to most vehicles when wet. This is an especially fine autumn colors drive.

Camping: Four national forest campgrounds, with unlimited opportunities for primitive, undeveloped camping.

Services: All services in Beaver; limited services in Junction and along the US 89 corridor.

Nearby Attractions: Kimberly/Big John Scenic Backway, Butch Cassidy's boyhood home, Historic Marysvale, Big Rock Candy Mountain, Fremont Indian State Park.

The Drive

Beaver Canyon Scenic Byway (Highway 153) climbs from the town of Beaver into the Tushar Mountains and Fishlake National Forest. The scenic byway ends after about 17 miles of forest and mountain driving to a high point at Eagle Point Resort. This drive continues the route east across the spine of the **Tushars** (the state-designated Kimberly/Big John Scenic Backway), descending to Junction in the Sevier River Valley. From Junction, the drive turns north on US 89 along the scenic **Sevier River** to the junction with I-70.

This 62-mile drive provides a nice diversity of scenery and roadside attractions, from the beautiful and seldom-visited Tushar Mountains to the gentler landscapes and rustic communities of the Sevier River Valley.

The initial scenic byway section of this drive is paved and suitable for all vehicles. Traffic in the canyon is nearly always light, though the road is rather narrow near the mouth of Beaver Canyon. Because of heavy snow in the canyon, snow tires or chains are required from Nov 1 through Mar 31; the road may be inconvenient for larger vehicles during that period. Because Highway 153 east of Puffer Lake is unpaved (and technically closed during winter), it is a good idea to

Beaver Canyon & the Sevier River Valley

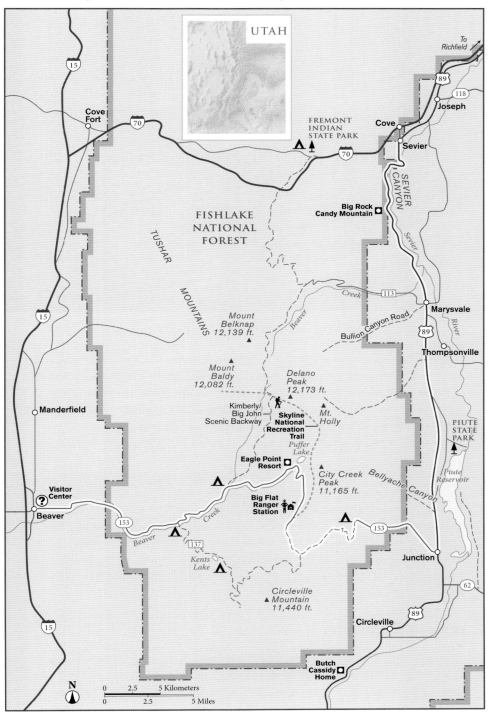

UTAH

To Richfield

15

70

Cove Fort

89

118

Joseph

FREMONT INDIAN STATE PARK

Cove

70

Sevier

SEVIER CANYON

Big Rock Candy Mountain

Sevier

FISHLAKE NATIONAL FOREST

TUSHAR

Creek

113

Beaver

Marysvale

15

Mount Belknap 12,139 ft.

Bullion Canyon Road

89

MOUNTAINS

Thompsonville

River

Mount Baldy 12,082 ft.

Delano Peak 12,173 ft.

Manderfield

Kimberly/ Big John Scenic Backway

Skyline National Recreation Trail

Mt. Holly

PIUTE STATE PARK

Puffer Lake

Piute Reservoir

Eagle Point Resort

Visitor Center

City Creek Peak 11,165 ft.

Bellyache Canyon

Beaver

Big Flat Ranger Station

Creek

153

153

Junction

Beaver

137

Kents Lake

62

Circleville Mountain 11,440 ft.

15

89

Circleville

N

0   2.5   5 Kilometers

0   2.5   5 Miles

Butch Cassidy Home

Beaver Canyon starts off as a narrow cut in the rock but soon opens up in dramatic fashion.

check in Beaver about the current status of this road. In dry conditions, travel east of Puffer Lake, across the ridge of the Tushars and down into the Sevier Valley, which will be no problem for passenger cars and smaller campers. The first stretch of the unpaved road beyond Puffer Lake is briefly steep and narrow, which will make travel impractical for RVs and trailers, as will the switchbacks into the Sevier River Valley.

Unlike the Wasatch Plateau, to which the Tushar Range bears a resemblance, this isn't a true plateau but the remains of a series of stratovolcanoes that were in a period of massive eruption about 24 million years ago. The region is rich in minerals and was the site of a small mining rush around the turn of the 20th century. These are some of the highest summits in Utah, with Mounts Baldy, Belknap, and Delano all higher than 12,000 feet. The entire range is seldom visited, making this a good place for high-level hiking, bicycling, and backpacking trips "far from the madding crowd."

Historic Beginning

The drive begins in **Beaver** at the foot of the Tushars' west slope. Beaver seems to be living in the past. It is full of inexpensive motels and attractive old buildings and boasts at least one of those small-town drugstores from the 1950s or

1960s—the sort of place that appears to have just a little bit of everything and about anything a person would need to get along . . . back in the 1950s or 1960s.

In the 1870s and 1880s, Beaver was the most important community in southern Utah. Today it is one of the best examples of a larger southern Utah pioneer town, with many stone and brick buildings (dozens of Beaver homes are on the National Historic Register). Most of the town's residents are descendants of the original settlers sent here by Brigham Young from Parowan in 1866. The **Beaver Co-Op** (1872) was one of the largest stores south of Salt Lake City, profiting from mining and transportation. The beautiful old courthouse, now a community museum well worth a visit, dates from 1877.

One hundred years earlier, the Dominguez-Escalante expedition took advantage of this relatively verdant site to refresh themselves on their long journey in search of a short route from New Mexico to California. Beaver was the birthplace of Utah's favorite outlaw, **Butch Cassidy,** and the boyhood home of **Philo Farnsworth,** credited as "the father of television." If you're a history buff, allow at least an hour to poke around this old town.

From downtown Beaver, 200 North (next to the old high school) becomes Highway 153, clearly marked for Eagle Point and Puffer Lake. A large LDS church and the adjacent **Beaver Canyon Campground/RV Park** mark the eastern limit of town. Half a mile farther, note the famous old racetrack on the left. After another mile you've left all residential and commercial development behind and you are in a very pretty mountain canyon with Beaver Creek flowing alongside the road. A little under 5 miles from downtown Beaver you enter **Fishlake National Forest.** The road surface is fine, but the road is narrow, and down here in the forest the views are closed in.

The byway quickly twists and climbs 4,000 feet through groves of mountain mahogany and ponderosa pine, passing four hydroelectric plants on its way. Two miles from the entrance to the national forest is **Little Cottonwood Campground;** it's 2.5 miles farther to Ponderosa picnic site. Just past Ponderosa is the turnoff on the right for FR 137. This good dirt road provides access to some attractive high mountain lakes and nice camping sites at **Little Reservoir, Kents Lake,** and **Anderson Meadow Reservoir** before connecting with the unpaved main backway farther east.

The byway climbs steeply from here, and about a mile past this turnoff (mile 11.4 from town) is **Mahogany Cove Campground.** Above here the views of steep, forested hillsides above and below really open up in spectacular fashion. Three miles beyond Mahogany Cove you will reach **Merchant Valley Dam,** which supplies water for the power plants below. Above the dam is a beautiful flat alpine meadowland crisscrossed with ATV trails.

Kimberly/Big John Flat Road Scenic Backway

The road levels off through the meadowland. About 2 miles above Merchant Valley Dam is a turnoff on the left, well marked for Big John Flat, a designated scenic backway. This 22-mile section of the unpaved **Kimberly/Big John Flat Road Scenic Backway** climbs over the Tushar Mountains and leads up to the old Kimberly mining district. Kimberly developed rather late as a mining camp, when the Annie Laurie Mine was established in 1899. Between 1901 and 1908 the town residents numbered 500 here, and the mill was processing 250 tons of ore per day. Today all that remains are a handful of log ruins and the remains of the Annie Laurie mill.

The Kimberly/Big John scenic backway ends at I-70 near **Fremont Indian State Park,** where you can see more than 500 examples of rock art, both incised petroglyphs and painted pictographs, messages in stone from the people who inhabited this canyon from the times of the earliest hunter-gatherers until recent pioneer days. For a small fee, you can wander around the informative museum,

The last paved stretch of road climbs steeply at the top of the southern Tushar Mountains.

which also has brochures with extensive details about the rock art sites. The sites themselves are spread out over several miles along the frontage road parallel to I-70; most are near the road or accessible by short hikes.

The unpaved backway is generally suited for any vehicle with decent clearance (not for large RVs or trailers). The road is closed in winter.

About a mile farther along the Beaver Canyon drive is a turnoff on the right, signed for **Beaver High Adventure Base**, a Boy Scout camp. This road descends a little less than a mile to beautiful **Three Creeks Reservoir** in a splendid alpine setting. It's a good fishing spot and a great place for a picnic.

Just past the turnoff for Three Creeks you will leave the national forest, and you begin to encounter private homes as you approach **Eagle Point Resort.** After another mile you reach the development, once very low-key but increasingly built up, that's grown around the base of the ski area. Just past the end of this development you reach **Puffer Lake** cabins and the end of the paved road.

From the pavement's end, Highway 153 is actually the southern and eastern section of the Kimberly/Big John scenic backway. The well-maintained dirt road beyond Puffer Lake is fine (when dry) for conventional vehicles and truck-top campers. This road is technically closed in winter, which can last from November until mid-June. After the first couple of miles, this route descends, presenting no real obstacles for most vehicles. If you are still concerned about the suitability of your vehicle for the road ahead, check with the folks at the Forest Service office in Beaver. If for no other reason than the near total absence of people on the east-side descent (either as development or traffic), continuing on to Junction is highly recommended.

Climb steadily and steeply for just under 2 miles to a very beautiful high-meadow area where the views broaden out. You will see the trailhead here for **Trail 129,** one of several fine trails that depart the road from this high point. This meadowland is designated as a wildlife feeding area, so you will likely see deer and elk. Not surprisingly, you'll meet many hunters in the fall. Exactly 3 miles from the end of the paved road you intersect a road on your left signed for the **Skyline Recreation Trail.** The Skyline trail is the showcase trail for this section of Fishlake National Forest. It runs approximately 8 miles north and west from Highway 153 to intersect the northern segment of the Big John Road. Along the way, it climbs high to skirt the highest peaks of the Tushar Range.

At this point Highway 153 is close to 10,000 feet. There are excellent primitive campsites up here. Just be sure to camp where there is an existing fire ring, so as not to add to the already abundant selection. While there's been a dearth of bathroom opportunities for a while, several of the campgrounds here have pit toilets that are open year-round.

The route becomes a well-maintained gravel road that runs through high alpine meadows.

Two miles farther and the road begins its serious descent. After about 2.5 miles of descent, you will reach a major dirt-road intersection with FR 137 on the right, signed for **Kents Lake** (12 miles to the lake or 25 miles back to Beaver via this route, which connects with Highway 153). Junction is 11 miles east of here on Highway 153. After a couple of miles of gradual descent on sometimes-washboarded road, you emerge from the forest and meadows to a spectacular overlook of the Sevier River Valley. Ahead is the long descent to Junction (which can be seen down in the valley).

The descent on this side of the Tushars is visually striking for the nearly complete absence of trees. There are a few aspens but not much else up high and not much more below. This gives unrestricted views into the valley as you descend the hairpin gravel switchbacks (with no pull-outs and major consequences for miscalculation, the driver will have to keep his or her eyes on the road). It is 5 more miles of switchbacks and some exciting, steep dropoffs to the farming and ranching community of Junction, on US 89. With the steepest part of the descent behind you, you pass a road doubling back on the left for City Creek Campground, with a handful of nice undeveloped sites tucked away in a shady grove.

Junction and nearby Circleville were settled in 1864. Livestock was important from the start and remains so today. The county seat of Piute County, Junction's 1893 redbrick courthouse is one of the most attractive in the state. Poking around here won't take long since there's not much to see, but this is a fine example of idyllic, small-town ranching America—with some decrepit newer structures serving to emphasize the older buildings' sturdiness. Junction has a gas station, an antiques/general store, and a small motel that may or may not be open; more lodging is available in Circleville or Marysvale.

Butch Cassidy Country

Now that you've made it this far, you might as well make the 6-mile side trip south to Circleville, where that outlaw Butch grew up.

Folks in **Circleville** are no doubt a lot prouder of their favorite infamous son than of a particularly nasty incident that took place over the mountains from Beaver at just about the same time Cassidy was born. During the Black Hawk War, Circleville was the site of the massacre of an entire Paiute village in 1866. Following the outbreak of hostilities, all of the male members of a neighboring village were placed under armed guard, while the women and children were locked in a cellar. Some of the braves attempted to escape, and all of them were shot and killed. After some discussion on how to handle the women and children, they were led up singly from the cellar and their throats cut. It's a vivid reminder that relations between white settlers and Native people were not always peaceful.

An old settler's cabin, 2.5 miles south of Circleville and clearly visible on the right from the highway, is **Butch Cassidy's boyhood home.** Cassidy, born **Robert Leroy Parker,** lived here on his father's ranch from age 13. It was here that the boy met Mike Cassidy, who had run with a group of horse thieves before taking a ranch-hand job with the Parkers. Cassidy taught the youngster all he needed to know about growing up tough and independent, and the boy must have idolized him, for he later took his old friend's name as an alias.

Mike Cassidy left for Mexico one step ahead of the law. Shortly after, young Parker stole some horses and lit out for Colorado. Sometime later he teamed up with two other adventurers and robbed a train in Grand Junction and a bank at Telluride, emerging as the soon-to-be-famous bandit Butch Cassidy.

Cassidy and his notorious band, "the Wild Bunch," robbed banks and stagecoaches, held up mining payrolls, and rustled cattle throughout the region around the turn of the century. He was said to have been a likable fellow, a Robin Hood–like character who was known to have been helped out many times by ordinary citizens in his evasion of the law. There is even a story of the Piute County judge in nearby Junction buying Butch beers when he came to town.

Cassidy and his partner, **the Sundance Kid,** were allegedly killed in a shootout with a company of cavalry in Bolivia. Yet stories of his reappearance in this region, and subsequently in the Pacific Northwest, persisted for years. According to the research of at least one historian, he lived out a quiet life in Spokane before dying of pneumonia in the 1930s.

North of Junction, US 89 follows the Sevier River Valley. This is mostly BLM land on both sides of the road, scrub sagebrush desert used for grazing, so there is no development at all. Off to the left are the high peaks of the Tushar Range. On the right you occasionally catch a glimpse of the Sevier River and where it widens into Piute Reservoir a few miles north of Junction. At the northern end of the reservoir (5 miles north of Junction) is **Piute State Park,** with primitive camping and not much else.

From Marysvale to Rock Candy

It is 19 miles of wide-open ranch land to the pretty old town of **Marysvale.** A few substantial commercial buildings and the names of several of the streets branching off from US 89 are evidence that this was once a mining town of some importance. Marysvale began in the 1860s as a Mormon farm town. In 1868 ore strikes

The Sevier Valley stretches out below gravel switchbacks on the Tushars' east side.

in the Tushars, west of town, brought hordes of miners. It has always alternated between mini-booms and hard times; nearby uranium mining in the mid-1900s resulted in one of the highest rates of cancer in the world. Marysvale's selection of motels, RV parks, gas stations, and convenience stores are oriented around the current boom: off-road adventurers. Marysvale and other towns in the Sevier River Valley benefit from proximity to the **Paiute ATV Trail,** a system of more than 900 miles of off-road trails throughout central Utah.

Just north of Marysvale, US 89 follows the Sevier River as it winds through a very picturesque sort of desert canyon called **Clear Creek Canyon.** Here you will start to notice some really fantastic coloration and eroded shapes in the hills. The colors are the result of hydrothermal activity (much like the soft, yellow rock at Yellowstone), evidence that the volcanic activity of the Tushars is quite recent.

At about mile 4.5 north of Marysvale, watch on your left just above the road for the yellow-brown formation locals named for the folk song **"The Big Rock Candy Mountain,"** made famous by the late Burl Ives. They also named nearby

Big Rock Candy Mountain also looks a bit like a giant fudge sundae.

Lemonade Springs after the song, and the trickle that issues from this bizarre heap of soft yellow rock *does* look and even taste slightly lemony. The coloration comes from oxidized iron in the clay-rich earth (limonite), but clearly there must still be some sort of low-grade acid concentration up in these hills (the volcanic Tushars are known as a source of sulfur). The acidity is probably more closely related to battery acid than to citric acid, but "Lemonade Springs" is certainly more romantic sounding than, say, "Battery Acid Springs."

Just past the formation, a scenic pull-out gives the best view back toward the Big Rock Candy Mountain. From this vantage point, you may decide for yourself (and argue with your kids, no doubt) whether this does, in fact, look like a huge chunk of marbled candy. (Actually, they might have called it "the Big Chocolate and Caramel Syrup-Covered Ice Cream Sundae Mountain," but that's not very melodic.)

North of the low-key development around Big Rock Candy Mountain, the valley increases in beauty. The Sevier River flows immediately to the right of the road. At just under mile 12 from Marysvale, you reach I-70. To return to I-15, take I-70 west; to continue along US 89 north to Richfield, get on I-70 east. Fortunately, because this is Utah, even the interstate drives are scenic, the only difference being the speed at which the scenery rolls by.

Richfield is a full-on mini city, with fast-food restaurants, supermarkets, discount stores, and all the other manifestations of civilization as we know it.

16

Historical Sites & Wide-Open Spaces

Eureka to Delta

General Description: A 50-mile basin and range drive across broad, dry valleys and past rough desert hills filled with mining history.

Special Attractions: Tintic District mining towns, Great Basin desert views, rockhounding, Little Sahara Recreation Area, site of Topaz internment camp, Fort Deseret.

Location: Central Utah, on the edge of the Great Basin.

Drive Route Number: US 6.

Travel Season: Year-round. Can be very warm in summer.

Camping: Developed sites limited to campgrounds at Little Sahara, commercial RV park at Delta; undeveloped sites on public lands along the route.

Services: All services in Delta; limited services in Eureka.

Nearby Attractions: Nebo Loop Scenic Byway, Pony Express Trail Scenic Backway, Notch Peak Loop Scenic Backway.

The Drive

This is one of but a handful of drives in this guide that touch on the rough, desolate region of the **Great Basin,** the desert land that lies to the west of Utah's famed mountain and high plateau country. This is not an easy region to appreciate on first sight; it resists the modern tourist almost as staunchly as it did the early settlers who quickly learned simply to avoid it. Dry, cracked alkali flats and volcanic plains devoid of much vegetation, home to rattlesnake and tumbleweed, alternate with craggy mountains. But in its remoteness and its sheer resistance to man's attempts to domesticate it, it has a raw, imposing, and eternal power.

In some ways, this drive describes various attempts at coming to terms with the Great Basin; or, at least, Man's tenuous and sometimes failed efforts to put this rough land to some practical use. The drive runs from the old **Tintic Mining District** south along US 6 to Delta, the last outpost on the edge of the Great Basin and site of **Topaz Relocation Center,** a Japanese-American internment camp during World War II. Along the way, the route offers glimpses of the vast desert wasteland to the west, of the fascinating accumulation of shifting sand dunes at **Little Sahara,** and of a river that just gives up and dies here in the desert.

The 50-mile drive is on excellent, flat, paved road. It can be done in a day or as a detour to points south.

Historical Sites & Wide-Open Spaces

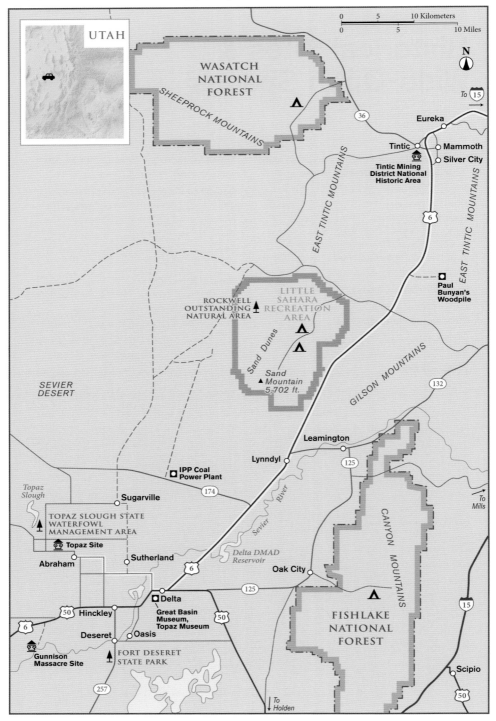

UTAH

WASATCH NATIONAL FOREST

SHEEPROCK MOUNTAINS

0   5   10 Kilometers
0   5   10 Miles

N

To 15

36

Eureka

Tintic
○ Mammoth
○ Silver City

Tintic Mining District National Historic Area

EAST TINTIC MOUNTAINS

6

EAST TINTIC MOUNTAINS

Paul Bunyan's Woodpile

ROCKWELL OUTSTANDING NATURAL AREA

LITTLE SAHARA RECREATION AREA

Sand Dunes

▲ Sand Mountain 5,702 ft.

GILSON MOUNTAINS

132

SEVIER DESERT

To Mills

Leamington

Lynndyl

125

IPP Coal Power Plant

174

Sevier River

CANYON MOUNTAINS

Topaz Slough

Sugarville

TOPAZ SLOUGH STATE WATERFOWL MANAGEMENT AREA

Topaz Site

Abraham

Sutherland

Delta DMAD Reservoir

6

Oak City

125

125

15

FISHLAKE NATIONAL FOREST

50

Hinckley

6

Deseret

Oasis

Delta
Great Basin Museum, Topaz Museum

50

Gunnison Massacre Site

FORT DESERET STATE PARK

257

To Holden

Scipio

50

Mining History

To reach the drive's starting point at Eureka, exit I-15 at Santaquin and take US 6 west. (You could also join this drive from Fairfield or Tooele in Drive 23 via a handful of paved or unpaved roads; if you choose the unpaved option, make sure you have a detailed map.) The drive from Santaquin to Eureka passes small farming towns and old mining sites. West of the hamlet of Elberta the landscape becomes more dramatic, as we leave agriculture behind and enter the rough desert hills called the **Tintic Mountains,** named for a Ute Indian chief.

In 1869 ore strikes in these hills resulted in the establishment of the **Tintic Mining District.** Within 30 years this became one of America's most important mining districts, with most activity centered around Eureka, Mammoth, Diamond, and Silver City—some of the most rough-and-tumble towns in the West. The population here soared to an estimated 8,000 just before the turn of the century. Mining slowed in this century but continued through the 1950s and has recently resumed here. Altogether, the district produced an estimated $570 million in silver, gold, copper, lead, and zinc.

Present-day **Eureka** has a very authentic "mining town that's seen more prosperous days" appearance. The town of about 650 sort of toddles along, supported by the few regional mining jobs left, a recently completed Superfund cleanup effort to mitigate the effects of old mines (which resulted in high levels of contamination in soil throughout town), and a slow trickle of tourist business. This is a quiet, funky place and your last opportunity for fuel and food for a long way.

For a good overview of the mining history in the Tintic area, stop at the excellent **Tintic Mining Museum** on Main Street. As with the many Daughters of Utah Pioneers museums in small towns across Utah, call one of the numbers listed on the front door and someone will come down to open up for you. If you don't have cell service here, just ask at any open business in town. Also peek into the old **Porter Rockwell cabin**; Rockwell was a bodyguard to Brigham Young whose violent exploits are famous in Mormon lore.

As you leave Eureka at its southern end, note the old gallows frames used for lowering miners into the tunnels and for extracting ore. The most prominent of these, just on the right as you leave town, has a nice interpretive plaque that explains how the underground mining operations were carried out.

A mile or so past Eureka, US 6 trends slightly to the left—ignore the fork to the right, signed for Tooele. Ahead of you stretches out the wide, dry expanse of the Great Basin. At this point the highway travels due south through a broad valley ringed with rough, arid desert hills. A little more than 2 miles past Eureka is the well-marked turnoff on the left for **Mammoth.** Though there is not much to see here, it is worth the short (less than a mile) side trip up this paved road to the shabby but interesting cluster of houses in a spectacular hillside setting. Mammoth was the site of the Tintic District hospital just after the turn of the century.

It is just under a mile to a similar turnoff on the left, this one to the defunct town of **Silver City.** Depending on the status of the current small-scale mining operation up this road, you may or may not be able to reach the cement foundations that remain at this town site, which sits on private property. The short drives up these two canyons are worthwhile to give a sense of how the mining in this district was spread out among many small canyons, each with its own little community, all centered around the larger town of Eureka. Although some folks like to climb on the old mining equipment and otherwise investigate these old sites, the abundance of unsecured shafts and toxic slag piles make them unsafe for kids (and probably adults, too). As with any accessible mining area, watch out for open mine shafts and don't even think of trying to enter one.

Woodpiles & Beaches

Driving south along US 6, it may seem surprising that this is not a state-designated scenic byway. The landscape is pristine, wild, high prairie dotted with rough hills covered with sagebrush, pinyon, and juniper. The views are terrific and, except for the relics of old mining operations, there is no sign of development. The road is excellent, flat, and fast.

About 15 miles south of Eureka is the turnoff, on the left, signed for **Paul Bunyan's Woodpile**—unless vandals have removed the sign, which sometimes happens in this part of the world. As with some other brown BLM signs around Utah, you might find the sign along the road to the attraction, after you've made the turn. A cluster of lava columns, each about a foot in diameter, the "woodpile" formed about three million years ago and now resembles a gigantic stack of petrified wood. You will have to get out of the car to see it, but the short walk can be a nice break.

To get there, drive 3.3 miles on a decent but somewhat rough dirt road to a gate. Park below the gate. You can see a little of the woodpile from the trailhead. The moderate trail is about 1 mile long. Recent fires burned out the formerly wooded area and marred the trail, so the exact trail may be hard to find. It's fairly easy to pick your way through a small drainage and up a hill to look across the ravine at the woodpile or to hike a little farther to the woodpile itself.

A few miles to the south on US 6 is Utah's largest dry beach. Most of the sand at **Little Sahara Recreation Area** was left by the Sevier River, which flowed into

Paul Bunyan's Woodpile is an isolated remnant of long-ago volcanic activity.

Lake Bonneville, the prehistoric sea that filled this part of the Great Basin until about 15,000 years ago. Southwest winds picked up particles of sand, then were deflected upward by Sand Mountain until they lost impetus and dumped the sand here, forming this isolated, 124-square-mile system of free-moving dunes. The dunes are still moving to the north and east at a rate of between 5 and 9 feet per year.

From the well-marked Little Sahara turnoff, it is 4.4 miles to a left turn, then 1.5 miles to the visitor center, the hours of which vary greatly. It is open Friday through Sunday during spring, summer, and fall; the staff also has helpful information about other local sites. When the entrance booth is staffed, they may or may not let you in to take a quick look without paying the $18 day-use/camping fee.

Campgrounds here are very nice, with water and toilets, though the constant roar of dune-buggy and motorcycle engines can be annoying to those in search of peace and quiet in the desert.

If the noise gets on your nerves, you can escape to the **Rockwell Outstanding Natural Area,** a 9,000-acre vehicle-free zone set aside within the recreation area to preserve a sense of the natural ecosystem. The surroundings are mostly BLM land, which means pack-it-out primitive camping is allowed just about anywhere that's not fenced off.

If you decide to skip the visit to Little Sahara, you will get an idea of what it is like as you continue south on US 6, when **Sand Mountain** comes into view on the right. This fascinating geological oddity (it is an isolated, gigantic dune) appears either black or sandy gray, depending on the light.

Just after you pass Sand Mountain, look off to the right, farther south and west, and you will see one of the world's largest coal-fired electric plants. **Intermountain Power Project**'s immense power plant supplies electricity for communities as far away as Southern California. About 12 miles past Little Sahara, the road passes the first cultivated fields as you approach the small community of **Lynndyl,** a quiet farm town tucked away in a cluster of trees.

South of the oasis of Lynndyl, you return to the desert. In about 3 miles you will pass under the very impressive network of power lines that issue from the power plant. Note that the Sevier River now flows to the left of the road on the final leg of its long journey from the high snows of the Markagunt Plateau to its eventual dissipation in the dry wasteland to the southwest of Delta. Strange to see a river that, rather than flowing into some other body of water, just runs out of energy and dies.

Shortly after crossing the Sevier, you pass the small Delta airport and then the golf course, announcing you are in Delta's northern suburbs.

The modern town of **Delta** is not particularly scenic, but it is a friendly and convenient service center and the last community of any size for anyone striking out across the Great Basin. There are a couple of supermarkets, a few family-style restaurants, and a surprising number of motels that cater to rock hounds and birders (Delta is surrounded by designated waterfowl-management areas).

Delta was not a pioneer Mormon community, but the area has a long history. Remnants of Folsom Early Man culture, dating back nearly 8,000 years, have been found in the nearby Sevier Desert. In 1853 Captain John Gunnison and six of his men were killed by a Native American war party while surveying a possible transcontinental rail line. There is a monument to the massacre, but little else, a few miles west of **Hinckley** on US 50/US 6 and then south at the well-marked dirt road to the monument. **Fort Deseret** is about 4 miles south of Hinckley. If you are expecting an elaborate pioneer stockade, this simple adobe structure will be a disappointment. The 10-foot mud walls were put up in a big hurry at the start of the Black Hawk War in 1866, when Brigham Young advised all of the Mormon settlements in central Utah to prepare for hostilities. The Native Americans never came, so the fort was never tested. (Probably a good thing, from the looks of it.)

Delta came into being in 1907 after construction of the **Yuba Dam,** east of here on the Sevier River, made it practical to irrigate new fields here.

Desert Attractions

Beyond Hinckley there is little but rough, dry, inhospitable, and thoroughly glorious Great Basin desert for more than 80 miles, until you reach the Nevada line. Most tourists who make that drive are on their way to Great Basin National Park, just over the border.

In spite of the town's rather prosaic birth, there are things to see in the Delta area apart from the imposing desert scenery to the west. Delta's **Great Basin Museum,** at 45 West Main Street right in the middle of town, is a good source of information on regional history and geology. Trilobites from **Antelope Springs** and topaz crystals from **Topaz Mountain** are among the more popular rockhounding finds. The 50-mile desert/mountain **Notch Peak Loop Scenic Backway** heads north of US 50/US 6 about 43 miles west of Delta. Usually drivable in passenger vehicles, it offers good opportunities for rockhounding and trilobite hunting. Check in at the Great Basin Museum for tips on other likely spots and pick up its useful little guide.

Delta's more recent significant historical claim to fame was a regrettable affair that took place here more than half a century ago. During World War II, 8,700 Japanese Americans were uprooted from their California homes and forcibly moved to an internment camp named **Topaz Relocation Center,** set in a marshy area on the edge of the Sevier Desert.

Little remains of the Topaz internment camp's baseball field except some of the original fencing used for a backstop.

Today, the exceptional **Topaz Museum** (55 West Main; topazmuseum.org) sits right next to the Great Basin Museum, with exhibits created based on input from both locals in Delta and Japanese-American families of those imprisoned. Its many informational plaques and photographs, along with artifacts and even a restored recreation hall out back, capture well how detainees made the most of a terrible situation—and serves as a reminder of the costs of unfounded fear.

The Topaz site itself is worth a visit. To reach the site, continue west on US 6 from downtown Delta, go straight where US 6 curves to the left, and follow signs for Sutherland (the power plant will be visible straight ahead). Just follow this obvious main road (now called 1500 North) for 2 miles until you see a prominent sign indicating Sutherland to the right, Abraham and Topaz straight. You're essentially working your way northwest on the most obvious main roads within a grid. At 7000 West, make the clearly marked right turn for Topaz. Go north on 7000 West for 2.5 miles to a stop sign and the end of the pavement. Continue north on good, graded gravel to the intersection with 4500 North. As the sign indicates, turn left onto this off-and-on paved road.

At this point you are in the general vicinity of the relocation center, and you begin to get a sense of just how unpleasant this must have been for the thousands

The Topaz Museum displays artifacts from a sad chapter in the area's past.

of Japanese Americans banished to this alkali wasteland. At mile 3.7 watch for the unmistakable memorial on the left.

In recent years, members of the Japanese-American community have bought the land where the camp once stood, ensuring its preservation as a monument to the tragedy. From the monument, a labeled driving tour along the grid of roads constructed for the camp leads to remnants of buildings—shops, the newspaper office, a baseball field—and a lingering mood of desolation and rough times. Whether you visit the Topaz site or not, do stop in at the museum.

The quickest way to reach the I-15 corridor from the Delta area is to drive 27 miles east on US 50 through undulating, brush-covered hills. Salt Lake City is a little under 3 hours of direct driving from Delta.

17

Nebo's Mountain Majesty

Payson to Nephi

General Description: A high-alpine 38-mile drive along the eastern flank of 11,928-foot Mount Nebo.

Special Attractions: Payson Lakes Recreation Area, Mount Nebo Wilderness Area, Devil's Kitchen Geologic Interest Site, hiking, fishing, backpacking.

Location: Central Utah, in the Wasatch Range.

Drive Route Number & Name: FR 015, Nebo Loop Scenic Byway.

Travel Season: Memorial Day to Thanksgiving, depending on snowfall. This is a spectacular autumn colors drive (late September until early October).

Camping: Five national forest campgrounds, two commercial campgrounds at Nephi.

Services: All services in Payson and Nephi. No services on route.

Nearby Attractions: Tintic Mining District, Little Sahara Recreation Area, Provo/Utah Lake, attractive communities of the Sanpete Valley.

The Drive

This really isn't a loop, despite its official name. The 38-mile **Nebo Loop Scenic Byway** is a north–south mountain drive that runs between the regional centers of Payson and Nephi. This popular excursion provides spectacular close-up views of imposing Mount Nebo, impressive vistas of Utah Valley and the Wasatch Mountains, and abundant opportunities for high-level alpine hikes. It is a relatively short drive that makes a nice half-day outing.

The Nebo Loop byway is fully paved and fine for all vehicles. A bit of climbing to its 9,000-foot high point, heavy weekend traffic, and a few tight turns may cause headaches for larger rigs, but there are no real problems with the road. Traffic can be heavy on weekends, especially during the autumn colors season. The road closes during winter. In general—and for photographers in particular—this drive might best be done in morning, since it is predominantly to the east of Mount Nebo.

While the byway can be driven in either direction, it seems to be most popular as a north–south drive, setting out from **Payson** (which might be a good reason to do it the other direction during high season). Payson is a quiet community of about 17,000 with a fine collection of attractive old brick homes on Main Street north of the sleepy business district. Main Street is one-way, running south; at its south end is a nice, shady town park with a wading pool, ideal for a picnic.

Nebo's Mountain Majesty

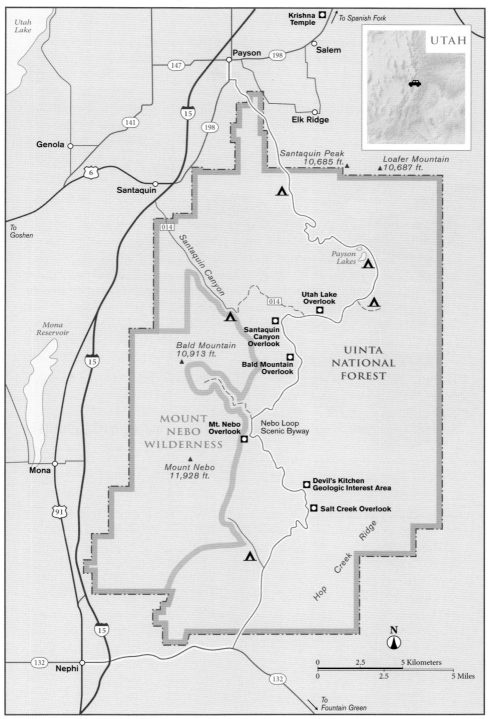

Before you tackle the loop, you may want to make a quick jaunt to **Spanish Fork,** just north of Payson, to see one of Utah's most unusual structures. The **Sri Sri Radha Krishna Temple** is open to the public and makes for an intriguing look into a way of life new to most Utah residents (and Americans in general). After some misgivings, the mostly Mormon locals embraced the temple, which was completed in 2001. The traditional Indian-style building is at 311 West 8500 South, just off Highway 198 (State Street). Tours are given 10 a.m. to 6 p.m., and if you're lucky, you might stumble upon a traditional feast, celebration, or Hare Krishna chant.

US 6 is Payson's 100 North. Follow it east through town until you see (on the right) the large, ornate old **Peteetneet Academy.** You really cannot miss this outstanding architectural gem, one of the most elaborate old schoolhouses in the state. The red and beige brick building, named for an Indian chief who befriended early Mormon settlers and formerly home to a private school, is now a regional museum and cultural center (open weekdays 10 a.m. to 4 p.m.). Peteetneet Avenue, on the right (also called 600 East), is well marked for the Nebo Loop Scenic Byway.

Head south through a nondescript residential area. Two LDS churches within four blocks should give you an idea of the sort of place Payson is. Within a mile you will be on a narrow but paved country lane, winding southward and upward away from Payson. At about mile 3.5 the road comes up and out of the canyon into really gorgeous mountain meadowlands. This lovely, open interlude lasts but briefly before the road enters another narrow, steep canyon that is heavily wooded with a stream cascading on the right. A mile farther you enter **Uinta National Forest.**

Just inside the national forest boundary, on the right, is the small (12 sites) and secluded **Maple Bench Campground** with an information kiosk about the area. More maple-themed campgrounds (Maple Dell, Maple Lake) follow. You'll pass a number of trailheads for pleasant hikes, including the short and easy **Grotto Falls** walk, about 7 miles from the mouth of the canyon, which ends at a pretty waterfall and natural wading pool.

Mount Nebo Views

By about 10 miles from Payson, you have gained enough elevation that the trees have thinned out and the views have become more expansive. At mile 12.7 is the turnoff on the right for **Payson Lakes,** a developed Forest Service campground

The Krishna Temple's Indian-style decoration is unexpected in this mostly Mormon part of the world.

Roadside overlooks provide views from Nebo to Utah Lake and its surrounding settlements far below.

with nearly 100 tent and RV sites (it's 0.5 mile from the main road). It's very popular with local families. One bonus is that all the sites are wheelchair-accessible, as is a paved lakeside nature trail. This may be a good spot to stop for a break, especially since the shortage of bathroom facilities from here on out make the flush toilets near the lake very appealing.

A mile and a half past Payson Lakes is the turnoff on the left for **Black Hawk Campground,** which is 2 miles from the byway. Just past this turnoff you should begin to notice that you are very high up on the northeast flank of Mount Nebo. At mile 15 there is a nice overlook on the left called **Beaver Dam Creek Overlook.** A plaque here describes the confrontation in 1865–67 between Ute chief Black Hawk and the Mormon settlers, famous throughout central Utah as the Black Hawk War.

Past this overlook, the views of Nebo's summit are impressive. Mormon settlers named **Mount Nebo** ("Sentinel of God") for the biblical peak where Moses died, the highest mountain east of the Jordan River. It seemed appropriate, since this Nebo lies to the east of Utah's Jordan River, which runs from Utah Lake to the Great Salt Lake (well, okay, it's a bit to the south as well). At 11,928 feet, Mount Nebo is the highest peak in the Wasatch Range and one of the highest in the state. The **Mount Nebo Wilderness** protects 28,500 acres of rugged alpine terrain surrounding the peak.

The road continues to climb. At just past mile 17, **Utah Lake Viewpoint** provides a very nice view off to the northwest. From here you can see clearly most of the Utah Valley far below, with Utah Lake (only 18 feet deep at its deepest) to the northwest and Mount Timpanogos, the massive snowy peak to the northeast of Provo.

Past here, the drive features several scenic overlooks, which don't seem like enough to truly drink in all the changing views. Some of them are "unofficial," there mostly for construction crews and the many cowboys who herd cattle here; those are often rough gravel and could take out your undercarriage if you're not careful. The "official" overlooks, most on the west side of the road, are generally paved. The **Bald Mountain Overlook** is particularly impressive, with several excellent trailheads. Now that you have used your vehicle to gain all this elevation, this is a good place to embark on a mountain hike and find views for which you would normally have to work a lot harder. Near the high point of the drive, the road follows a steep ridge with dramatic dropoffs, then hits a series of twisting curves, all with spectacular vistas.

At about mile 25 the road begins to descend, and it really is remarkable just how close to the east face of Nebo the road brings you. There is an especially fine overlook just past mile 25. At mile 29, be sure to stop at the very interesting **Devil's Kitchen Geologic Interest Site.** A short interpretive trail leads to a surprising sight. Here, in the heart of this most Alp-like mountain landscape, is a little scene lifted from the red sandstone canyons to the south. A geological oddity, Price River conglomerate is an easily eroded, brightly colored material that stands out in sharp contrast to the surrounding alpine forest. The hoodoos, spires, and columns look like they belong in Bryce Canyon.

The byway descends along Salt Creek and, at just under mile 38, reaches the intersection with Highway 132. Here you leave the national forest, and the scenic drive is essentially finished.

Turn right at this intersection to go to Nephi, 3 miles to the west, and I-15. A left here takes you into the **Sanpete Valley,** where several very pretty old Mormon towns merit a side trip (it's also easy to connect this way to US 89 and Drive 18). The first of these is **Fountain Green,** 8 miles from the intersection with Highway 132, a classic Sanpete Valley Mormon village. Fountain Green, traditionally tied to sheep raising, holds a sheep festival every July, and it is common to see the animals grazing in backyards throughout the town. Sanpete County is also one of the nation's top turkey-producing areas, which explains the abundance of poultry barns along this route. A processing plant in Moroni, just down the road from Fountain Green, handles the millions of turkeys the valley's cooperative farms raise each year (this is also probably where your turkey-manure garden compost originated). Other Sanpete communities are described as a side trip from Fairview on Drive 18.

A motorcycle navigates the steep, narrow pavement on the Nebo Loop's southern section.

Nephi is an orderly little city of 6,000 that has a well-used look about it; many travelers stop here to fuel their cars and their bellies before making the trek to central and southern Utah. The town occupies an interesting position geographically. The base of the towering Nebo massif is lovely spruce/pine forests and dramatic alpine terrain, but Nephi also sits at the eastern edge of the rough desert plains and dry, rocky hills of the Great Basin. It could be the ideal place for someone who cannot decide between desert and mountain activity and scenery.

Settled in 1851, Nephi was named for the first of the prophets of the Book of Mormon (Moroni was the last). The place saw plenty of traffic even before the Mormon pioneers moved in. First Fremont Indians and then Utes lived in this valley. The Dominguez-Escalante expedition came through here in 1776, Jedediah Smith visited in 1826 and 1827, and John C. Fremont passed by in 1843–44.

The town prospered as a farm and ranching community, then got a major economic boost when a rail line came down from Salt Lake City during the 1870s, making Nephi an important agriculture and livestock shipping point. One of Utah's premier rodeos, the **Ute Stampede,** celebrates Nephi's cow-town heritage.

18

Huntington & Eccles Canyons—Lakes, Stones & Desert Bones

Huntington to Fairview & Scofield

General Description: A traverse of the Wasatch Plateau's alpine terrain (55 to 75 miles).

Special Attractions: Beautiful alpine driving, access to backcountry drives and hiking, quaint Fairview, historic mining towns.

Location: Central Utah, in the Manti–La Sal National Forest. The drive includes Highway 31 from Huntington to Fairview, and Highways 264 and 96 from the intersection with Highway 31 to the old mining town of Scofield.

Drive Route Numbers & Names: Highways 31/264/96, Huntington Canyon

Scenic Byway/Eccles Canyon Scenic Byway.

Travel Season: While roads are officially open year-round, snow closures are common from November until May.

Camping: Four national forest campgrounds, state-park and commercial campgrounds at Huntington and Scofield.

Services: All services in Huntington and Fairview; limited services in Scofield.

Nearby Attractions: Cleveland-Lloyd Dinosaur Quarry and Scenic Backway, Skyline Drive Scenic Backway, attractive old Sanpete towns along US 89, Manti Temple.

The Drive

The **Wasatch Plateau** is one of Utah's most important geographical features, marking the division between the vast Colorado Plateau and the Great Basin. This drive combines the Huntington Canyon and Eccles Canyon Scenic Byways and provides an excellent introduction to the spectacular Wasatch Plateau high country. The length of your drive will vary from 55 to 75 miles, depending on which options you choose. The route is paved, two-lane highway, suitable for all vehicles, with generally light traffic on both branches of the drive except during hunting season. Expect icy roads and even temporary snow closures in winter; snow tires or chains are required October 1 through April 30.

Huntington Canyon is the longest canyon on the Wasatch Plateau, and Highway 31 is the only paved road across the plateau. The Eccles Canyon drive, which branches from the high point of the Huntington Canyon drive (approximately 10,000 feet elevation) down to **Scofield Reservoir,** is impressive; lonely and desolate in all the best ways, it is perhaps the best part of this drive and not to be missed.

Huntington & Eccles Canyons

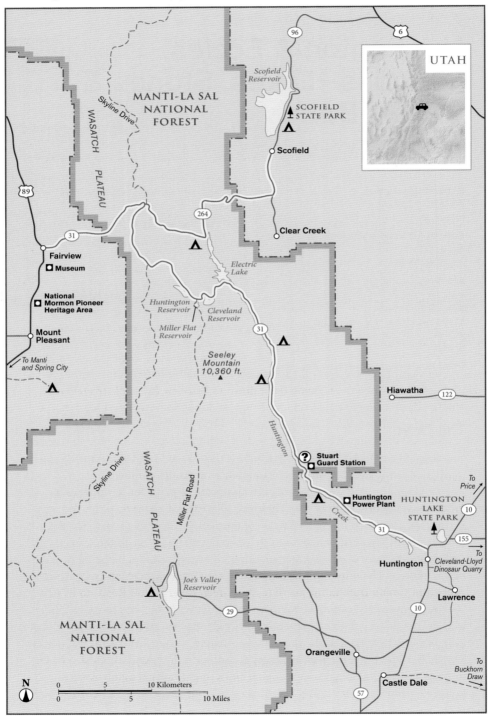

These strange sculptures, part of a sprawling roadside garden, are one of a few unique sights along Highway 10 south of Huntington.

The only real decision you will have to make is whether to finish the standard route of the Huntington Canyon drive down to Fairview (which I strongly recommend). In a conventional vehicle, I suggest doing both right and left forks of this drive, ending in either Fairview or Scofield, depending on which side of the mountain range you wish to finish this drive on. In a large RV, or pulling a trailer, you may not want to drive down one fork, then reascend to do the other. If you must choose one over the other, I recommend the Scofield branch.

In either case, the drive begins in **Huntington,** one of a few farming and mining towns along Highway 10. Highway 10 skirts the east side of the Wasatch Plateau and, to the south, the west side of the geologic uplift known as the **San Rafael Swell.** This makes it a relatively convenient alternative to the US 6/US 191 corridor from Price to southern Utah and the starting point for some of the state's best backways. The unpaved **Cottonwood Wash/Buckhorn Wash** road, which runs from **Castle Dale** in the north (as the Green River Cutoff Road) to I-70 in the south, gives drivers a more intimate encounter with the San Rafael Swell. It leads to 2,000-year-old pictographs and petroglyphs, fantastic desert scenery, and the turnoff for the Wedge Overlook's views of aptly named **Little Grand Canyon.** The main route is maintained by Emery County and drivable with most vehicles in good weather, although some rougher spots might make it unadvisable for low-slung vehicles or RVs. Inquire about conditions and grab a free off-road route map and guide booklet at the regional visitor center in Price or at the **Museum of the San Rafael Swell** in Castle Dale. Take plenty of water if you go.

For a shorter drive with a taste of the swell and its secluded mysteries, take the paved Moore Cutoff Road (County Road 803), which starts just south of Ferron on Highway 10 and ends at I-70. It features petroglyphs and dinosaur tracks. The Utah Geological Survey website (geology.utah.gov) has a ton of information about formations in this region, including mile-by-mile descriptions of roads such as this.

Prehistoric Starting Point

Close to Huntington is an attraction that all area visitors, especially those with children, should take in: the **Cleveland-Lloyd Dinosaur Quarry.** The source of more than 30 complete skeletons and more than 12,000 individual bones from 70 different prehistoric animals, the quarry area encloses the greatest concentration of Jurassic-age dinosaur bones ever found.

The visitor center at the Cleveland-Lloyd Dinosaur Quarry includes a fully reconstructed allosaurus skeleton.

About 147 million years ago, the plain to the east of current Huntington was a shallow, muddy-bottomed lake. Dinosaurs were trapped in the boggy areas, and many bones accumulated here. The lake eventually dried up, and later geological activity deposited layer upon layer of strata over the site. Wind and water eroded these upper levels, bringing the fossilized bones close enough to the surface to be discovered by local ranchers. Word of these finds reached scientists at the University of Utah, who staged the first of many official digs in 1929.

There is a small visitor center and museum, an attractive picnic area, and a few self-guided interpretive trails. Go early if you'd like to venture very far in this sunbaked land on a warm day. Among the many dino exhibits at the visitor center is a complete allosaurus skeletal reconstruction. The BLM-administered site is open 10 a.m. to 5 p.m. on weekends (Fri through Sun) most of the year, and daily in summer. From Huntington, take Highway 155 to Cleveland, then follow signs to the quarry. The road to the quarry is unpaved but well maintained and suitable for all vehicles. Getting back to civilization can be tricky because this area is criscrossed with unpaved roads that all look about the same; just stay pointed north and west as much as possible and you'll connect with the highway eventually.

From Huntington, Highway 31 heads north and west through farmland and ranchland before trending upward into the mouth of a narrowing sandstone canyon with Huntington Creek flowing on the left. Just at the mouth of the canyon, about 8 miles from town, is a large, coal-fired electrical generating plant. After the power plant this drive takes on a mountain/canyon aspect as it enters **Manti–La Sal National Forest.**

Several basic National Forest Service campgrounds (none with drinking water) are located just beside the road. Just past Bear Creek campground is a turnoff to the left for the **Crandall Canyon Mine,** one of many active coal mines in the area. There's nothing interesting to see in the canyon, but it was the site of a major recent disaster: in 2007, six miners were trapped when a mine shaft collapsed. Three rescue workers were killed and another six injured when the tunnel they were digging also collapsed. The six trapped miners were never recovered. The US government later levied a $1.6 million fine on the mine owners for safety violations that helped cause the disaster. A few miles south of here, in Orangeville, is a memorial to 27 miners killed in the Wilberg mine fire 25 years earlier. Such incidents serve as a grim reminder of mining's highest costs.

There are many nice picnic spots and places to fly fish, and the upper reaches of Huntington Creek for the final 4 miles to Electric Lake are designated "fly fishing only." Near the Old Folks Flat campground, once the site of an annual LDS gathering, is the **Stuart Guard Station,** which now acts as a seasonal Forest

Dirt bikers pause from riding the Skyline Drive Scenic Backway to take in the view from the top of the Sanpete Valley Overlook.

Service station. Between Memorial Day and Labor Day, this is a great place to take a break and ask any questions about the area (it's open 9 a.m. to 5 p.m.).

At mile 23 you reach a scenic pull-out at **Electric Lake,** named for its function as the storage reservoir that supplies the steam turbines at the Huntington generating plant.

This is an air-conditioned place. Most summers the snows here last into July (making this a good place for a summertime snowball fight), but when summer does come to these high meadows, it comes full bloom. Few places in the American West rival the Wasatch Plateau for abundance and variety of wildflowers.

The road stays high as it reaches the southern tip of Electric Lake, then passes Cleveland and Huntington Reservoirs, winding level at elevations of about 9,500 feet with impressive views of the Sanpete Valley, San Pitch Mountains, and Mount Nebo to the northwest.

Just after Cleveland Reservoir, Miller Flat Road heads south on 29 miles of mostly level maintained gravel to **Joe's Valley Reservoir,** a popular recreation site that can also be reached by paved road from the Orangeville/Castle Dale area.

In 1988 the skeleton of an 11,000-year-old woolly mammoth was found just below the dam at the head of Huntington Reservoir. This important find is on display at the **College of Eastern Utah Prehistoric Museum** in Price (a replica is on display at the Fairview Museum).

The road finally tops out above 9,700 feet after winding along up high for about 7 or 8 miles from Electric Lake. Just before this high point, you will encounter a turnoff on the right, signed prominently for Scofield. This is an unpaved branch road, not the main Eccles Canyon road to Scofield. Shortly after that right, there is a left for the southern part of the Skyline Drive.

Skyline Drive

The **Skyline Drive** is one of the Wasatch Plateau's featured scenic attractions. This unpaved road, a designated scenic backway, winds along the steep spine of the Wasatch Plateau for more than 100 miles, much of it above 10,000 feet. The most spectacular stretch of this drive is the 30 miles running from Highway 31 south to the Joe's Valley–Ephraim Road, fairly consistently between 10,500 and 10,800 feet in elevation. Some parts of this drive run along hogback ridges barely wider than the road itself, with outstanding views of lakes, cirques, and Sanpete Valley towns below. Far to the east are the plateaus of the Tavaputs; 50 miles to the north are the summits of the Wasatch Front.

Portions of the Skyline Drive are passable in conventional vehicles in summer, but high-clearance is often required. If you intend to explore this very beautiful high-level road, check first in Huntington or Fairview (or any National Forest ranger station) for conditions.

Pause to take in the top-of-the-world views before Highway 31 starts to descend. Here you can see much of the Sanpete Valley as well as Mount Nebo to the north. An interpretive panel helps identify the many raptors that glide aloft here. Perhaps not surprisingly, this area is also very popular with kite skiers in winter. Just past this point is the well-marked turnoff on the right to Scofield, which is the right-hand branch of this driving route. You can take this right and skip ahead to that leg or continue the descent to Fairview. Also here is the turnoff on the right for the northern part of the Skyline Drive, which is slightly less striking than the southern end but often better maintained.

The descent on Highway 31 to **Fairview** runs through a beautiful forest of aspen and fir. After 7 miles, you reach the ramshackle outskirts of the greater Fairview metropolitan area.

Do not be misled by the suburbs. With lots of old brick homes, this is a classic little Mormon country town. Take a few minutes to drive around the side streets, where you are liable to see sheep grazing in yards, kids riding horses, and other such bucolic sights. Toward the south of town is a well-used rodeo arena.

The **Fairview Museum of History & Art,** at 100 North and 100 East, is huge, with everything from a mastodon replica to lots of Mormon pioneer artifacts. It really is a must-see for anyone interested in the history of the Sanpete Valley, or

in small-town western life in general. There are excellent exhibits of 19th-century furniture, pioneer spinning wheels, agricultural machines and tools, and Native American basketry and pottery. A new building south of the original houses rocks and other artifacts as well as an impressive collection of art by Sanpete Valley painters and sculptors. Outside the museum are displays of cook wagons, farm implements, and coaches. Admission is free, and it's open year-round Tues through Sat, 11 a.m. to 5 p.m. (Apr through Oct), and noon to 4 p.m. (Nov through Mar). Donations are appreciated.

Mormon Country

The Sanpete Valley is the best area in the state to see the cultural remnants of 19th-century Mormon settlement. From Fairview, consider taking a drive south on US 89 through the picturesque old Mormon communities of **Mount Pleasant, Spring City,** and **Ephraim** to the regional center of **Manti.** Spring City was first settled in 1852, abandoned during the Walker Indian War (1853–54), resettled in 1858, abandoned again during the Black Hawk War (1866), then resettled for good the following year. Its numerous 19th-century buildings, many of which are now galleries or art studios, have earned Spring City the nickname "the Williamsburg of the West." Ephraim (home of **Snow College**) and Manti are both attractive and substantial communities, settled early in Utah's pioneer era and preserving the architecture of the period. Manti is the site of perhaps the most beautiful of the state's 13 Mormon temples, and the third oldest, after St. George and Logan.

From Fairview, 400 North (Highway 31) heads back up and over the Wasatch Plateau. As you will have gathered from the earlier descent, the ascent of Highway 31 up Fairview Canyon is much steeper (to 8 percent grade) and narrower than Huntington Canyon. It is 8 miles to the Scofield/Skyline north intersection.

Just after this turnoff, make sure you angle to the right with the main road (100 yards past the turnoff); if you go straight here, you will head north on the Skyline Drive. Once past the Skyline Drive turnoff, the well-marked road to Scofield is straight ahead. You are now on the **Eccles Canyon Scenic Byway.**

The road descends through lovely meadows and high summer pastures, well watered with creeks and ponds. Land up here alternates between national forest and tracts of private property, so there are high ranch pastures and the private homes of a few very fortunate individuals (if you see signs for "MIA Shalom" and wonder what that refers to, it's an LDS girls' camp). **Flat Canyon Campground**

The Stuart Guard Station in Huntington Canyon is now a seasonal Forest Service information post.

This tramway stretches for 2 miles down the valley, annually carrying millions of tons of coal from the Skyline Mine.

is about 3.5 miles from the start of the Eccles Canyon drive. Just past the campground the road begins to descend steeply for a couple of miles to the northern end of Electric Lake before making a short final ascent and descent in earnest—via the first of a few hairpin turns on this drive—at about 11 miles from the start of the Scofield drive.

The terrain up here has a real alpine look, or perhaps more like somewhere in Norway. Beyond Electric Lake there is no mark of Man up here except this road—completely desolate, in the best way. Because this is just about at timberline, the tree cover is very thin, so views are quite open. In late July and early August, these meadows are alive with California corn lily, wild geranium, green gentian, scarlet gilia, purple lupine, wild delphinium, wild sweet pea, alpine sunflower, woodland star, forget-me-not, bluebell, charlock, hyssop, blue penstemon, and columbine. This is perhaps one of the area's prettiest alpine drives.

At this point you descend into **Eccles Canyon.** At mile 13 you reach the first of several large coal mines in the Scofield region. Note on the left the interesting coal tramway along the hillside, stretching for 2 miles down the valley. Just at the lower terminus of this very impressive transport system is the Skyline Mine, which produces between 3.5 and 5 million tons of coal each year. On the right is the turnoff for the old mining town of **Clear Creek,** a nice diversion 3 miles up this branch canyon on good road. The town is rather rundown and forlorn, though there are a few well-maintained homes amid many ruined miners' shacks and some evidence that this was once a robust little community.

Scofield

About 3.5 miles beyond the Clear Creek turnoff is the hamlet of **Scofield,** nicely situated at the southern end of Scofield Reservoir. Utah's officially designated Eccles Canyon Scenic Byway technically ends at the turnoff, but while not as picturesque as the high meadows and alpine terrain above, mining operations and mining towns can be visually interesting. This drive is definitely worthwhile all the way to Scofield.

While Clear Creek is in the sort of narrow valley we generally associate with mining towns, Scofield occupies a wider, more open setting. The pretty pasturelands at the town's south end somewhat mask its mining-town look. The town is rundown in a picturesque way: old stone and brick buildings, characteristic miners' cabins, and the usual trailer homes. The hodgepodge does include a gas station and grocery store.

Scofield is famous in mining history annals as the site of one of the worst mine disasters of all time. On May 1, 1900, an explosion at the Winter Quarters Mine ignited clouds of coal dust, sweeping flames through the shafts and setting off two dozen kegs of blasting powder. Nearly 200 bodies were recovered, some of them children as young as 13. One Scofield family lost six sons and three grandsons that day. The tragedy at Scofield was often cited as an example in efforts to enact and enforce child labor laws.

The **Scofield Cemetery** sits on a bench to the west of town. Note the number of gravestones bearing the date May 1, 1900. In all, nearly 150 victims of the great tragedy are buried here.

Below the town of Scofield, this drive declines in interest and beauty. **Scofield Reservoir** is pretty uninspiring—just a big hole full of water—although it is full of fish. **Scofield State Park,** with a full-service campground, is 5.5 miles farther along.

The rest of the way to US 6 is unspectacular. Once past the minor residential development at Scofield Reservoir, the road leaves the canyon and heads across sagebrush-covered ranchland. It is 10 miles to the highway, where a left turn takes you quickly to I-15. If you go this way, stop at the impressive new train-themed rest area a few miles west of Soldier Summit on US 6, which also serves as a regional information center. A right on US 6 will take you to Helper, where you can pick up Drive 19 in progress from Duchesne.

19

Indian & Nine Mile Canyons—Natural History Meets Ancient Art

Duchesne to Price & North to Myton

General Description: A highly diverse 145-mile drive combining lovely forested canyons, the traverse of old Native American and settler trails, and many cultural and historical attractions.

Special Attractions: Ashley National Forest, Indian Canyon, historic attractions and museums in Helper and Price, Nine Mile Canyon, rock art sites.

Location: Central Utah.

Drive Route Number & Names: US 191/Indian Canyon Scenic Byway, Nine Mile Canyon Scenic Backway.

Travel Season: Generally year-round. The foliage in Indian Canyon is especially brilliant in fall.

Camping: State park campground at Duchesne, one national forest campground on US 191, commercial campground in Nine Mile Canyon, RV parks at Helper, Price, and Wellington.

Services: All services in Price and Helper, most services in Duchesne, basic services in Wellington and Myton.

Nearby Attractions: Reservation Ridge Scenic Backway, Huntington Canyon and Eccles Canyon Scenic Byways, Cleveland-Lloyd Dinosaur Quarry.

The Drive

The two travel corridors described by this drive were two early ways in and out of the remote Uinta Basin region. Until the mid-1880s the only way into the basin was on horseback. The old stage road, which followed an ancient Native American trail through Nine Mile Canyon and over the ridge into the Duchesne River Valley, was instrumental in the development of the basin by connecting the established railroad community of Price with the frontier military post at Fort Duchesne. In 1886 the canyon road was widened and improved by troopers of the African-American Ninth US Cavalry (famously known as the **buffalo soldiers**), and it served as the only real route into the Uinta region for more than 25 years.

This region remained true Wild West frontier longer than almost anywhere else in the American West. **Butch Cassidy,** who was known to have used the Nine Mile Canyon road for eluding posses, made perhaps the most daring robbery of his career, in 1897, at the paymaster's office of the Pleasant Valley Coal Company just north of Helper.

Indian & Nine Mile Canyons

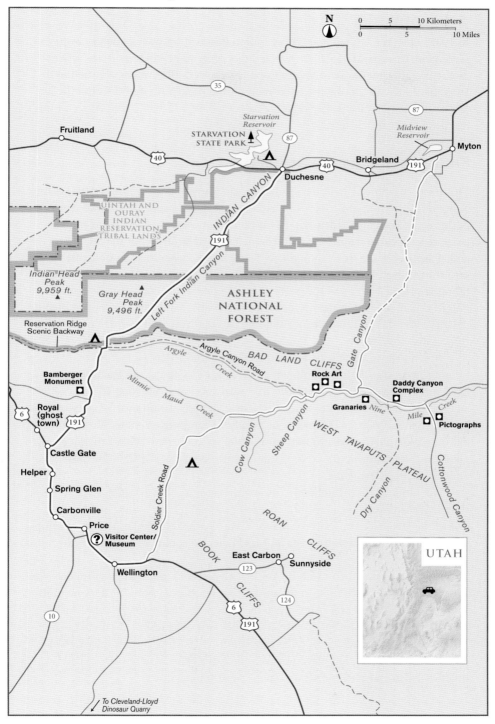

N

| 0 | 5 | 10 Kilometers |
| 0 | 5 | 10 Miles |

35

87

Starvation
Reservoir

Fruitland

STARVATION
STATE PARK

Midview
Reservoir

Myton

40

87

40

Bridgeland

191

Duchesne

UINTAH AND
OURAY
INDIAN
RESERVATION
TRIBAL LANDS

191

INDIAN CANYON

Indian Head
Peak
9,959 ft.

Gray Head
Peak
9,496 ft.

Left Fork Indian Canyon

ASHLEY
NATIONAL
FOREST

Gate Canyon

Reservation Ridge
Scenic Backway

Argyle Canyon Road

BAD LAND CLIFFS

Argyle

Creek

Rock Art

Daddy Canyon
Complex

Bamberger
Monument

Minnie

Maud

Creek

Granaries

Nine

Mile

Creek

Royal
(ghost
town)

6

191

Cow Canyon

Sheep Canyon

WEST TAVAPUTS PLATEAU

Pictographs

Cottonwood Canyon

Castle Gate

Soldier Creek Road

Helper

Dry Canyon

Spring Glen

Carbonville

ROAN

Price

Visitor Center/
Museum

BOOK

CLIFFS

UTAH

Wellington

East Carbon

123

Sunnyside

CLIFFS

10

6

124

191

To Cleveland-Lloyd
Dinosaur Quarry

In 1905, when the Uintah and Ouray Indian Reservation was opened to white settlement, thousands of settlers traveled this route to new homes in the wilderness. Even after the Indian Canyon Road (current US 191) was established in 1915, mail still came along the older road during the winter months until the late 1920s, as it is 1,700 feet lower than the high road over Indian Creek Pass and was less prone to snow closure.

From Mountains to Canyons

This drive combines Utah's designated Indian Canyon Scenic Byway with nearby Nine Mile Canyon Scenic Backway, creating a 145-mile loop. The initial segment of this route is an alpine drive up beautiful Indian Canyon, 45 miles of wilderness scenery with a handful of picturesque farms and ranches at the Duchesne end. This part of the drive should take 1 to 2 hours, depending on how often you stop for pictures. The Nine Mile Canyon Backway is approximately 78 miles and requires at least 3 hours to complete. For a long time, the backway was mostly unpaved, but a recent uptick in fossil fuel exploration and extraction prompted its paving. Dust and vibration from rumbling trucks threatened the precious rock art throughout the canyon.

Plan on spending at least an hour in **Helper** and **Price**—much more if you intend to visit the highly recommended College of Eastern Utah Prehistoric Museum at Price. It is possible to do the entire loop as a very long all-day excursion from Salt Lake City, but a more practical strategy would involve an overnight stay in Helper, Price, or Duchesne, or a night of camping en route. This would allow ample time to poke around historic Helper and Price. US 191 makes an appealing alternative to the traffic (and high accident rate) of US 6 for those traveling to southeastern Utah.

The route starts at **Duchesne,** a town that seems off the beaten track even today. According to one account, Duchesne was named for a nun, making this one of the few places in Utah named for a non-Spanish Catholic. There are campgrounds at nearby **Starvation State Park**. You also could fairly easily connect this trip with Drive 20.

From Duchesne turn south on US 191, signed for Castle Gate (44 miles). The turn is easy to miss; it's right in the center of town, across from the very helpful visitor information center. After a prosaic start past scrubland, the road climbs gradually up the canyon for 25 beautiful miles past old-fashioned ranches along Indian Creek. The final 3 or 4 miles of ascent to 9,100-foot **Indian Creek Pass** climb steeply. At the high-elevation section of this drive, you're surrounded by miles of aspen and pine forests and high-elevation meadows.

Highway 191 between Duchesne and Helper rises into beautiful, heavily forested territory that's very different from the surrounding deserts.

Just after leaving **Ashley National Forest,** watch for a dirt road on the right, signed as **Reservation Ridge Scenic Backway.** This mountain backway winds for about 45 miles along Reservation Ridge, with broad views out over **Strawberry Reservoir** and Ashley National Forest, before meeting US 6 near **Soldier Summit.** The single-lane four-wheel-drive road is closed from mid-Nov to mid-May.

The descent on 191 to the west of Indian Creek Pass is steeper than the east side. About 7 miles past the summit, note the small but attractive monument on the right, dedicated to **Governor Simon Bamberger.** This monument to Utah's first non-Mormon governor (an immigrant German Jew) was erected here by inmates allowed to work on state roads according to a state law enacted in 1911. Road work might not be fun, but prison is probably worse.

Diverse Mining Towns

The scenic aspect of this part of the drive comes to an abrupt end at the coal processing plant at the intersection of US 6 and US 191, just north of Helper. Turn left here for Helper and Price and a short touristic interlude based on social and industrial history.

During the 1880s the Denver and Rio Grande Western Railroad discovered and developed the vast coal deposits of Carbon County. Since then, the ups and downs of the coal mining industry have determined the character of life in Carbon County, a place distinctly different from the rest of mostly Mormon Utah.

Helper, 2 miles from the intersection of US 191 and US 6, was named for the "helper" engines attached to heavily loaded trains for the long haul up to Soldier Summit. Helper was also known as "the town of 57 varieties," due to its ethnic diversity. By the early 20th century, about one-third of all Carbon County coal miners were Italian, and there were also large numbers of Southern Slavs, Finns, and Greeks. All of this gives the Helper-Price area a distinct quality, more like other western mining districts (places that shared this sort of ethnic diversity) than the agriculture-based LDS settlements.

It's worth poking around Helper's historic district. The town still shows indications of the wealth that was floating around here at a time when people knew how to build on a grand scale. After years of economic ups and downs, it's now on an upswing thanks to artists and entrepreneurs who've been beautifying the place. Helper's chief tourist attraction, and the best place for a quick overview of the recent regional history, is the **Western Mining and Railroad Museum,** at 296 South Main St.

The best place for an overview of the prehistory of the region is down the road in **Price.** Like Helper, Price has a large non-Mormon population, and its **Hellenic Orthodox Church** is reputedly one of the oldest continuously occupied Greek churches in America. But the big attraction here, and a must-see for anyone interested in things prehistoric, is the **College of Eastern Utah Prehistoric Museum**'s excellent collection of dino stuff. In the **Hall of Dinosaurs** stand four complete dinosaur skeletons; the museum also exhibits a complete woolly mammoth skeleton, unearthed in Huntington Canyon in 1988. Kids can measure their feet against dinosaur tracks preserved in coal.

There are also displays of Fremont Culture artifacts, including a very impressive collection of rock art photographs and reproductions. The museum, at 155 East Main St., also houses a regional travel council office with information about Nine Mile Canyon as well as other attractions throughout central Utah. This is a great place to ask about the many unpaved but rewarding backways near here, pick up maps, and grab a free copy of the Nine Mile Canyon tour guide. The museum is open Mon through Sat 9 a.m. to 5 p.m. Admission is $6.

When it's time to tear yourself away, drive south from Price 7.5 miles on US 6 through the town of **Wellington.** Its pleasant city park is a nice picnic spot. About 2 miles past Wellington turn left at the well-marked road for Nine Mile

This monumental statue in front of the library in Helper is
a symbol of mining's importance in the region.

Canyon Scenic Backway. After about 1.5 miles of nondescript suburbs, you will pretty much be in the wilderness. WARNING: As the sign indicates, you'll go 75 miles with no services on this route. Bring lots of water and snacks, and fuel up in Wellington.

Nine Mile Canyon

The most logical reason a canyon longer than 40 miles should be named Nine Mile Canyon is the 9-mile triangulation survey of the area made by John Wesley Powell's mapmaker during the landmark 1869 Powell expedition. Maps presented to Congress clearly indicate Nine Mile Creek.

Long known to Ute and earlier Fremont Culture Indians, this historic trail still has the feel of the past. Sometimes said to be the world's longest newspaper or art gallery, it contains thousands of images of antelope, bison, and other animals—including some figures that may or may not be human. For a deeper dive into the archaeology of this fascinating place, pick up Jerry Spangler's book *Nine Mile Canyon: The Archaeological History of an American Treasure.*

The drive will take 3 to 4 hours, depending on your pace and how much time you spend searching for the fascinating rock art that abounds here. There are many attractions along this drive; I will try to give accurate mileages, all measured from the start of the scenic backway. For very detailed information and photographs of petroglyphs and other attractions, pick up a guide pamphlet available from castlecountry.com, the visitor center, and many other locations around Price. (If you're using the brochure, many of the mileages seem just a tad off—short by about .2 miles in most cases.)

Note: Please keep in mind that there is a mix of public/private land along this drive. There are many attractive old cabins, some on BLM-administered land but most on private ranches. It is especially important to honor the PRIVATE PROPERTY signs here, where the distinction between public and private is sometimes indistinct.

Ten miles from the Scenic Backway sign you will pass a ruined cabin in the vicinity of **Soldier Creek.** Elk and deer are often plentiful here. At the mouth of Soldier Creek Canyon the road begins to climb. At about mile 16 you come into the wide valley called **Whitmore Park.** There was a stage station at the west end of this valley, probably near one of the several corrals. The road curves as the canyon narrows.

The College of Eastern Utah Prehistoric Museum features lots of dinosaur displays.

Rock Art Abounds

Cross the bridge over **Minnie Maud Creek** at mile 21. Half a mile farther is a BLM "Welcome to Nine Mile Canyon" sign describing the canyon. Shortly thereafter, you pass Nine Mile Ranch, the only lodging or developed camping in the canyon. At about mile 26 you should begin to notice the first major **petroglyph panels** on a rocky point to the left of the road. In fact, you can see carvings all along the road from here if you look carefully at the dark, varnished areas of the rock. Once you get good at finding them, they seem to be everywhere.

At mile 27.2 is a county park with restrooms. The old town site of **Harper** is a little past mile 30. About 1 mile past the remains of Harper is a balanced rock to the left of the road. Just beyond this rock, on the left, is an excellent panel of rock art. View these from the road; they are on private property.

The cavalry troops who improved the road in 1886 also raised the telegraph line through the canyon on surplus metal poles left over from the Civil War. Many of these slender poles, with small arms branching off, can still be seen today. Just past mile 33 is the attractive stone house built by canyon resident and longtime telegraph operator Ed Harmon.

The first major dirt road intersection on your left is the Argyle Canyon Road, which stretches all the way to Highway 191. In good weather, it can make for a shortcut for those in high-clearance vehicles, but if you're coming from the north, that would mean missing the best part of the Highway 191 drive as well as Helper and Price. Soon after, a BLM sign indicates the road up **Harmon Canyon** to the right. Just after the sign, on the left and about 30 feet above the road, are some of the canyon's best petroglyphs.

After another 1.5 miles, stop at the prominent tall cottonwood that spreads its boughs across the road. Look up to the left, about 200 feet from the road, and note the very distinct snake design. For the next few miles the walls to the left will be full of ancient art.

At about mile 38 is the site of the **Nutter Ranch,** a substantial cluster of log houses and newer concrete block buildings, all marked as private. This ranch served for some time as the headquarters for Preston Nutter's Utah cattle empire. Nutter had more than 25,000 head of cattle ranged on land from here south to the North Rim of the Grand Canyon. As the midway point between Price and the garrison at Fort Duchesne, this was also the telegraph relay station—the stone building and log cabin next to the cliff were used for this purpose.

At 0.25 mile past the ranch is a bit of route confusion at a major split in the road. The sign reads straight ahead for Prickly Pear Canyon, Dry Canyon, and Cottonwood Canyon; left for Myton. Go straight (continuing in Nine Mile Canyon), and shortly past the split you may see the remnants of a Native American granary. At mile 44, you'll see a big pull-out for the **Daddy Canyon Complex.** This area includes a short hike to a couple of stretches of rock art as well as restrooms.

The road forks after this; continue up the canyon to the right for the remains of a Fremont pit house on the right (reachable via a short hike—the route can be hard to distinguish, but the ruins are not far up the hill. When in doubt, take a right turn). A few hundred yards farther along, another very short and more level walk, this time on the left side of the road, leads to the Big Buffalo—an enormous buffalo indeed. Continue another short distance to the well signed Great Hunt panel, a short walk away, with a densely populated depiction of a human form with a bow and arrow as well as plentiful bighorn prey.

Petroglyphs in Nine Mile Canyon are often right beside the road.

From here, you have two options: Return the way you came, or make the turn for Myton on a paved road that soon becomes gravel. Many drivers turn around here and head back to Price the way they came rather than continuing to Myton on a less scenic and often washboarded road. Either way, consider a short hike on the **Gate Canyon trail,** located at milepost 43.6 on the road to Myton, which follows an original 1886 road segment that was bypassed for the later route.

Although the Gate Canyon road to Myton is officially the north end of the Nine Mile Canyon Byway, the road actually departs Nine Mile Canyon, climbing

up and out of the drainage to cross into the Duchesne River Valley. From the intersection, the road winds and bounces up a dry canyon for 6.5 miles until it reaches a high point with expansive views off to the north. The road then descends back into the sage-covered scrubland below. At about mile 15 from the intersection are ruins of an important watering stop. **Outlaw Ambush Point** (site of an aborted stage robbery attempt by some Butch Cassidy pals) is 1 mile from the Myton intersection; the site of **Gate Arch** is 0.5 mile farther. The natural arch that once stood here was dynamited in 1905 out of fear that it might collapse on a passing wagon.

The pavement resumes at about 27 miles from where it left Nine Mile Canyon. Two and a half miles past the start of the pavement, turn left at the yield sign to reach US 40 after another 1.5 miles. Turn left to reach Duchesne (8 miles) and the fastest return to the Salt Lake Valley. Turn right toward Myton, Roosevelt, and Vernal for Drive 20.

The Great Hunt panel is just a short walk from the road.

20

Flaming Gorge–Uintas Scenic Byway

Vernal to Manila & Dutch John

General Description: A 150-mile drive along the eastern edge of the Uinta Mountains and along the southern rim of Flaming Gorge Reservoir, providing outstanding views of the river gorge and the High Uintas as well as roadside geology lessons.

Special Attractions: Utah Field House of Natural History/Dinosaur Garden, Dinosaur National Monement, Steinaker and Red Fleet State Parks, Ashley National Forest and Uinta Mountains, Flaming Gorge Reservoir and Dam, Sheep Creek Canyon, Swett Ranch.

Location: Northeast Utah. The drive begins in Vernal, runs north to Flaming Gorge Reservoir, then explores branches to Manila and Dutch John.

Drive Route Numbers & Name: US 191/Highway 44, Flaming Gorge–Uintas Scenic Byway.

Travel Season: Year-round. Ice and snow may create hazards during winter.

Camping: Eleven campgrounds in Flaming Gorge National Recreation Area, 5 campgrounds in Dinosaur National Monument, numerous national forest campgrounds along US 191 and Sheep Creek Loop, commercial campgrounds in Vernal.

Services: All services in Vernal and Manila; limited services at Red Canyon, Flaming Gorge Lodge, and Dutch John.

Nearby Attractions: Diamond Mountain/Jones Hole Hatchery, High Uintas Wilderness Area, Red Cloud/Dry Fork Scenic Backway, Browns Park Scenic Backway.

The Drive

Like so many of the places described in this book, Flaming Gorge presents a vivid lesson in geology at its most dramatic and most varied. This drive presents terrific contrasts: the rugged **Uinta Mountains;** beautiful alpine forests; a brilliantly colored, 91-mile reservoir at the bottom of a dramatic river gorge; and high desert country to the north. Plus dinosaurs!

Because of difficult terrain, poor access to the Uinta Basin, and extremes in weather, this was never a popular region for agriculturally minded settlers, either Native American or white pioneer. In terms of permanent settlement, the place is simply . . . defiant. Still, throughout history it has been a favorite hunting ground for Native Americans and mountain men, a popular hideout for outlaws, and a place for early explorers to marvel.

Today the area is a favorite for tourists and recreationists, and a relatively undisturbed home for wildlife. Flaming Gorge National Recreation Area offers

Flaming Gorge–Uintas Scenic Byway

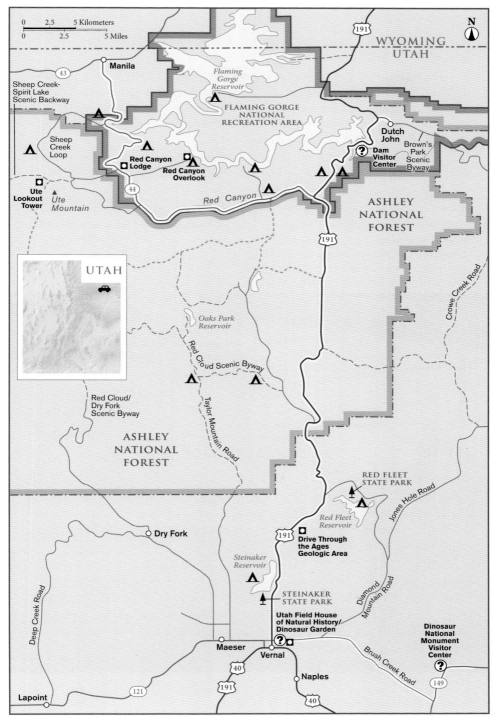

0   2.5   5 Kilometers

0   2.5   5 Miles

N

WYOMING
UTAH

Manila

Flaming
Gorge
Reservoir

Sheep Creek-
Spirit Lake
Scenic Backway

Dutch
John

FLAMING GORGE
NATIONAL
RECREATION AREA

Brown's
Park
Scenic
Byway

Dam
Visitor
Center

Sheep
Creek
Loop

Red Canyon
Lodge

Red Canyon
Overlook

Ute
Lookout
Tower

Ute
Mountain

Red   Canyon

ASHLEY
NATIONAL
FOREST

191

Crowe Creek Road

UTAH

Oaks Park
Reservoir

Red Cloud Scenic Byway

Red Cloud/
Dry Fork
Scenic Byway

Taylor Mountain Road

ASHLEY
NATIONAL
FOREST

RED FLEET
STATE PARK

Jones Hole Road

Red Fleet
Reservoir

Dry Fork

191

Drive Through
the Ages
Geologic Area

Diamond Mountain Road

Deep Creek Road

Steinaker
Reservoir

STEINAKER
STATE PARK

Utah Field House
of Natural History/
Dinosaur Garden

Maeser

Vernal

Brush Creek Road

Dinosaur
National
Monument
Visitor
Center

149

40

Naples

Lapoint

121

191

40

visitors two information centers, more than 600 camping and picnic sites, and more than 100 miles of trails.

The official state-designated **Flaming Gorge Scenic Byway** runs from Vernal north on US 191 to Greendale Junction, then takes the left (west) branch (Highway 44) to Manila. I've added a recommended side trip of the eastern branch, continuing north on US 191 to Dutch John, and an especially recommended drive along the **Sheep Creek Geological Loop.**

This is a long drive, at least **150 miles** as a round-trip from Vernal, with many options for interesting side trips, many described in detailed brochures you'll see at tourist-oriented spots all over town. This is really scenic driving country. With stops to enjoy the scenery, count on at least 5 hours to complete the drive, far more if you want to explore Dinosaur National Monument, which alone is worth a full day or more.

The quarry at Dinosaur National Monument encloses a collection of about 1,500 dinosaur bones as well as informative displays.

There are options for finishing this drive, depending on whether you want to return to Vernal. All main roads along this drive are paved, in excellent condition, and appropriate for all vehicles; traffic is generally light. Snow can be a problem in the winter, though the main road is kept clear year-round. Ask about current back-road conditions and routes at the **Ashley National Forest office,** 355 North Vernal Ave. in Vernal.

Dinosaurs Aplenty

Begin this drive in **Vernal,** the dinosaur capital of the world and a town with a distinct "on the edge of civilization as we know it" atmosphere. Few cities in America developed as late in our social history as Vernal did, or remained so isolated. This was still a pioneer outpost until well into the 20th century, partly because there was very little early LDS interest in settling the region, due to an unfavorable report by an exploration party sent forth by Brigham Young in 1861. These days, it rides the boom-and-bust cycle of oil and gas extraction, with attendant businesses everywhere and trucks constantly rumbling through town.

Opened in 2004, the new **Utah Field House of Natural History** interprets the region's historical, pre-history, ecological, and geological diversity. A mural showing the geological features of the Uinta region, from the Precambrian (2.7 billion years old) to the Pleistocene (11,000 years old) is especially useful in understanding the foundations of the drive through Flaming Gorge. The neighboring **Dinosaur Gardens** display 14 life-size statues of the region's ancient inhabitants (including a 90-foot diplodocus and 18-foot-tall tyrannosaurus), all in an outdoor setting of native rock and foliage. Don't miss these two educational and entertaining attractions.

Now that you're in the mood for dinosaurs, it would be a shame to drive all the way out to Vernal and *not* visit **Dinosaur National Monument.** One of the world's greatest prehistoric boneyards, it also boasts scenic drives of its own. This highly recommended side trip begins in **Jensen,** 12 miles east of Vernal via US 40 or Brush Creek Road (500 North in Vernal). Drive 4 miles north on Utah Highway 149 from the middle of Jensen to the entrance to the national monument and another 2 miles to the visitor center. From there, a shuttle carries visitors from a large lot near the park entrance to a real dinosaur bone quarry with helpful exhibits explaining the 1,500 bones found here.

At the visitor center you can pick up a handy self-guided-tour brochure for the highly recommended 10-mile **"Tour of the Tilted Rocks."** It leaves the visitor center and leads to hiking trails, rock formations, massive Fremont-style petroglyphs and pictographs, excellent views of the Green River, and the **Josie Bassett cabin** built by one of the area's most notorious cowgirls. Josie and her sister, Ann,

A replica of a giant woolly mammoth peers through a window into the Utah Field House of Natural History.

were friendly with Butch Cassidy's Wild Bunch boys, who used this remote place as a stopping-over point on the Outlaw Trail.

Most of the **Harpers Corner scenic drive,** on the east end of the monument, is in Colorado; its trails, old cabins, and overlooks are also worthwhile if you have the time. Note that there are no services at the monument, so be sure to grab fuel and snacks before you go.

Another recommended side trip from Vernal is the **Jones Hole Scenic Backway.** The drive traverses a variety of local ecosystems, from desert sagebrush to alpine aspen grove, before dropping into a narrow canyon at **Jones Hole,** where an important national fish hatchery supplies trout for Utah, Colorado, and Wyoming. This is one of the few fully paved scenic backways in the state. The road is narrow, however, and may be difficult in winter conditions. The backway starts 4 miles east of Vernal, departing from Diamond Mountain Road. The 80-mile (round-trip) drive takes at least 2 hours, plus time for sightseeing.

The regional travel office in Vernal can give you very nice brochures describing this drive and others in the region.

Beautiful Recreation

Flaming Gorge National Recreation Area is about 41 miles north of Vernal. Head north on Vernal Avenue (US 191), and just beyond the outskirts of town (about 3.5 miles from the town center) you will see on the right a small information board for **"Drive Through the Ages Geological Tour."** Stop to read the short route description and pick up the brochure about the signed geological attractions that line the route; signs along the road indicate when you pass from one formation to another.

Just past this board you will pass four blue/white geological information signs in rapid succession, the first of many. Soon on the left is the very attractive **Steinaker Reservoir.** The landscape is still sage-covered here, but toward the north end of the lake it becomes wooded. Near this end of the lake, another sign indicates a Jurassic Morrison formation—the **graveyard of the dinosaurs** for which Vernal is famous. The road is remarkably well marked with geological info signs nearly every 100 yards.

Steinaker State Park (with camping and hiking) lies at the north end of the reservoir. About 4 miles past the reservoir is a sign on the right for **Red Fleet State Park,** which has especially nice hiking trails and camping. Just north of the reservoir, a short paved road on the right takes you to a pull-out marking the start of a fun 2.5-mile hike to dinosaur tracks on the lake's sandstone shore—and you can jump in the lake to cool off.

US 191 continues to climb, with a handful of pull-outs offering views of jagged escarpments off in the distance. Fourteen miles north of Vernal, on the left, is the turnoff onto FR 018, the unpaved **Red Cloud/Dry Fork Scenic Backway,** also signed for East Park Reservoir. Four miles along FR 018, the route forks: The right fork goes north to **East Park Reservoir** (with nice secluded camping), the left fork is the backway drive to **Dry Fork.** This is a lovely forest and mountain drive on one of the few roads that provide access to the lower part of the Uinta Mountains. Driving conditions on this backway vary greatly, from paved to quite rough. Check for current conditions in Vernal, especially if you're not in a high-clearance vehicle. Driving time for the 45-mile loop is about 2 hours.

At around mile 17 on US 191, the sagebrush flats turn to pinyon and juniper. A few miles farther and this has become an alpine drive, with aspen the predominant roadside tree. The Uintah/Daggett county line is the high point of this drive at 8,428 feet.

The road passes two nice national forest campgrounds, **Red Springs** and **Lodgepole,** then enters Flaming Gorge National Recreation Area at about 33 miles north of Vernal. A mile and a half farther is the intersection at Greendale Junction; right is the continuation of US 191 to Flaming Gorge Dam and the town of Dutch John. We'll go straight here, designated Highway 44 and signed for Manila.

About 3 miles past this intersection is the turnoff on the right for **Red Canyon Overlook** and **Red Canyon Recreation Complex.** One mile up the overlook road is **Red Canyon Lodge,** where you will find a restaurant, cabins, groceries, gas, fishing, horseback rides, a gift shop, and a kids' fishing pond. Also up this road are 2 campgrounds, a visitor center, and picnic area. It is 3 miles to the overlook.

Red Canyon Overlook presents probably the most spectacular view of Flaming Gorge Reservoir. From this elevation, 1,700 feet above the reservoir, the water appears in deepest hues of blues and greens. And that 1,700 feet is straight down, with the cliffs below the overlook almost perfectly vertical.

It is about 12 miles of forest driving to the south end of the Sheep Creek Canyon loop, just past **Deep Creek Campground,** on the left. This recommended side trip is described on the return from Manila, but if you intend not to return this way, you might want to do the loop from here, reversing the direction of the description. One reason for not doing the Sheep Creek Canyon loop on your way north is that it means missing the great view from the turnout and overlook about 2 miles farther north on Highway 44, just at the start of the long descent to Manila. Or you can just dash out to the overlook and backtrack to do the loop.

Manila & Dutch John

Tiny **Manila** is the county seat and largest community of Daggett County; Dutch John is the only other "town" in a county that probably has a larger population of bears than people. The official state census for the county is 950 (but that probably includes the bears). Small as it is, Manila still provides most basic traveler services.

From Manila you can do a big windblown loop north through Wyoming to the town of Green River (Highway 43 becomes Wyoming Highway 530), then back down US 191 along the east side of Flaming Gorge. Or you can double back from here to the Sheep Creek Canyon Geological Drive and Greendale Junction. Another option to consider is to head west on Highway 43 (this soon becomes WY 414) on good roads across the northeast flank of the Uintas to reach I-80 at Fort Bridger, Wyoming. This is the quickest route back to Salt Lake City (a little more than 3 hours from here) along flat, high desert farmland.

Retracing Highway 44 south from Manila, it is just under 6 miles to the northern entrance, on the right, to the **Sheep Creek Canyon Geological Drive.** This 15-mile side trip (one-half to 1 hour) is highly recommended. The road is almost entirely paved, though not in great condition. It should be fine for all but the longest rigs. There are several campgrounds and picnic areas along the way, including a very attractive campground immediately on entering the loop road. Two miles up Sheep Creek Road, on the hill to the right, is the burial site for Cleophas Dowd (1857–97), who homesteaded here from 1885 until 1897, when he was killed by his associate, Charles Reaser. Two of his children are also buried here.

At mile 3, just past Sheep Creek Ranch (where you may see llamas grazing), you enter the **Sheep Creek Geological Area.** Sheep Creek Canyon was split by the Uinta Crest Fault, which exposed 18 distinct layers of strata. All along this drive are nice markers describing the stunning geological formations. Along the fault line, spikes and wavy layers of rock jut up from the canyon floor.

This is a really stunning canyon, with outstanding formations. As you gaze at them, look for the Rocky Mountain bighorn sheep that frequent the canyon. Just past mile 6 the road climbs out of the canyon (nothing radical) and leaves the official geological area. The road has turned into a very nice alpine drive.

At just under mile 10 is the turnoff for **Ute Tower Fire Lookout** (signed FR 221 for Spirit Lake and Brown Lake), the last of its kind in Utah. To get to the lookout, turn right, then a quick right again at the signposts. Follow FR 221 a little more than 1 mile to FR 5 on the left. It is about 1.5 mile of rough unpaved road up FR 5 to the tower, which is open to the public on Fri and Sat in summer. Built as a Civilian Conservation Corps project, it is still in service during fire season. There are no public facilities and no water.

At mile 13 you return to Highway 44, turning right/south. It is about 14 miles from the south entrance of the loop to the intersection with US 191, where you will turn left/north for Flaming Gorge Dam and Dutch John. This road is sometimes closed in winter.

Dam Tours

Whether you are interested in visiting the dam or not, you should at least drive up to see the **Swett Ranch.** Oscar Swett homesteaded this land in 1909 and developed the ranch over the next 58 years. Swett sold the ranch in 1968, and the Forest Service bought it in 1972, preserving it as an example of a traditional Utah family ranch. Half a mile north on US 191 is the turnoff on the left for Swett Ranch. The ranch is 1.25 mile up this reasonable dirt road, which may not be suitable for large RVs and trailers. Swett Ranch is open 10 a.m. until 5 p.m. daily from Memorial Day to Labor Day.

It's a little more than 5 miles farther along US 191 to the visitor center at **Flaming Gorge Dam.** "Dam tour guides" lead groups into the dam and power plant, beginning with an elevator descent to the riverbed. The visitor center is open 9 a.m. to 5 p.m., and short tours are given daily mid-Apr through mid-Oct.

If you have time, it is worth the effort to continue this drive about 12 miles out to the viewpoint beyond Antelope Flat, where you will get a sense of how John Wesley Powell must have felt in describing his first impression of the gorge: "The river enters the range by a flaring, brilliant red gorge that may be seen from the north a score of miles away." The gorge really can appear to glow red from down here, due largely to its composition of red quartzites and red shale.

The town of **Dutch John,** about 3 miles beyond the dam, was built in 1957 to accommodate workers at the dam. Today it is a strictly practical commercial center of fair usefulness but little touristic interest. About 2.5 miles past Dutch John, watch for the turnoff on the left for Antelope Flat. From the top of this eastern branch of the Flaming Gorge drive, it is possible to continue on US 191 north to Green River, Wyoming, and quick I-80 returns (another 3 hours on interstate) to Salt Lake City.

For a more adventuresome return to Vernal, the partly paved **Browns Park Scenic Backway** leaves US 191 about 10 miles north of Dutch John and runs east and south to join the paved Jones Hole Road. This route passes through some of the finest scenery in northeastern Utah and near a handful of significant wildlife areas and gives a glimpse of the region's pioneer era at such historic sites as the **Jarvie Ranch.** The 55-mile backway, suitable for most cars in dry conditions, requires at least 2 hours. Inquire first at a Forest Service office in Vernal or Dutch John and pick up a driving-tour brochure.

Red Canyon Overlook provides perhaps the most spectacular views of Flaming Gorge Reservoir.

21

Mirror Lake Scenic Byway

Kamas to the Wyoming Line

General Description: It's 65 miles of the most pristine alpine country to be seen from any paved highway in the country.

Special Attractions: Mountain lakes and meadows, superb views, wildlife, camping, hiking, fishing.

Location: Northern Utah. The byway runs between Kamas and the national forest boundary, just south of the Wyoming state line.

Drive Route Number & Name: Highway 150, Mirror Lake Scenic Byway.

Travel Season: Varies, depending on early snowfall and late snowpack. The highest part of the road can remain closed until early July. By early October it is likely to close with any good storm.

Camping: There are 24 national forest campgrounds and ample opportunity for primitive camping.

Services: All services in Heber City and Evanston, Wyoming; basic services in Kamas; no services along the route.

Nearby Attractions: Broadhead Meadow Scenic Backway, North Slope Scenic Backway.

The Drive

This is one of the most spectacular mountain drives in the West. Here you can explore the largest east–west trending range in the Western Hemisphere. The **Mirror Lake Scenic Byway** is one of only two highways that penetrate Uinta Mountain range enough to give an idea of just how grandly deserted this region is (the other is the west branch of the Flaming Gorge Byway, Drive 20).

Without their yearlong snow mantle, the **Uintas** would not be particularly attractive peaks. They are hardly "Alp-like," being much broader, and they lack the elegant, steep summits and sharp ridgelines of, say, the Tetons to the north. But the Uintas form a proper wilderness, barely penetrated by roads of any sort. On the Mirror Lake Scenic Byway you will come face to face with Nature, and you may feel rather in awe of the power of untamed places—as you should. Hikers get lost every year in this rugged terrain; always come well prepared with food, water, and extra clothing if you want to hike here, and tell someone where you're headed.

Trailheads along the Mirror Lake road lead to some of the best alpine hikes and backpacking trails in America. There are also more than two dozen designated campgrounds and many picnic areas just off the byway. A $6 fee, collected at either end of the byway, helps pay for maintenance of these much-loved amenities and is good for up to three days. For really detailed information on trails,

Mirror Lake Scenic Byway

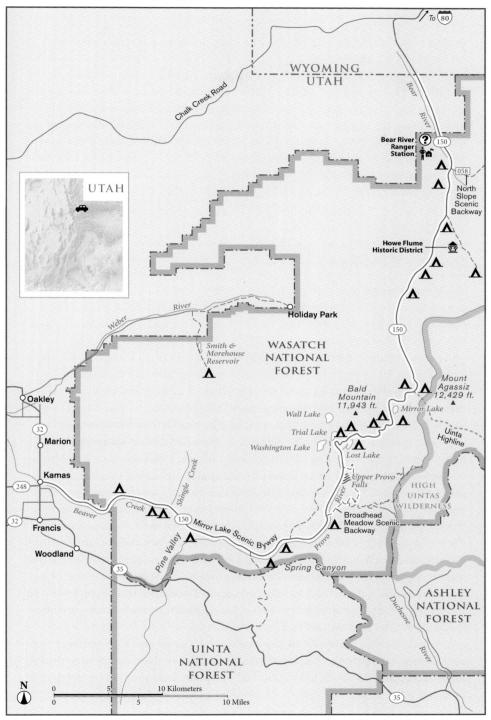

campgrounds, and other recreational opportunities, stop at the Forest Service information office in Kamas.

The Mirror Lake Scenic Byway is entirely paved, with numerous turnouts, and it's drivable in any size vehicle. Traffic is usually moderate midweek, heavy on weekends. This is a great drive for families, with many picnic spots and short hikes making for an easy introduction to the natural world. It has been known to snow (hard) in the middle of summer at 10,687-foot **Bald Mountain Pass,** and the weather can be extremely unpredictable at any time; be prepared for emergencies, and be sure to bring along warm clothing. September is a beautiful time for this drive, with generally clear, cool days and cold nights. This byway is generally closed from mid-October until May, though exact dates depend entirely on snowfall.

Gaining Elevation

The drive begins in the pleasant mountain ranching village of **Kamas.** To reach Kamas from Salt Lake City, take I-80 east to the US 40 (Heber City) exit, then watch for Highway 248 on the left, 5 miles south of the interstate. Kamas is about 8 miles from the intersection.

East of where it intersects with Main Street, at the only real intersection in town, Center Street becomes Highway 150. The Forest Service office is just after you turn onto Highway 150, about half a block on the right. From here it is 32 miles to Mirror Lake and 72 miles to Evanston, Wyoming.

It is 2.5 miles from the outskirts of Kamas to **Kamas Fish Hatchery** on the right and another 2.8 miles to the entrance to **Wasatch-Cache National Forest.** A rapid succession of campgrounds lies just inside the boundary. At **Shingle Creek Campground** the byway leaves Beaver Creek and climbs steadily, crossing the North Fork of the Provo River. Picnic areas, overlooks, and campgrounds line the road.

A little more than 8 miles beyond Shingle Creek, on the right, is a pull-out at the west portal of the **Duchesne Tunnel.** The 6-mile tunnel, completed in 1952, diverts 600 cubic feet of water per second from the east-flowing Duchesne River, augmenting the flow that irrigates the valleys behind the Wasatch Front. This is the first real indication of just how important the Uintas are in supplying water to the region. Four major rivers—the Weber, Bear, Duchesne, and Provo—originate in small mountain lakes in this corner of the Uintas.

Watch next for **Slate Gorge Overlook** about 5 miles past the Duchesne Tunnel. A short trail leads to a view of a 20-foot waterfall in a narrow canyon created from overlapping layers of billion-year-old Precambrian shale (shale is not exactly slate, but pretty close).

Near the overlook is the turnoff on the right for the **Broadhead Meadow Scenic Backway.** This unsurfaced and rocky road branches off to the left (north) from the unpaved Murdock Basin Road about a mile in and then ties back into Highway 150 just south of **Upper Provo Falls.** The route loops for 4.5 miles through lodgepole pine forests and past an alpine meadow through which runs a crystal-clear trout stream. Near the start of this route you can see a new forest regenerating after a large fire in 1980. This very scenic but rough drive is recommended for high-clearance vehicles only.

Be sure to stop at the **Provo River Falls Overlook** and to hike the short trails down to see the lower falls; it's about 100 yards on well-maintained trail. The falls—actually a series of pretty falls—are about 0.5 mile after the signs indicating the Provo River crossing and the Upper Provo Bridge campground on the right. This makes a wonderful picnic spot.

The byway continues to climb into a beautiful alpine world of glacial tarns and lovely meadows beyond the upper limit of the forest. You are now near the top of the Mirror Lake Byway and in one of Utah's finest outdoor recreation areas. Hiking and bicycling trails wind across the ridges, and high mountain trout lakes are scattered throughout this cool, breezy tundra.

Uinta Wilderness

It is 2.5 miles from Provo Falls Overlook to Lily Lake Campground, then 2.5 more miles of ascent from Lily Lake to 10,678-foot **Bald Mountain Pass,** the high point of this drive. Be sure to stop at the **Bald Mountain Overlook** just below the pass. The 11,947-foot Bald Mountain is only a bit more than 1,000 feet higher than the road. Views out over the surrounding river valleys toward the distant mountains of the Wasatch Range are even more striking. The 2-mile **Bald Mountain Trail** leads from the pass to the summit of Bald Mountain, where the views are terrific. Bring a jacket—it's cold up there!

On the north-side descent from the pass, it's 0.75 mile to **Hayden Peak Overlook.** A bit farther along, **Mirror Lake, Moosehorn,** and **Butterfly Campgrounds** (all higher than 10,000 feet) are the highest-elevation campgrounds on this drive. Mirror Lake is especially attractive, shaded by fir trees in a beautiful meadow. Pass Lake is 0.25 mile north of the Mirror Lake turnoff. From Pass Lake, the road winds up for a few miles to its final high point, 10,347-foot **Hayden Pass,** before descending on the north side of the range. From Hayden Pass there is a nice, mostly flat 1.5-mile (round-trip) trail to very pretty Ruth Lake. On the other side of the highway is an access point for the 78-mile **Uinta Highline Trail,** which stretches all the way from Mirror Lake to the Red Cloud/Dry Fork Scenic Byway near US 191 (described in Drive 20). Following the spine of the Uintas, it doesn't

Shepherds' old-fashioned outfits are sometimes parked in the foothills of the Uintas.

often drop below 10,000 feet in elevation. Just after crossing into Summit County, watch for the Forest Service sign on the right commemorating Richard Kletting, who helped to establish this forest reserve (Utah's first) in 1897.

The byway follows the **Hayden Fork** of the Bear River down through deep green spruce and fir forest. Watch for moose on the north slope of the Uintas, as this forest is home to the state's largest concentration of them. Other animals abound as well, and it would be unusual not to see wildlife along this drive. Short trail walks along the Hayden Fork are likely to yield animal sightings, especially in the late afternoon and early evening. Beaver are plentiful in this stream.

Bear River Ranger Station is open from the middle of May (though you will probably not reach it from the south that early) through October (closed Tues and Wed). The view back toward the south and east is especially fine early in the summer when the Uintas are still snow-covered.

Just north of the national forest boundary, on the right, is the turnoff for FR 058, the **North Slope Scenic Backway.** This extremely scenic drive strikes due east along the north slope of the Uinta Range, passing China Meadows to its end at **Stateline Reservoir.** A number of spurs branch off the main road and lead to Boy Scout campgrounds, summer homes, and old Forest Service guard stations. The main road passes many points of historical interest, including sites of tie-hack cabins. (Tie-hack workers cut logs for the Transcontinental Railroad, then built flumes to move the logs downstream. There's a rebuilt cabin at the Bear River

Ranger Station.) At the end of the backway, you will be as close to 13,528-foot **King's Peak** (Utah's highest) as you can get in a vehicle.

The 38-mile drive on partially improved dirt/gravel road involves a fair bit of ascent and descent and is impassable in any vehicle when wet. In good conditions, it is possible to use this route (continuing north from Stateline Reservoir) to reach Fort Bridger, Wyoming. Check at Bear River Station for current road conditions and a detailed description of this sometimes rough but very worthwhile drive.

The national forest boundary is the official end of the Mirror Lake Scenic Byway; the drive north leaves the forest and continues across high prairie and ranchland. If you loved the drive, you might consider retracing your route. Otherwise, the quickest route back to the Salt Lake Valley from here is via Evanston, Wyoming, on I-80. The Wyoming state line is 6 miles north of the forest boundary; it's 23 miles farther to Evanston. Evanston has all services.

22

Touring Timpanogos

Provo to Heber City, via the Alpine Loop

General Description: A 32-mile alpine canyon drive, with attractive branch drives to Cascade Springs and Timpanogos Cave.

Special Attractions: Bridal Veil Falls, Heber Creeper Railroad, Sundance Mountain Resort, spectacular views of Mount Timpanogos, Timpanogos Cave National Monument, Cascade Springs, autumn colors on the Alpine Loop Scenic Backway.

Location: North-central Utah.

Drive Route Numbers & Names: US 189, Provo Canyon Scenic Byway, Highway 92, Alpine Scenic Loop Backway, FR 114, Cascade Springs Scenic Backway.

Travel Season: Provo Canyon is open year-round; the Alpine Scenic Loop and Cascade Springs roads are usually closed by snow from late October until late May.

Camping: Two state park campgrounds, numerous national forest campgrounds in American Fork Canyon, two national forest campgrounds in Provo Canyon, commercial campgrounds at Provo, Heber City, and Midway.

Services: All services in Provo and Heber City; limited services in American Fork.

Nearby Attractions: Camp Floyd and Pony Express Trail, Utah Lake and Provo attractions, Park City and Deer Valley resorts, Mount Nebo and Mirror Lake scenic drives.

The Drive

This drive combines the **Provo Canyon Scenic Byway** with two beautiful scenic backways: the **Alpine Scenic Loop** and the **Cascade Springs Scenic Backway.** Taken together, these three short drives offer an extended look at the lovely alpine landscape and forests blanketing the foot of rugged Mount Timpanogos.

The 32-mile Provo Canyon Scenic Byway links Utah Valley with the higher alpine valley around Heber City. The byway follows US 189 along the Provo River in craggy Provo Canyon, past the famous Bridal Veil Falls, and through lovely trout-fishing flats on its way to Deer Creek Reservoir at the lower end of the Heber Valley.

The 20-mile Alpine Loop Scenic Backway runs between the Provo Canyon Scenic Byway and the mouth of **American Fork Canyon,** just below **Timpanogos Cave National Monument.** This paved (but steep and narrow) road presents outstanding views of 11,750-foot **Mount Timpanogos** and is a popular autumn colors drive. A paved branch road from the Alpine Loop leads to the limestone terraces and pools at Cascade Springs, then continues (unpaved) down to the Heber Valley.

Touring Timpanogos

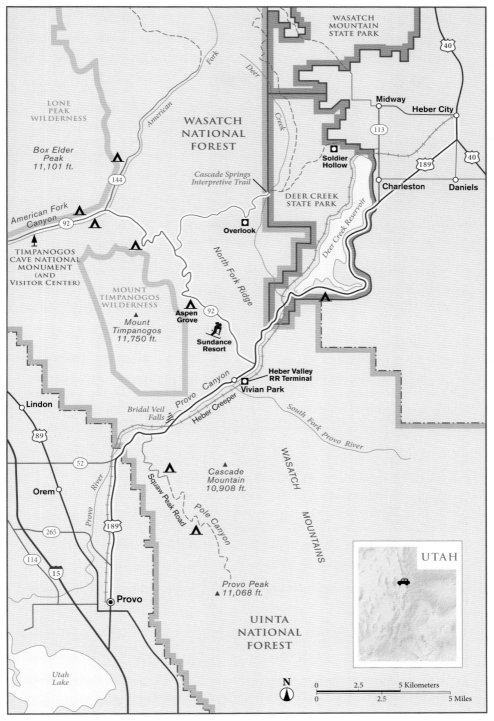

WASATCH MOUNTAIN STATE PARK

LONE PEAK WILDERNESS

Box Elder Peak 11,101 ft.

WASATCH NATIONAL FOREST

American Fork

Deer

Creek

Midway

Heber City

144

113

Soldier Hollow

40

40

189

American Fork Canyon

92

Cascade Springs Interpretive Trail

DEER CREEK STATE PARK

Charleston

Daniels

TIMPANOGOS CAVE NATIONAL MONUMENT (AND VISITOR CENTER)

Overlook

North Fork Ridge

Deer Creek Reservoir

MOUNT TIMPANOGOS WILDERNESS

Mount Timpanogos 11,750 ft.

Aspen Grove

92

Sundance Resort

Heber Valley RR Terminal

Vivian Park

Provo Canyon

Lindon

Bridal Veil Falls

Heber Creeper

South Fork Provo River

WASATCH

89

52

Provo River

Squaw Peak Road

Cascade Mountain 10,908 ft.

MOUNTAINS

Orem

265

189

Pole Canyon

114

15

Provo Peak 11,068 ft.

Provo

UINTA NATIONAL FOREST

UTAH

Utah Lake

N

0   2.5   5 Kilometers

0   2.5   5 Miles

Trails lead all the way to the top of Timpanogos (at upper left), one of the tallest of the Wasatch Mountains.

As might be expected of a drive with such complexity and diversity, there are a number of alternatives from which to choose, depending on your interests, your vehicle, and your time constraints. The entire Alpine Loop/Cascade Springs segment of this drive may be closed by snows from October until late May, and these narrow, steep, twisting roads are impractical for vehicles longer than 30 feet (trailers are not allowed on these roads), so wintertime travelers and drivers of large rigs will be limited to the Provo Canyon section.

A recommended route: Ascend the lower part of Provo Canyon, take the Alpine Loop Road past Sundance, drop down to Timpanogos Cave, then back over to Cascade Springs and down to Heber. For a round trip, descend back down Provo Canyon. Provo Canyon (US 189 past the Highway 92 turnoff) is scenic enough, though certainly not as scenic as the Alpine Loop side trip.

Provo

This drive begins at the mouth of Provo Canyon at the northeast edge of Provo's sprawl. **Provo** is Utah's third largest city (after Salt Lake City and West Valley City) and the central community in Utah's second-largest metropolitan area. The attractive and fertile position between freshwater Utah Lake and the foot of the Wasatch Mountains was noted by the Dominguez-Escalante expedition in 1776. A

Drivers tend to stick to the middle of the Alpine Loop road, even on its many blind curves.

French-Canadian fur trapper, Etienne Provost, had a serious run-in with a party of Snake Indians 50 years later (eight of his men were killed) and moved on after first giving his name to the river that flows into Utah Lake.

When the Mormon pioneers made their way here in 1849 (just two years after establishing their first settlements in the Salt Lake Valley), they somehow passed over the names of sundry Book of Mormon prophets and church leaders in deciding on a shortened version of the fur trapper's name for the new community. Today Provo is best known as the home of **Brigham Young University,** which was founded as Brigham Young Academy (high-school level) in 1875. The current institution of more than 30,000 students is one of the nation's largest religiously affiliated universities.

University Avenue in Provo, which runs past Brigham Young University, is also US 189. Follow it north (signed for Heber City). As with other canyon drives along the Wasatch Front, you are in the mountains as soon as you enter the mouth of the canyon. The Timpanogos Utes used Provo Canyon as the route between their winter home around Utah Lake and their Heber Valley summer hunting grounds. This was also the route followed by the first Mormon settlers of the Heber area, who took a surprisingly long time to establish themselves in that beautiful alpine valley in 1858.

Provo Canyon is surprisingly pristine, considering how close it is to a major urban area. This is, however, a very popular pleasure drive as well as a significant commuter corridor (as evidenced by the interstate-width pavement through much of it), so expect a fair amount of traffic.

A very small national forest campground, **Hope Campground,** is about 5 miles up Squaw Peak Road (paved), 1.25 miles past the mouth of the canyon, on the right. At about mile 3 on US 189 is the turnoff on the right for the **Bridal Veil Falls** parking lot, trails, and base facilities. The beautiful falls cascade 600 feet in two large steps. Until 1996, a tramway, said to be the steepest in the world, climbed 1,228 vertical feet to a ledge overlook just above the falls. In January 1996, a massive avalanche tumbled all the way to the other side of the canyon and wiped out the tram's base station. Now the remains of the restaurant at the top are only visited by intrepid climbers, including ice climbers who flock to the frozen falls in winter. If you just want to view the falls, an excellent viewpoint about 0.25 mile farther along on the right gives a better look than from the base.

Two and a half miles beyond the falls is **Vivian Park,** a very popular picnic and fishing spot that is also the southern terminus for the "Heber Creeper" Railroad, properly called the **Heber Valley Railroad.** The original version of this line, the Utah Eastern Railway, ran between Heber City and Provo from 1899 until the 1960s. It got its nickname from the slow pull up Provo Canyon. Today it runs as a scenic tourist attraction, with vintage railway coaches pulled by an authentic 1904 steam locomotive. There are usually at least two runs per day (Tues through Sat) from Mother's Day through Oct, with Christmas-themed rides in Dec. The 3-hour journey winds up Provo Canyon and around the west edge of Deer Creek Reservoir to Heber; you can buy tickets and board the train at Vivian Park. For schedule information see hebervalleyrr.org.

Redford's Resort

About a mile beyond the park is the turnoff on the left for Highway 92, clearly marked for Sundance. This is the start of the highly recommended **Alpine Scenic Loop Backway.** The continuation from here of the Provo Canyon Scenic Byway, east on US 189, is certainly scenic but offers little of extraordinary interest. The rest of Provo Canyon continues as an alpine canyon drive to **Deer Creek Reservoir,** where the landscape turns into high sagebrush flat—no trees, just rolling hills and grass until Heber City. The state park at Deer Creek offers a modern campground (with showers). Deer Creek and nearby Jordanelle Reservoirs are important recreational resources but uninspiring as scenic attractions.

The Alpine Scenic Loop Backway (Highway 92) is entirely paved but too steep and too narrow for large RVs; trailers are not permitted on this road. The Alpine

Scenic Loop and Cascade Springs roads are usually closed by snow above Sundance Resort from late October until late May.

At mile 2.2 is the turnoff for the **Sundance Mountain Resort** parking. Sundance is one of Robert Redford's pet projects, a combination of environmentally responsible mountain resort development and an institute for advancement of the cinematic and other arts. It's a pleasant place to stop for lunch or a summer ski-lift ride (return via lift, hike, or mountain bike). There are nice views of Mount Timpanogos from here, but they get more dramatic as the road climbs past Sundance development.

A little more than 2.5 miles past Sundance you will encounter more development in the form of a BYU alumni campground and the nearby trailhead for some of the popular Timpanogos hikes, including the grueling but highly rewarding all-day (or overnight) 14-mile summit hike, which gains 4,500 feet in elevation. You also enter **Uinta National Forest** here; there's a $6 use fee for the national forest, good for three days. The road becomes increasingly narrow as it winds up through lovely groves of aspen and pine. Do not park your vehicle along this road except at the designated pull-outs (which are numerous), as some do. Also, be aware that many drivers here seem determined to drive down the center of the narrow road, even in the face of oncoming traffic. Given the lack of a shoulder and the steep dropoffs, this can be disconcerting.

At mile 6.2 from Sundance is the turnoff for Cascade Springs (described on return); about 0.25 mile farther along is a large pull-out/parking area at the high point of the Alpine Loop Drive, a popular start point for hikes and mountain bike rides. At this point you must decide whether you will descend American Fork Canyon to Timpanogos Cave National Monument or head to Cascade Springs.

Cave Sights

From here it is a long descent into **American Fork Canyon.** This road winds down—much like on the uphill side—for about 5.5 miles to the canyon bottom, passing numerous roadside cascades. In the wooded canyon bottom, there are nice campgrounds and picnic spots for about 2 miles along the American Fork River. It is 2.5 miles from here to **Timpanogos Cave National Monument.**

At Timpanogos, three limestone caves display an impressive variety of stalagmites, stalactites, draperies, flowstones, and helictites, sometimes reflected in clear cavern pools. The first of these caves was discovered in 1887 by a rancher from nearby American Fork who, according to local legend, was tracking a mountain lion across ledges high on the south slope of the canyon.

Depending on snow conditions in the canyon, the caves are usually open from mid-May through September. The number of visitors to the caves is limited and restricted to scheduled tours. If you want to do the tour, go to recreation .gov in advance to reserve a spot with a credit card. Otherwise, get there early and go immediately to the ticket window to reserve your spot. Tours for the day are often sold out by noon during the summer. You do not ascend to the caves until just before your designated tour time, which might be hours from the time of your ticket purchase. So, if you want to tour the caves, come here before stopping for your picnic lunch. There is a fine nature trail on the opposite slope of the canyon—a good way to kill some waiting time.

It is a paved but very steep 1.5-mile hike to the caves from the visitor center/ ticket office—give yourself plenty of time, especially if you're not used to this altitude. The 0.5-mile tour through the caverns lasts about an hour, so count on at least 3 hours for the round-trip. Read through the detailed informational brochure prior to starting up to the caves.

It is 3 miles farther to the mouth of American Fork Canyon. Unless you are bailing out on this drive and want to get back to the Salt Lake/Provo areas, you may as well turn around at the cave; if you are not interested in the cave, there is really no reason to descend on the American Fork side of the pass (except for the better picnic sites and abundant camping along the stream on this side).

Watering Holes

Return to the high point of the Alpine Loop and FR 114 on the left, the road to Cascade Springs. This paved backway begins with a 2.5-mile descent from the Alpine Loop, then climbs for a mile before starting a long descent with open views off to the south and east. Timpanogos and Mount Nebo loom grandly, and the mountainsides blaze with color in the fall. The **Deer Creek Overlook** allows you to enjoy what are really the first "open" vistas along this drive.

At mile 6.8 you reach **Cascade Springs,** a good place to get out and stretch your legs. An easy 0.5-mile boardwalk-and-asphalt path loops through the springs. Self-guided nature walks feature lots of plaques describing the marsh grasses, birds, water flow, and the way the land is altered by water. This is an especially nice site for kids: They can get out on these nature trails and actually learn some things about the effects of water.

Beyond Cascade Springs the road goes through to the Heber Valley, if you do not want to return to Provo Canyon. Although the first 0.75 mile of this gravel road is rather steep switchbacks and might be a tad rough, it is fine for family sedans and pickups or campers provided it is dry and you are not too heavily loaded. Remember to go slowly and avoid hitting your brakes, if possible, on the loose gravel—it's a long way down, with no guardrails. If conditions are poor,

The road into the Heber Valley consists of switchbacks and loose gravel. Heed this sign or you might end up getting to the bottom much faster than anticipated.

you will know within the first mile whether you can make it; after that, it's all downhill.

The descent provides lovely views of the Heber Valley. After 1.5 miles you will catch a glimpse of **Deer Creek Reservoir,** and just past mile 5 you reach the farms of Midway. When you hit the T at the hard-surfaced road (mile 5.5), turn right. The road winds through attractive farmland and pastureland until it makes a left and hits Highway 113. Turn left here for Midway/Heber, right to return to Provo.

The well-watered **Heber Valley** is commonly referred to as "Utah's Switzerland," both for its dramatic alpine scenery and for the many Swiss immigrants who settled in Midway. The very useful information center is at the north end of Main Street (US 189/US 40).

The nearby old mining town of **Park City**, about 20 minutes north of Heber, has been thoroughly transformed into a popular year-round resort area. Once you have penetrated the dense perimeter of condo development, the charming remade Main Street offers glimpses of its mining past.

The quickest return to the Salt Lake Valley from Heber City is north for 19 miles on US 40 (Heber City's Main Street) to I-80, then 22 miles west.

West Desert Ramble

Fairfield to Tooele to Dugway to I-80

General Description: A 120-mile basin and range drive that reveals elements of Utah's mining, Pony Express, and Mormon history as well as the dramatic alpine terrain of the Deseret Peaks Wilderness Area and the forbidding desert wilderness of the Great Basin.

Special Attractions: Stagecoach Inn/ Camp Floyd, Mercur and Ophir mining camps, Deseret Peak Wilderness Area, Stansbury Mountains, Skull Valley, Great Basin views, Iosepa.

Location: North-central Utah, just west of Salt Lake City.

Drive Route Numbers & Names: Highways 73, 36, 112, and 199; Middle Canyon Scenic Backway; South Willow Canyon Scenic Backway.

Travel Season: Generally year-round, with much less to do in winter. Both backways are closed in winter, while drifting snow can sometimes be a problem throughout this drive.

Camping: Six national forest campgrounds on South Willow Creek Road, one BLM campground at Johnson Pass, primitive camping along some segments of the drive.

Services: All services at Tooele; most services at Grantsville; gas and food at Stockton.

Nearby Attractions: Pony Express Trail Scenic Backway, Bingham Mine, Great Basin drives, Great Salt Lake, Deseret Peak, Wendover, Bonneville Salt Flats.

The Drive

This 120-mile drive offers a combination of scenery and attractions designed to give an impression of the sparsely settled valleys on the edge of the Great Basin and to the immediate west of the Salt Lake Valley. The drive provides access to two recommended scenic backways, which are described as side trips: **Middle Canyon Scenic Backway** and **South Willow Canyon Scenic Backway.** Also accessible from this drive is the fascinating, if desolate, **Pony Express Trail Scenic Backway.**

Parts of this drive are almost "anti-scenic." The landscape south of Rush Valley and west of the Stansbury and Onaqui Mountains is harsh to the point of brutality but also dramatic in its ruggedness. This drive is a very good (and relatively easy) introduction to the Great Basin region as a day excursion from Salt Lake. It is perhaps appropriate that two short side trips from this drive offer glimpses of both copper and gold mining operations: Utah is still one of the nation's top producers of both.

There are several ways to begin and end this drive. The drive organized here, a full-day excursion from the Salt Lake Valley, is designed to take advantage of

West Desert Ramble

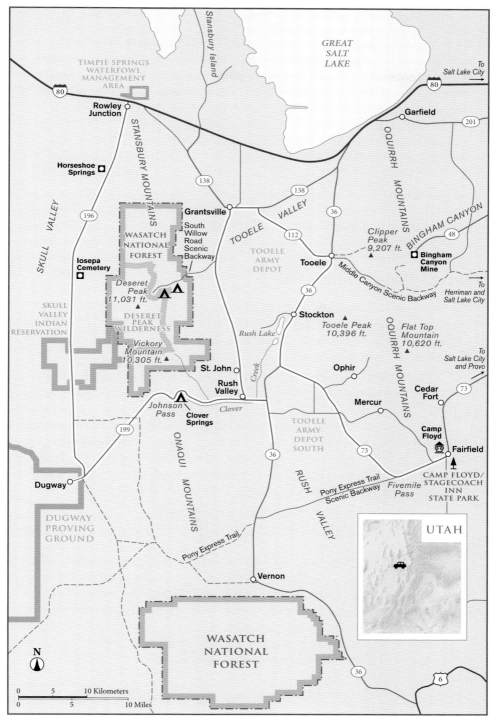

GREAT SALT LAKE

To Salt Lake City

TIMPIE SPRINGS WATERFOWL MANAGEMENT AREA

Stansbury Island

80

Rowley Junction

Garfield

201

Horseshoe Springs

STANSBURY MOUNTAINS

138

TOOELE VALLEY

138

36

196

Grantsville

South Willow Road Scenic Backway

112

OQUIRRH MOUNTAINS

BINGHAM CANYON

Clipper Peak 9,207 ft.

48

WASATCH NATIONAL FOREST

TOOELE ARMY DEPOT

Bingham Canyon Mine

SKULL VALLEY

Iosepa Cemetery

Tooele

Middle Canyon Scenic Backway

To Herriman and Salt Lake City

Deseret Peak 11,031 ft.

DESERET PEAK WILDERNESS

36

Stockton

Rush Lake

Tooele Peak 10,396 ft.

Flat Top Mountain 10,620 ft.

To Salt Lake City and Provo

SKULL VALLEY INDIAN RESERVATION

Vickory Mountain 10,305 ft.

St. John

Creek

Ophir

OQUIRRH MOUNTAINS

Cedar Fort

73

Rush Valley

Mercur

Johnson Pass

Clover Springs

Clover

199

ONAQUI MOUNTAINS

TOOELE ARMY DEPOT SOUTH

36

73

Camp Floyd

Fairfield

CAMP FLOYD/ STAGECOACH INN STATE PARK

Dugway

Pony Express Trail Scenic Backway

Fivemile Pass

RUSH VALLEY

DUGWAY PROVING GROUND

UTAH

Pony Express Trail

Vernon

WASATCH NATIONAL FOREST

36

6

N

0   5   10 Kilometers

0   5   10 Miles

the morning light on the east faces of **Deseret Peak Wilderness Area** peaks and afternoon/evening light on its west side. Shorter versions of this drive might start at either Tooele or Grantsville (accessed quickly via I-80 from Salt Lake) or might remain to the east of Deseret Peak with a possible return to Salt Lake over Middle Canyon Road. You could also connect to this drive from Drive 16 to the south.

All of the valley roads, and those up to Mercur and Ophir, are paved and suitable for all vehicles. Parts of the Middle Canyon and South Willow roads are unpaved and unsuitable for trailers, larger RVs, or low-slung cars. With few services along this route, it's a good idea to bring lots of water and possibly a backcountry water filter to take advantage of remote springs. The best source of information about unpaved roads, camping, and recreation anywhere in Utah's Great Basin is the BLM field office at 2370 South Decker Lake Blvd. in West Valley City, on the Salt Lake Valley's west side.

On the Pony Express Trail

The drive begins at **Fairfield,** reached easily from the second Lehi/Highway 73 exit on I-15, a short drive south of Salt Lake City. Before you reach Fairfield, you'll pass through the sprawling **Eagle Mountain** suburban development's big, boxy houses. As you drive west on Highway 73, you are following the old Overland Stage and Pony Express route and are at the start of what was generally considered one of the most dangerous and difficult sections of the long trail across the desert.

In 1858 General Albert Johnston arrived here with 3,500 federal troops out of government fears over a Mormon insurrection. Johnston established **Camp Floyd,** which was, at the time, the nation's largest single concentration of soldiers. The town of Fairfield grew prosperous on business generated by the troops, and it reportedly had 17 saloons. The combined population of town and camp was more than 7,000, making this the second largest community in the territory. The camp disbanded and the town depopulated in 1861 on the outbreak of Civil War hostilities back east.

The Central Overland Stage and the Pony Express had stops here, where John Carson built his popular inn. This inn has been restored as the centerpiece of a low-key historic site—it's open 9 a.m. to 5 p.m. Mon through Sat, and admission is $3 per person—that also includes the Camp Floyd cemetery. The adjacent park makes a nice picnic spot if you get a late start.

Continue west on Highway 73 to where a good paved road comes in on the left, well-marked as the **Pony Express Trail Scenic Backway.** Take this left to continue on the fascinating but desolate Pony Express trail. This backway runs through Faust, over Lookout Summit, to Simpson Springs and Fish Springs, then across Antelope Valley into Nevada. The first 15 miles or so, to Faust, are paved, followed by well-maintained gravel suitable for all vehicles in dry conditions.

The drive traces the Pony Express trail across western Utah, one of the roughest stretches on its entire 1,900-mile route. Along the way, **Fish Springs** is a true desert oasis, an 18,000-acre marshland rich in waterfowl and the nation's most remote National Wildlife Refuge. The Pony Express trail is a much-recommended side trip if you have the time (and lots of water and a full tank of gas—there are no services for quite a while). The BLM distributes a brochure describing historic sites en route, available at BLM offices in Salt Lake; it may also be found in Lehi or Fairfield, and the kindly folks staffing Camp Floyd may also have information on the route as well as road conditions.

Highway 73 west of Fairfield and south of Mercur gives a really good taste of Great Basin driving and a real sense of the immense desert expanses out here. The Oquirrh Mountains form the eastern boundary of Rush Valley, with the Stansbury and Onaqui Mountains on the west. Back and to the left is the rough, empty terrain crossed by the Pony Express; it is still essentially unchanged today. In early light, the east face of Deseret Peak is especially dramatic from east of the valley.

Highway 73 curves to the north just past the Pony Express turnoff, entering the well-watered Rush and Tooele Valleys. The proximity of these desert valleys to the original Mormon Salt Lake Valley settlement made this an early choice for satellite settlements. Mormons herded livestock here shortly after their 1847 arrival in Utah, permanently settling the Tooele Valley by 1849.

Mining History

About 9 miles from the Pony Express turnoff is the turn on the right for **Barrick/ Mercur Gold Mine.** Once Utah's leading producer of gold, the former strip-mining operation has now become a reclamation project.

Prospecting soldiers from Fort Douglas in Salt Lake City discovered rich silver ores in these canyons in the 1870s (Brigham Young forbade his followers from mining, which could lead to sin and discord, so early mining in Utah was done by soldiers and railroad workers). In 1879 a German prospector found gold in cinnabar, a form of mercury ore, and named his claim "Mercur." It was another 12 years before an effective chemical method was developed to extract gold from Mercur's ore, but by the turn of the century, this was a major boom town. Mercur's population was at a peak of about 6,000 when a fire destroyed most of the town in 1902. The mining at Mercur went into decline, the mill closed in 1914, and the place was a ghost town by 1917. There was a short-lived revival during the 1930s, but the Federal Mine Closure Act shut it all down again during World War II.

OPHIR
POST OFFICE

OPHIR UTAH

THIS ONE ROOM HOUSE WAS
LIVED IN BY MEN WHO WORKED AS
TEAMSTERS OR MINERS. WHEN IT
BECAME VACANT IN THE 1930'S IT
SERVED AS A CLUBHOUSE FOR
THE BOYS OF OPHIR. IT WAS
MOVED TO ITS PRESENT LOCATION
FROM MINERS STREET AND WAS
RESTORED TO REPRESENT THE
OPHIR POST OFFICE, WHICH HAD
BEEN TORN DOWN. THE POST
OFFICE BOX, WINDOW, AND DESK
ARE FROM THE ORIGINAL OPHIR
POST OFFICE.

2012   PLAQUE DONATED BY

The astronomical rise in gold prices during the 1970s created the latest rebirth of "the town that can't stay dead." But mining stopped for good in 1995. Displays at the **Oquirrh Mountain Mining Museum** in the **Deseret Peak Complex** on Highway 112 in Tooele give some sense of both Mercur's history and of the nature of modern gold processing—which makes a visit to the museum more rewarding than one to the vacant town site. The museum's hours are sporadic, but you can get someone at the complex's information booth to open it for you.

Just north of the Mercur road you get really excellent views of the **Tooele Army Depot,** and you may wonder, "Gee, what sort of nastiness goes on down there?" This is, indeed, a weapons storage and development depot, which makes the prospect of buying a lot with a view above this valley much less attractive. It is a little more than 4 miles to the road to Ophir, on the right. **Ophir** is a pleasant 3.75-mile diversion, a quiet community of summer homes (only a handful of people live here full-time). In the 1870s a silver mining boom put the population at nearly 6,000. Now, the town is a quaint combination of parks, old mining cabins, and other remnants of a bygone era. The historic district, complete with quite a few restored buildings from the old days, and surrounding hillsides are a great place for history buffs to explore; keep in mind much of those are private land.

Just north of the Ophir turnoff you will see **Rush Lake.** Like the Great Salt Lake, this lake has no surface outflow, draining solely by underground seepage and evaporation. In wet years, Rush Lake is very popular with sail boarders (in dry years, it barely exists at all). Highway 73 ends 4.5 miles north of the Ophir road at the intersection with Highway 36. A little more than 2.5 miles north of here, note on the left the marker topped with a red metallic pennant (nicely perforated with bullet holes). An early military camp was established here in 1854 by the first detachment of soldiers to enter the Rocky Mountain region. Access to Rush Lake is through tiny **Stockton** (with gas station and old-timey cafe), 4.5 miles north of the Highway 73/Highway 36 intersection.

Beckoning Backways

It is 10 miles from here to **Tooele,** a proper metropolis with its own sprawling suburbs. Tooele is the modern version of the old community at Fairfield, economically tied to the local military depot. The best suggestions for the source of the name Tooele is that it is a corrupt form of the name of an early Native American chief, Tuilla, or of the Spanish/Aztec word *tule,* for bullrush.

Tooele is also the starting point for **Middle Canyon Scenic Backway,** a nice mostly paved diversion. Drive north on Main Street to Vine Street, the

Visitors can tour preserved buildings in the old mining town of Ophir.

A steep drive (or hike) from the end of the maintained road in Middle Canyon leads to views into the giant Bingham Canyon Mine on the other side.

main east–west street in the heart of Tooele. (There may or may not be a sign for Middle Canyon Scenic Backway, so just watch for Vine Street.) Just as you turn right (east) on Vine, note the very attractive stone building on the left, built in 1867 as the **Tooele County Courthouse,** now the museum of the Daughters of Utah Pioneers. A few blocks farther along is the very interesting **Tooele County Museum.** Past the prominent Catholic Church on the right, the road winds up, out of town, and into wooded Middle Canyon. There is a $3 day use fee.

There are nice picnic spots on both sides of the road, and it is obvious this is where the Tooelites go to escape the valley heat. At about mile 5.5 the canyon opens up a bit, and this becomes an attractive mountain drive, still on good paved road. At mile 6.7 the hard surface ends; do not bring trailers or RVs beyond this point. The road beyond here has steep switchbacks, so inquire in Tooele about conditions. At mile 8.2 you reach the high point on this main road. On the left is a steep dirt road that goes up another 2.5 miles to one of the most spectacular views in all of Utah. From the viewpoint, the massive **Bingham Copper Pit** is right below, and across the valley is the Wasatch Front, with Salt Lake at its feet. From here you can see all the way north to Ogden and south to Provo and Mount Nebo.

On the east (Salt Lake) side of the pass, the gravel quickly becomes pavement descending **Butterfield Canyon** through forests (and about 7,553 Kennecott Copper Co. NO TRESPASSING signs). This road may or may not be open, so don't plan to use it unless you check in advance. Both it and Middle Canyon are closed in winter.

Deseret Peak Close Up

Back down in the Tooele Valley it is about 7 miles on Highway 112 from the northwest suburbs of Tooele to the intersection with Highway 138. Merge left here and Highway 138 becomes Main Street, **Grantsville,** whose small downtown has gas stations, a motel, a supermarket, and a **Donner-Reed pioneer museum**, only open on Saturday. The ill-fated Donner-Reed party was already a month behind schedule when it arrived here and was delayed further on the harsh desert trek to the Sierra Nevadas.

Given the lack of civilization for the next leg of this drive, it's a good idea to fuel up here, especially if you intend to explore the Pony Express Trail or otherwise go off-road. Continue west on Main Street right through town until West Street, on the left, well marked for Wasatch National Forest Recreation Sites, North Willow Canyon, and South Willow Canyon.

It is about 4 miles from Grantsville to **South Willow Creek Canyon Road,** a highly recommended backway that provides access to Deseret Peak, on the right. The road is narrow but partly paved and well maintained. It climbs gradually but steadily, with Willow Creek running far below and to the left. Soon you leave the scrubland behind and enter the pinyon/juniper forest. The road deteriorates after a few miles. It is also very narrow, and because of the surrounding vegetation, it is sometimes difficult to see other vehicles—of which there will not be many.

At just past mile 3 the pavement ends and you enter **Wasatch-Cache National Forest** on good graded gravel, passing **Cottonwood Campground** at mile 4 and **Intake Campground** 0.5 mile farther. Just past Intake is a seasonal ranger station; after that the road (still well maintained) begins to climb more steeply. This is about the limit for RVs and trailers unless you have good low gearing. At just past mile 5 you pass a Boy Scout campground, then the road proceeds through an impressive narrow cut in the limestone walls (not surprisingly, this spot is popular with climbers). The road gets rougher after this, though it's still fine for most passenger vehicles.

At around mile 6 you reach Lower and Upper Narrows campgrounds, then another narrow passage. From here the road climbs out of the canyon, the landscape becomes very alpine, and the views of Deseret Peak start getting really terrific. At mile 6.7 you reach **Loop Campground,** a nice place to stop; campsites are $15 a night. The road toward the end is rough but reasonable for anything but the largest RVs. It is definitely worth driving up here to experience one of the most pristine forests accessible by car. The road ends just after mile 7.

Uncrowded hiking trails above Loop Campground take you through gorgeous forest right to the snows of **Deseret Peak.** The 4-mile (each way) hike to the peak itself is arduous, gaining a whopping 3,500 feet en route, but many shorter branches will take you around its base. (If you happen to hear an occasional explosion, do not be alarmed; that will just be the folks down at the Tooele Army Depot blowing off their big firecrackers.)

Desolation & Dugway

Continue south on the main road (sometimes called Mormon Trail Road—you didn't think the Mormon Trail came this far west, did you?). Twelve miles south of the Willow Canyon road is the very spread-out community of **Rush Valley.** This road becomes Main Street, which doesn't look particularly "main." In fact, it looks no different than any of the other streets in this strictly residential community. There are no businesses here, just well-spaced homes. Part of the reason for this sprawling aspect is that Rush Valley was originally two separate towns, St. John and Clover. Main Street ends at Highway 199, which may or may not be signed for Dugway to the right.

Highway 199 climbs a pass that marks the gap between the Stansbury and Onaqui Mountains. After about 4 miles you reach **Clover Springs Campground.** This is a nice—but very basic—campground, with outhouses and a spring right in the middle of the campground. Filter the water before drinking any.

The 2 miles from Clover Springs to Johnson Pass get cooler and greener as you climb higher into these truly beautiful desert mountains. The road here is well maintained, and several scenic pull-outs give nice views of the Tooele Army Depot's ominous-looking bunkers to the southeast. Starting the descent on the west side of the pass you will pass a single building, formerly a cafe, then descend to the cluster of homes that constitute Terra. This is also approximately where the pinyon forests end, signaling your arrival in Skull Valley. Just ahead is the notorious, sinister, top-secret, you-don't-even-want-to-know-what-goes-on-here **Dugway Proving Ground.**

About 7.5 miles from **Terra,** you may notice ahead in the distance, like some sort of mirage, the biggest, most elaborate LDS church you would ever not expect to see out in the middle of nowhere. This church serves the Dugway Proving Ground, around which quite a substantial community has grown, even supporting its own high school (nicknamed the Mustangs, after the wild horses in the region). You cannot go on the military base, although the very friendly security officers at the entry post will let you patronize their pop machine and give you all the directions and information you need about the country outside the base.

Dugway is a bit of a mystery, and a somewhat shadowy one at that. Built in the 1940s as a chemical and biological warfare test center, the base ignited controversy in the 1960s when many nearby sheep mysteriously died. Today it seems safe enough to drive by with the windows down . . . probably.

Just between the intersection with the base road and the entry to the base is the good dirt road to the south that meets the Pony Express trail 10 miles south of here. The restored express station and campground at **Simpson Springs** is about 10 miles down this road, making this a reasonable overnight option. You might want to bring your own water—there's water at the campground Mar to Nov, but you can only imagine what might be in it.

The road north from Dugway to I-80 stretches out before you almost menacingly. The land out here is desolate and forbidding. The bleak valley off to the left goes by the friendly name of **Skull Valley,** which seems appropriate enough. At this point you are parallel with the southern limit of the Cedar Mountains. Way off to the right, south of the Cedars, is one of several BLM wild horse areas.

Deseret Peak Wilderness marks the southern boundary of the Stansbury Mountains and is part of the Wasatch National Forest system. A few miles north of Dugway, you begin to see the rugged outline of Deseret Peak, which, at 11,031 feet, retains snow for all but a few months of the year.

About 3 miles onto the small **Skull Valley Goshute Indian Reservation** is the Pony Express gas station and convenience store, which may or may not be open. This is completely in the middle of nowhere (and rather north of the old Pony Express trail, which ran more than 20 miles south of here).

Sad History

It is 8 miles from the reservation to the site of **Iosepa.** Not much remains of the old colony that existed here for nearly 50 years. Mormon missionaries found eager converts in the Hawaiian Islands in the 1850s and 1860s, and church leaders decided to settle a community of about 100 converts here in desolate Skull Valley. Iosepa was essentially a plantation owned by the LDS Church; the Hawaiians were little more than indentured servants, not owners of the land at which they scratched away. Despite their absolute, even blind, loyalty to the church in spite of this deprivation and hardship, they were never considered equals to the European settlers.

A minor leprosy outbreak in 1896 gave Iosepa the distinction of having one of the few leper colonies on American soil and further distanced the Islanders from the Euro-American Mormons. When the Mormon Temple on Oahu was finished in 1917, the colony of Iosepa was dissolved.

It is a strange story set in a strange place. Not much remains of the patch of green that once clung to Skull Valley's rocky east bench. The several hundred fruit and shade trees planted here have succumbed to Nature, which, once the irrigating hands of the tenants departed, turned the land inexorably back into desert.

The town site is on a private ranch today, but you may still access the old cemetery, where there is an especially fine memorial and historical marker describing the settlement of the area. Drive about half a mile up the dirt road between two farmhouses (keep in mind you are on private property) and head toward the large pavilion visible from the road. Built by the **Iosepa Historical Association,** it is now the site of commemorative events every Memorial Day.

Horseshoe Springs flows seemingly out of nowhere into the parched Skull Valley desert.

Just north of Iosepa, the valley on the left is surprisingly well watered, supporting several small ranches with fields under irrigation. The land around here is a mix of private ranches and public land; it remains undeveloped mainly because there is really not much reason to develop this remote, dry place. But it is certainly scenic in its own very rugged way. The sheer walls of Deseret Peak tower above the road on the right; the lower and drier Cedar Mountains form the western border of Skull Valley off to the left.

About 5 miles north of Iosepa is the turnoff on the left for **Horseshoe Springs Wildlife Management Area,** where water flows in the wilderness and everything is lush and green. Horseshoe Springs, long a Goshute watering hole and a stop for later explorers including Jedediah Smith and emigrants headed to California, is worth a short stop to see pretty ponds, lush vegetation, and lots of birds. This is also a nice example of a cooperative management project carried out on BLM-administered land. Local groups have developed a low-key interpretive site here with a short boardwalk; if vandals haven't made off with them, signs will describe the place's long history.

There is no actual town of **Rowley Junction,** just a long-deserted truck stop and an interstate entrance. Wendover's casinos, and the famed Bonneville Salt Flats racetrack, are 75 miles to the west; Salt Lake City is 45 miles east across desert landscapes with many views of the Great Salt Lake.

24

The Two Cottonwood Canyons

Salt Lake City to Brighton & Alta

General Description: Two short alpine canyon drives from Salt Lake City up into the Wasatch Front.

Special Attractions: Mount Olympus and Twin Peaks Wilderness Areas; Solitude, Brighton, Snowbird, and Alta ski resorts; excellent hiking trails and rock climbing.

Location: North-central Utah, at the southeastern edge of the Salt Lake City metropolitan area.

Drive Route Numbers & Names: Highways 190 and 210, Big Cottonwood Canyon/Little Cottonwood Canyon Scenic Byways.

Travel Season: Year-round, though winter driving in the canyons can be slow and hazardous; snow tires or chains required November 1 to May 1. Even for nonskiers, these drives are worthwhile on clear winter days.

Camping: Two national forest campgrounds in each canyon, commercial campgrounds in Salt Lake City.

Services: All services in Salt Lake City; limited services (food and lodging) at the four ski resorts.

Nearby Attractions: Guardsman Pass Scenic Backway, Mill Creek Canyon, Salt Lake City attractions.

The Drive

This drive combines two short designated scenic byways into one drive, still moderate in length. Both canyon drives can be completed in half a day, making one or both a reasonable excursion for Salt Lake City visitors who have but a few hours to spend exploring the area's scenic treasures.

The two canyons are similar in character: Both lie primarily within the **Wasatch-Cache National Forest,** each has two small pockets of development around ski resorts (though the Big Cottonwood Canyon resorts are considerably smaller than those of Little Cottonwood Canyon). Both drives ascend narrow canyons with streams rushing beside the road. The roads in both canyons are paved (except for graded gravel from Alta to Albion Basin), excellent in condition, and drivable in all vehicles. Snows come early and remain late—local ski resorts are justly proud of their 500-inch average annual snowfall—and winter driving can be difficult, especially in Little Cottonwood Canyon.

Both canyon drives nicely mask the fact that they're in the backyard of a major metropolitan area, giving the traveler the impression of being far, far away from the urban grind. They are remarkably unspoiled, especially given the aggressive real estate development in the Salt Lake Valley. Due to their proximity to the city, both canyons are very popular for picnics and after-work excursions. Traffic

The Two Cottonwood Canyons

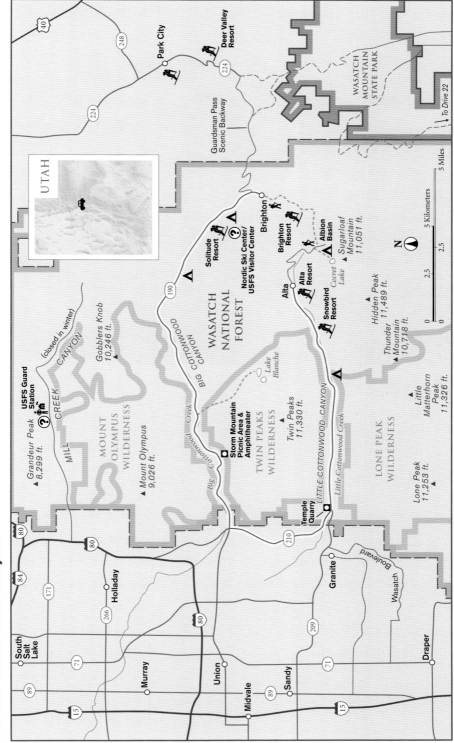

UTAH

40

248

Park City

224

Deer Valley Resort

224

Guardsman Pass Scenic Backway

WASATCH MOUNTAIN STATE PARK

To Drive 22

Solitude Resort

Nordic Ski Center/ USFS Visitor Center

Brighton

Brighton Resort

Albion Basin

Sugarloaf Mountain 11,051 ft.

WASATCH NATIONAL FOREST

190

Alta

Alta Resort

Cecret Lake

Snowbird Resort

Hidden Peak 11,489 ft.

Thunder Mountain 10,718 ft.

N

5 Kilometers

5 Miles

0   2.5   5

Gobblers Knob 10,246 ft.

(closed in winter)

USFS Guard Station

Grandeur Peak 8,299 ft.

MILL CREEK CANYON

MOUNT OLYMPUS WILDERNESS

Mount Olympus 9,026 ft.

BIG COTTONWOOD CANYON

Big Cottonwood Creek

Lake Blanche

Storm Mountain Picnic Area & Amphitheater

TWIN PEAKS WILDERNESS

Twin Peaks 11,330 ft.

LITTLE COTTONWOOD CANYON

Little Cottonwood Creek

Little Matterhorn Peak 11,326 ft.

LONE PEAK WILDERNESS

Lone Peak 11,253 ft.

Temple Quarry

210

80

84

80

171

Holladay

266

South Salt Lake

71

89

Murray

Midvale

Union

80

89

Sandy

209

71

Granite

Wasatch Boulevard

15

Draper

15

By mid-summer, Albion Basin is alive with wildflowers.

can be high on both drives, especially on the weekend. Keep in mind that because this is part of the Salt Lake City watershed, swimming is prohibited, and pets are not allowed anywhere in either canyon (neither are livestock, which partly accounts for their pristine condition).

Watch for cyclists in both canyons; in some places, you may have to navigate past them on narrow roads. A state law, passed in 2005 after a cyclist was killed in Big Cottonwood Canyon, mandates that cars must stay at least 3 feet from cyclists.

Canyon Start

The **Big Cottonwood Canyon Scenic Byway** starts at the mouth of the canyon, at approximately 7000 South, off Wasatch Boulevard (Highway 210). Just watch for the signs for Brighton/Solitude ski areas. The route designation is Highway 190, and the drive to the top is 15 miles.

As soon as you pass the water treatment plant at the mouth of the canyon, you are in the mountains. Just 4 miles into the canyon, an interpretive site describes the **Storm Mountain Slide Area** and the effect of the fault zone that lies beneath the Wasatch Front and is visible here. Geological interpretive signs along the lower part of this drive help explain the dramatic forces that formed these rugged gorges in what is actually the extreme west bench of the Rocky Mountains.

A few dirt roads branch off from the highway, leading to summer homes owned by a few lucky families. At mile 10 you pass **Spruces Campground** (105 sites), after which you encounter the increasingly heavy but generally attractive development buildup indicating you have reached **Solitude,** the first of the canyon's two ski areas. At about this point you will notice that aspens have become the predominant roadside tree. **Redman Campground** (46 sites) is right above Solitude, at 8,300 feet.

Just past Redman, on the left, is the turnoff for **Guardsman Pass Scenic Backway** (Highway 224). The road travels 20-plus twisty miles over the pass into the Heber Valley, with alternate finishes in either Park City or at the visitor center in Wasatch Mountain State Park. This drive offers some of the best roadside views of the Wasatch Front's peaks and forests, but these twin factors of scenery and

The Guardsman Pass Scenic Byway gives drivers access to wide views of the Wasatch Front's east side.

accessibility usually draw too much traffic on weekends to give the kind of solitude you would expect of a backway. It closes in winter.

Because Big Cottonwood Canyon is broader than Little Cottonwood, it offers more hiking trails departing from the roadside, many leading into **Mount Olympus Wilderness** to the north and the **Twin Peaks Wilderness** to the south. The 9-mile (round-trip) Mill B South Fork Trail to Lake Blanche, departing the byway from just east of the Storm Mountain Area, is one of the best of these, but there are shorter hikes, too.

Brighton Ski Resort was named for Scottish emigrant William Brighton, who came to Utah with his wife, Katherine, as part of a Mormon handcart company in 1857. In 1874 the Brightons opened a small hotel to accommodate the traffic crossing the high passes between the mining towns of Alta and Park City. The attractive mountain setting made this a popular summer excursion site for Salt Lake Valley residents, so it developed as a folksy sort of alpine resort. Nonlift skiing started prior to the First World War. The first ski lift cranked up in 1939, making this the state's second oldest ski resort (after Alta).

The **Brighton/Silver Lake Trail** deserves mention as one of the better wheelchair-accessible nature trails in the state. This 1-mile loop around Silver Lake, right at the base of 10,000-foot **Mount Millicent,** provides boardwalks that cross meadow areas and paved pathways that run through forest groves. Fishing docks are easily accessible from the boardwalks. Keep an eye open for moose.

From the road's end at Brighton, return to Highway 210. On exiting the mouth of Big Cottonwood Canyon, turn left at the light and continue south on Highway 210. It is an easy 3.5-mile drive to the mouth of Little Cottonwood Canyon (you can hike or ski, but not drive, directly from one canyon to the other).

Little Cottonwood

As the name suggests, **Little Cottonwood** is narrower than Big Cottonwood, with steeper canyon walls. At a little more than 8 miles to its end at Alta, it is also considerably shorter. The canyon separates two wilderness areas: Twin Peaks Wilderness to the north and Lone Peak to the south.

The sheer granite walls at the mouth of the canyon are very popular with climbers, but there are few hiking trails, so the cars pulled off the road in the lower part of this canyon more likely will belong to climbers. These granite walls were also the source of the stone used to build the Salt Lake Temple.

Half a mile into the canyon, look up to the left and note the tunnel carved out of the granite. This vault, a network of tunnels drilled 700 feet into the mountain, contains millions of genealogical and LDS church records. Half a mile farther along, on the left, is a particularly popular parking area for rock climbers—and for watching them.

At mile 4.5, at **Tanners Flat,** is perhaps the most attractive campground in the Salt Lake area, with 43 sites. While there are no elaborate amenities here (no hookups or showers, though there are bathrooms), Tanners Flat is very nicely situated in a shady grove beside Little Cottonwood Creek.

At mile 6 is the lower entrance to **Snowbird resort,** the largest of the four ski areas in Salt Lake City's backyard. The main entrance for the lodge and summertime attractions is 0.5 mile farther up the canyon. While lift-serviced skiing has been known to continue into July after heavy snow years, the resort also maintains a full slate of activities throughout the summer, from concerts to beer festivals to an alpine slide and zipline; for more information check snowbird.com.

This is also one of the canyon's most active hiking and mountain-biking spots. Snowbird's aerial tramway to the summit of 11,489-foot **Hidden Peak** presents terrific views of the Wasatch Front and Salt Lake Valley, with particularly fine perspectives on Mount Timpanogos just to the south. The tram runs regularly through the year, except for a two-week servicing at the end of October.

From here up to Alta, the canyon is full of condominiums, though fortunately, the canyon's narrowness (and the constant threat of avalanches every winter) limits development.

An extensive mining camp once filled the end of this narrow canyon. Silver was discovered here in 1863, and over the next 10 years the highly transient population rose to as much as 5,000. By 1873 there were 186 buildings here, 26 of them saloons. So much mineral wealth was being pulled out of these mountains that two years later a narrow-gauge rail line was built to **Alta.** After the collapse of the silver market in 1893, Alta lay fairly dormant for the next 40 years. Between the World Wars, the basin at the end of Little Cottonwood Canyon attracted a new sort of pioneer recreationist, who climbed up to ski the ridges and steep powder-filled bowls in numbers such that it was deemed worthwhile to open the second ski lift in the West (after Sun Valley) in 1938. Thus the booming Utah ski industry was born.

The end of the paved road is at mile 8.5, with **Albion Basin Campground** about 3 miles farther on partly paved and excellent gravel road. Albion Basin is high and cool (the area gets 50 feet of snow each winter) and is famous for its brilliant array of wildflowers. It's a delightful place for camping, picnicking, hiking, or wildlife viewing—watch for moose. Several fine trails depart from Albion Basin. The **Lake Mary Trail** is an easy 3.5-mile hike over Catherine Pass to Brighton, at the head of neighboring Big Cottonwood Canyon. A short trail (just under 1 mile) leads to **Cecret Lake,** an absolute gem of a high-alpine glacial tarn surrounded by spectacular alpine views of cliffs, including 11,000-plus-foot Mount Baldy and Sugarloaf Peak.

Another Salt Lake–area canyon deserves mention: **Mill Creek Canyon** ($3 day-use fee, collected as you leave). While much smaller and quieter than its cousins to the south, it is a gorgeous drive that quickly enters national forest and leaves all commercial development behind. And unlike the Cottonwood Canyons, you can hike with your dog here—off-leash on odd-numbered days. With lots of hiking trails, many of which lead into the Mount Olympus Wilderness, Mill Creek Canyon makes it possible to go from Salt Lake City suburbs to wilderness trails in a mere 15 minutes.

25

Ogden River Scenic Byway

Ogden to Monte Cristo

General Description: A 30-mile canyon/alpine drive with an optional 30-mile descent to Woodruff in the Bear River Valley.

Special Attractions: Pineview Reservoir, Star Burgers at the Shooting Star Saloon, ski resorts, lovely mountain panoramas.

Location: North-central Utah. The byway travels east from Ogden to the eastern boundary of the Wasatch-Cache National Forest.

Drive Route Number & Name: Highway 39, Ogden River Scenic Byway.

Travel Season: Year-round through Huntsville. The highest part of the byway, where it approaches Monte Cristo Summit, is closed during winter (usually from December through April, depending on snow conditions). Dense and varied foliage makes this a popular autumn drive.

Camping: Twelve national forest campgrounds.

Services: All services in Ogden; most services at Huntsville and Woodruff.

Nearby Attractions: Trappers Loop Scenic Backway, Hardware Ranch Wildlife Management Area, Logan Canyon Scenic Byway, Bear Lake Scenic Byway.

The Drive

Like other drives that run east from valleys into mountains, the **Ogden River Scenic Byway** follows a narrow canyon away from the urban center and up into spectacular alpine landscapes. Along the way to its high point of nearly 9,000 feet at **Monte Cristo Summit,** it passes through a complex quartzite gorge, a beautiful high valley, and some of the finest mountain meadows and forest in northern Utah. Also along the way are significant man-made attractions that include a reservoir and prize-winning hamburgers. There's plenty of variety on this drive.

The road is paved the entire way and suitable for all vehicles. Weekend traffic in summer and during the ski season can be heavy between Ogden and Huntsville. Beyond Huntsville it is doubtful you will see much traffic along Highway 39, especially beyond the high point at Monte Cristo. Expect snow anytime after September. The road through the canyon above Ogden can be very difficult when icy and inconvenient for large RVs. East of Huntsville the byway is subject to winter snow closures. Inquire in Ogden or Huntsville as to the current status of this road.

Ogden River Scenic Byway

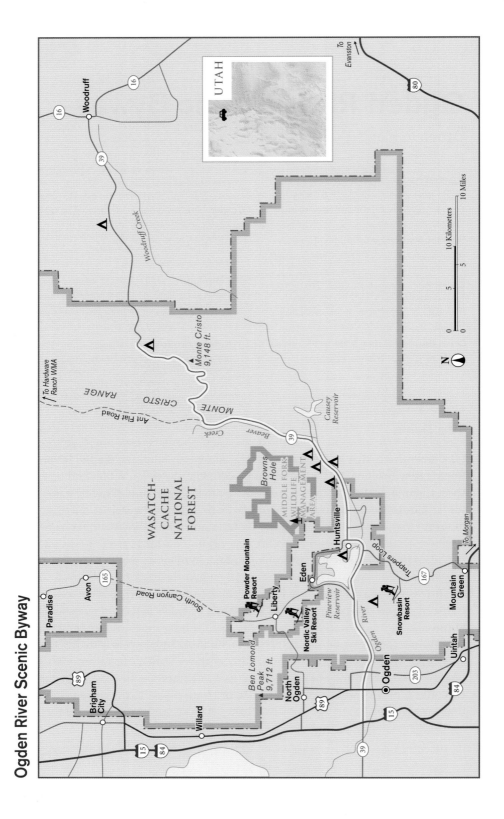

Railroad Heritage

Ogden is one of very few existing Utah communities founded by pre-Mormon pioneers. American and British trappers were active in the area from the early 1800s. Miles Goodyear established a trading post at the current site of Ogden in 1845, the first white settlement in the entire Great Basin. When the Mormons arrived two years later, Brigham Young promptly bought Goodyear out and resettled the area with his faithful followers. The city is named for British trapper and explorer Peter Skene Ogden, who never actually visited the site.

The city's growth was also tied to non-Mormon interests. Although the transcontinental rail line was joined at Promontory Summit, 60 miles away, the primary rail yard and depot were established early on at Ogden. The **old Union Station** (2501 Wall Ave.) houses the **Utah State Railroad Museum, Ogden Natural History Museum, John M. Browning Firearms Museum,** a collection of vintage automobiles, and an art gallery. Make a point of visiting this jam-packed collection of Ogden-area exhibits. Adjoining 25th Street has a long history, much of it colorful, which it celebrates now in a revived shopping, restaurant, and bar scene.

Highway 39 is 12th Street, north of the city center. Turn right (east) on Highway 39. Because the Wasatch Range abuts the eastern limit of the city, within 3 miles of downtown Ogden you are in near-complete mountain wilderness in a very narrow canyon beside a fast-moving stream. The chief (and rather significant) difference between this canyon drive and those from other Wasatch Front towns is that Ogden Canyon is mostly private property, while the others are mainly national forest. That makes this the eastern "suburbs" of Ogden. In places the road is lined with the private residences of those fortunate enough to have homes in this beautiful wooded canyon. Several attractive roadside restaurants might make nice stops.

In addition to resident traffic, this is a major conduit between Ogden and its lake and mountain recreation areas, so you might experience a fair amount of traffic in the canyon. The road is also narrow, with sharp curves, so large vehicles should exercise care and make use of the infrequent pull-outs to allow faster traffic to pass.

At mile 7 you pass the city water-treatment plant and enter **Wasatch-Cache National Forest.** Just beyond, you reach the dam and lower end of **Pineview Reservoir,** a major recreational resource for the Ogden area. The two campgrounds (total of nearly 100 sites) at the reservoir fill up quickly on weekends. If you are looking for a place to picnic, there are more peaceful spots along the Ogden River and at Causey Reservoir east of Huntsville.

Snowbasin & Trappers Loop

At mile 10 is the turnoff for the old road to **Snowbasin,** site of the 2002 Winter Olympics' downhill skiing events, which is now accessed via Trappers Loop. **Anderson Cove Campground** appears on the left. In another 0.5 mile, on the right, is the turnoff for Highway 167, the **Trappers Loop Scenic Backway,** clearly marked for Mountain Green.

Trappers Loop is recommended as a short side trip and is often used as a shortcut for those headed to Pineview from the south. It is named as the probable route followed by Peter Skene Ogden and his party of Hudson's Bay trappers. This is 9 miles of perfectly maintained paved road with really marvelous views of the eastern faces of the Wasatch Front's northern segment. The round-trip drive takes 30 to 45 minutes. There is gas and a convenience store in **Mountain Green.**

If you're headed for the Park City/Heber area, or just can't get enough of canyon driving, Trappers Loop leads to I-84, which in turn leads to lovely mountain towns and valleys along the **Morgan-Parleys Scenic Byway.** State Highways 65 and 66 drop south of I-84 from **East Canyon.** From there, it's easy to return to Salt Lake City via **Parley's Canyon** (I-80) or the highly recommended drive through **Emigration Canyon.** Even though Emigration Canyon was the one used by Mormon pioneers as they made their way to the Salt Lake Valley, it's remained less traveled than most canyons leading into the Wasatch Mountains. If Salt Lake City is your base for the Ogden Canyon drive, it's definitely worth taking the time to loop back via East and Emigration Canyons after exploring the area up north.

Development on the land adjacent to the Trappers Loop drive is in its early stages; this is how the land around Heber City

The Shooting Star Saloon, Utah's oldest, has been open in Huntsville since 1879.

and Deer Valley must have looked 30 years ago, before alpine-urban sprawl took over.

Retrace the Trappers Loop backway to Highway 39, where it is 1.5 miles to **Huntsville.** Most of this attractive community lies just off to the left of the highway, as signs indicate.

Huntsville's short diversions used to include an unlikely mountain attraction: a Trappist monastery, the **Abbey of the Holy Trinity.** Founded in 1947, the abbey housed a community of 25 monks of the Cistercian Order, better known in America as "Trappists," devoted to a simple life of prayer and manual labor. So far, locals have managed to keep the monks' sprawling farmland beside the road here undeveloped.

When the abbey closed for good in 2017, the monks donated $400,000 to a homeless shelter in Ogden—profits from years of selling bread and honey at its gift shop.

Burgers & Bucks

Now to move on from the sacred to the profane . . . well, perhaps not really *profane*, but tiny Huntsville's other major attraction is certainly of a much more secular nature. Actually, it's a barroom. If everyone in your party is over 21 years old (and heavily into beef), you really should stop in at the **Shooting Star Saloon** for a world-famous **Star Burger.** The fare is simple: beer and burgers. That's it. But the saloon's burgers are consistently judged among the nation's best. An institution since 1879, the Shooting Star claims to be the oldest operating saloon in Utah, and it is packed with artifacts including the massive stuffed head of a Saint Bernard called Buck. In accordance with state laws, children are not admitted.

Among more wholesome options, Huntsville also has a well-kept park celebrating the town's pioneer heritage. If you can tear yourself away from Huntsville's attractions, more fine scenery awaits up Highway 39. Just east of the turnoff to town on the left, there is a sign indicating a right turn to stay on Highway 39, headed east. Straight here goes to **Eden,** another small lakeside town and the gateway to **Nordic Valley** and **Powder Mountain** ski resorts, which have recently spawned a rash of vacation houses. We will take the right to continue up to Monte Cristo.

Most of the land around the lake is private, but just east of Huntsville the road reenters the national forest and you pass six national forest campgrounds in quick succession, with a total of about 150 campsites. These campgrounds are all nicely shaded by old cottonwood trees on the banks of the fast-flowing Ogden River. Just past the last of these campgrounds is the turnoff on the right for

Views from the mountains near Powder Mountain Resort stretch down to the town of Eden in the valley below.

Causey Reservoir and **Weber County Memorial Park,** a good place for a picnic or a swim.

Beyond the turnoff for Causey Reservoir, Highway 39 turns north and follows Beaver Creek up into the forested mountains. The forest here is primarily aspen, making this a truly spectacular autumn drive. This region is rich in animal life and is a likely place to spot moose and porcupines beside the road and beavers in the creek that bears their name.

About 6 miles along Beaver Creek is a turnoff on the left for **Hardware Ranch Wildlife Management Area,** 14 miles north on the unpaved and often rough Ant Flat Road. Hardware Ranch is primarily a winter elk preserve, though some of the animals remain through the summer and the visitor center and restaurant are open year-round. Check at the Forest Service office in Ogden on current road conditions or plan to visit the ranch when you're in the Logan area up north.

On to Woodruff

After 23 miles (and a long climb from Huntsville) you come up to a prominent pass as the road climbs almost to the summit of 9,148-foot **Monte Cristo Peak.** There will often be snow up here into June. The Forest Service fire guard station (still in use as a base for mountain rescues and sometimes available for rent in summer) and campground at Monte Cristo technically mark the end of the

Ogden River Scenic Byway. But you might want to continue down to Woodruff in the **Bear River Valley,** or at least far enough to drink in the broad views the eastern descent provides. This 30-mile continuation is as scenic as the ascent to Monte Cristo. One great attraction to the drive down to Woodruff is the near total absence of traffic.

Woodruff was settled in 1870 by pioneers from the current town of Bountiful. As is usual with these old LDS towns, there are a few nice old brick buildings, but the town is nothing extraordinary. There is a gas station, convenience store, a nice little park with picnic area, and a cute little rodeo arena. As expected, the most substantial building in town is the LDS church. Woodruff is a cold spot, averaging only 57 frost-free days per year and holding the record for the lowest temperature ever recorded for any Utah town, -50 degrees F.

From Woodruff, it is but a half-hour drive through pretty ranchland, with nice views of the Uinta Mountains to the south, to reach I-80 at Evanston, Wyoming, for the quickest return to the Salt Lake Valley. Another possibility is to use Highway 39 as a route to Bear Lake and Logan Canyon (Drive 27); this would be a much longer drive, but it would allow you to get to the lake or Logan while avoiding the doldrums of I-15.

26

Bear River Bird Refuge

Brigham City to the Refuge

General Description: A 22-mile drive through lush marshlands at the mouth of the Bear River.

Special Attractions: The Great Salt Lake, myriad varieties of marsh-dependent birds.

Location: North-central Utah, where the Bear River flows into the northeast corner of the Great Salt Lake.

Drive Route Names: Forest Street to Bird Refuge Road.

Travel Season: The refuge is open daily, year-round, from sunrise until sunset, although fewer birds inhabit the area in winter (November through February). Heavy spring rains may make the gravel roads impassable.

Camping: Public camping in the area is scarce. No camping is allowed on the refuge. Willard Bay State Park is 10 miles to the south; Mantua Reservoir, 6 miles east of Brigham City, has primitive campsites.

Services: All services are available at Brigham City; absolutely no services on the refuge itself.

Nearby Attractions: Ogden River Scenic Byway, Willard Peak Scenic Backway, Antelope Island/Great Salt Lake State Park, Harold Crane Waterfowl Management Area, Logan Canyon Scenic Byway.

The Drive

Utah sits right at the convergence of migratory waterfowl paths called the **Pacific and Central Flyways**: Each fall and spring hundreds of thousands of birds congregate in the marshlands formed where fresh water flows into the Great Salt Lake. This drive focuses on the most extensive of many waterfowl refuges established in Utah to protect migrating birds; a great variety of wildlife lives in these refuges year-round.

In terms of miles driven, this is a very short outing. It is 44 miles round-trip from Brigham City, which in turn is about 60 miles north of Salt Lake City; the refuge loop drive itself is 12 miles. But you can spend lots of time on this drive parking in convenient pull-outs and studying the incredible variety of life lurking in the pools and marsh grasses. Because the marshlands are ideal breeding grounds for mosquitoes and other pests as well as birds, be sure to use insect repellent if you plan to leave the car. Also be sure to bring water and a hat, since there's almost no shade.

In terms of scenery, this drive may seem limited when compared to drives that sweep past an ever-changing spectacle of alpine vistas or redrock panoramas. Views generally change more slowly in the broad basin that occupies the western third of the state. Here on this small corner of the Great Salt Lake, we are looking

Bear River Bird Refuge

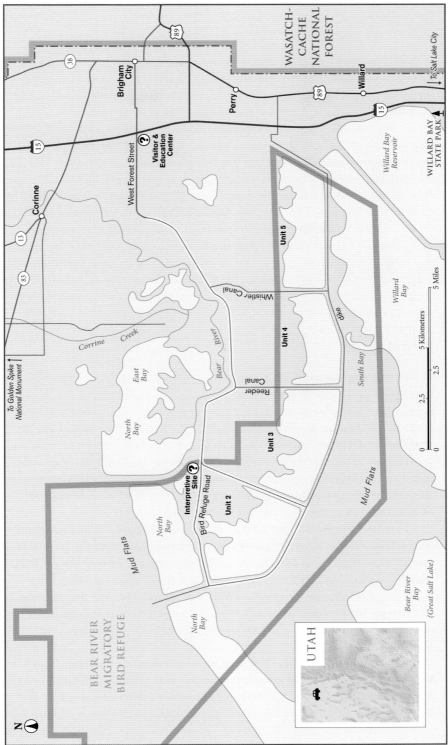

N

BEAR RIVER MIGRATORY BIRD REFUGE

To Golden Spike National Monument

Corinne

83

13

38

15

Brigham City

West Forest Street

Visitor & Education Center

Perry

89

Willard

89

15

To Salt Lake City

WASATCH-CACHE NATIONAL FOREST

Willard Bay Reservoir

WILLARD BAY STATE PARK

Corrine Creek

East Bay

North Bay

Bear River

Whistler Canal

Reeder Canal

Unit 5

Unit 4

Unit 3

Unit 2

dike

South Bay

Willard Bay

Mud Flats

Interpretive Site

Bird Refuge Road

North Bay

North Bay

North Bay

Mud Flats

Mud Flats

Bear River Bay (Great Salt Lake)

UTAH

0   2.5   5 Kilometers

0   2.5   5 Miles

at an encapsulated, confined space of water, marsh grass, and sky. It is the sort of drive in which you must focus in on small spaces rather than cast your view across the broad, expansive landscapes for which Utah is so well known. You will likely be rewarded by a different sort of fascinating beauty.

There is another, equally compelling reason for making this drive: the **Great Salt Lake.** As visually striking and as topographically and historically interesting as the famous lake is, it receives surprisingly little tourist attention. This is at least partly due to the lack of convenient, up-close viewpoints. Old lakeside resorts close to Salt Lake City are largely gone. Great Salt Lake State Park and the onion-domed attraction called **Saltair** (now used mostly as a concert venue) are attempting to revive the old tradition of using the south end of the lake for recreation. The causeway and state park at **Antelope Island** north of Salt Lake City provide an excellent opportunity for lake-oriented outings. And Drive 28 of this book will touch on the lake's largely forgotten north end. But for the most part, the lake is largely unapproachable and sadly ignored. This drive will give you some idea of its unique vastness and strange beauty.

Bird Refuge

The **Bear River Migratory Bird Refuge** lies about 16 miles west of Brigham City, where the Bear River enters the Great Salt Lake. The scenic part of this drive begins about 6 miles west of Brigham City on the long country road leading out to the refuge. It continues through a small corner of the refuge on a graded road along the top of a containment dike built out into the lake.

The last 10 miles out to the refuge, as well as the roads on the refuge, are well-maintained gravel, perfectly level and presenting no problems for any vehicle. Occasionally the gravel roads become difficult during heavy rain or snow. The 12-mile route along the dike, though narrow, is one-way.

Try to do this drive in the early evening, when the light on the mountains east of Brigham City is lovely and you can catch the sunset over the lake—a very special visual experience. (The refuge technically closes at dark; if you get stuck behind the locked gate, drive up to it slowly and it will open automatically.) Weekends often draw crowds to the refuge, while weekdays find the place remarkably empty. The birds are most active mornings and evenings. A pair of binoculars will be most useful. This is also a tremendous place for wildlife photography, especially with a telephoto lens.

To get to the refuge, take the Forest Street exit from I-15, or start from **Brigham City,** which is a nice town to visit. The two most prominent landmarks in downtown Brigham City are the ornate **Mormon Tabernacle** and the big, locally famous Welcome to Brigham sign that spans Main Street and proclaims

The new bird refuge visitor center also fosters education and research.

GATEWAY TO THE WORLD'S GREATEST WILD BIRD REFUGE. Brigham City is a quiet, unassuming community with some fine 19th-century homes and commercial buildings. The **Box Elder County Courthouse,** a block or two north of the famous sign, is especially attractive. Stop in at the Brigham City visitor center, on the right just north of the famous sign, for information.

From early summer into fall, the 15-mile stretch of US 89 south of Brigham City, sometimes called "Utah's Fruit-way," is dotted with old-fashioned fruit stands selling local produce. A handful of family-owned restaurants along here specialize in—no surprise—dessert. The peach harvest is celebrated in Brigham City with the **Peach Days festival,** usually the weekend after Labor Day.

To get to the refuge, take Main Street to Forest Street, just north of the "Welcome" sign. If you've bypassed Brigham City and taken the Forest Street exit from I-15, just head west on Forest. Follow this road under the interstate and onto country roads leading to the refuge.

While the refuge itself is a few miles west of the highway, the visitor center is only about a block from I-15. Completed in 2007, this information and education center is touted as one of the best wildlife-refuge amenities in the country. It includes displays, a short documentary film, bird-loving volunteer docents eager to provide information, and the last flush toilets you'll see for a while. A gift shop sells bird identification guides specific to the refuge. The building is surrounded by 1.5 miles of nature trail, mostly wheelchair-accessible boardwalk. The refuge itself is open daily from dawn to dusk; the visitor center is open Tues to Fri, 8 a.m. to 4 p.m. and the second and fourth Sat of the month, 10 a.m. to 4 p.m.

The drive is farther along this country road. The first 6 miles or so are mundane until you get far enough out onto the flats along the edge of the lake for the views to open up. Meanwhile, the views back toward the Wasatch Range also become more impressive. You will know you are getting close when you come up alongside the slow-moving Bear River.

River Scenery

The Bear River is the most confused river in America. It really doesn't seem to know for sure which way it's headed or where it will end up. Its source in the High Uintas is less than 90 air miles from where ends here at the Great Salt Lake, but this vagrant stream wanders 350 miles only to end up almost back where it started. Along the way it heads northward up through Wyoming and into Idaho, where it suddenly changes its mind and does an about-face, flowing south into Utah. In Utah it meanders aimlessly across the bed of what used to be ancient Lake Bonneville before finally finding its way here. It seems appropriate that the wayward Bear is the longest river in America that does not ultimately reach an ocean (though Utah's Sevier, which runs north from the Markagunt and Paunsaugunt Plateaus, then west to die in the wastelands of the Great Basin, is nearly as long). Of course, the reasons for the river's erratic course have to do with the dramatic geologic forces that formed this complex land of uptilt faults, dropped valleys, and barrier ranges—yet another geology lesson read upon the land.

This area outside the refuge, before the Bear River enters the lake and as it flows through about 10 miles of marshland, is just as good for bird watching as the refuge itself; in certain conditions it is actually the best place to view certain kinds of birds. John C. Fremont, one of Utah's earliest and most enthusiastic tourists, passed through this area in 1843 and was especially impressed by the abundance and variety of the waterfowl he discovered here. Fremont wrote in his journal: "The whole morass was animated with multitudes of waterfowl . . . with a noise like distant thunder."

The refuge was established by an act of Congress in 1928 after decades of water projects drained more than 90 percent of the Bear River marshlands, resulting in a catastrophic decline in the bird population. Waves of disease have also killed millions of birds over the years. Now, state and federal wildlife researchers monitor the area's birdlife and continue the search for cures for the severe diseases that afflict waterfowl.

Millions of birds make a stop here, and a much smaller number make it their full-time home. Between April and October, the white-faced ibis is one of the most commonly seen birds here; the largest single nesting colony in the world breeds in the marshlands of the Great Salt Lake. The **Eccles Wildlife Education Center,** opened in Farmington Bay south of here in 2018, also makes an excellent bird-watching detour on the lake; it's at the end of Glovers Lane in Farmington.

The single best time to see large concentrations of birds is in the early fall, although exact months vary according to species. The fall migration of ducks and geese numbers as much as half a million. The visitor center has a very useful pamphlet showing the statistics (as graphs) for 81 varieties of birds common to the refuge, indicating average monthly abundance.

Here are a few examples of what you might see on the refuge:

Bird Species	Highest Month	Average Peak Number
bald eagle	March	33
ruddy duck	April/May	20,000
snowy egret	July	2,800
short-eared owl	July	12
black-crowned night heron	August	600
great blue heron	August	780
pintail	September	180,000
cinnamon teal	September	33,000
American widgeon	Sept/Oct	67,000
Wilson's phalaropes	Sept/Oct	500,000
green-winged teal	October	120,000
tundra swan	October	40,000
marsh hawk	November	26
whistling swan	Nov/Dec	16,000

All that greets you at the refuge boundary is a sign and an open area containing a small pavilion, a simple information board, vault toilets, and a handful of benches. There is no water here, and no camping is allowed on the refuge. There is also no charge for entering the refuge.

A dramatic rise in the level of the Great Salt Lake in 1983 destroyed the refuge's few man-made structures, including a visitor center completed the previous year, and inflicted severe damage on the bird habitat. It took six years for the lake to recede enough for refuge staff and volunteers to start rebuilding the dikes, roads, and structures.

It may seem strange that hunting is allowed in several parts of the refuge, though only certain species at certain times of year, and only by permit. It controls

Pelicans love to gobble the plentiful fish at the mouth of the Bear River.

certain populations (mostly ducks and geese) that might otherwise get out of hand, while giving hunters a shot at some easy targets.

Animals at Home

As Mormons settled the Salt Lake Valley, migratory waterfowl became a prime source of market income. From 1877 until 1900, 200,000 ducks were harvested each year, mostly for restaurants back east. After the turn of the century, in some years a virulent strain of avian botulism killed more than half of the migrating birds that stopped to rest here, leaving the marshes clogged with their dead bodies. At the same time, widespread diversion of water from the Bear River for farming in the valley caused the marshes to dry up. By 1920 only 2,000 to 3,000 acres of the original 45,000 marshland acres remained. It was a classic example of "use-it-upedness" combined with a devastating aviary epizootic.

Today's Bear River Refuge is the result of efforts to counter and repair the destructive circumstances of the past. The refuge currently consists of 74,000 carefully managed acres of marsh, open water, and mudflats. A system of dikes and other water-control features maintains five 5,000-acre water impoundments in order to slow the flow of the fresh water into the Great Salt Lake. While the mysteries of avian botulism have not yet been solved, important research continues on the refuge, and advances have been made in controlling the disease.

The refuge drive is along the top of the dikes that border one of the impoundment ponds. The route is well marked and obvious. Once on the narrow dikes, it is impossible to go astray—if you do, you'll end up in the water. When you've completed the loop, you will go back out the way you came in (there are a couple of turnaround spots if for some reason you don't want to do the entire loop).

Along the 12-mile drive are periodic interpretive boards describing various features of the marsh habitat and its inhabitants. But the real attractions along here are the birds themselves. More than 200 species are regularly sighted here; of these, 62 are known to nest and breed in these marshes, making the refuge important for production as well. In addition to the many varieties of birds that frequent the refuge, this is home to 29 species of mammals (including otters), 12 species of fish, 5 species of reptiles/amphibians, and 177 species of plants.

This man-made causeway jutting out into the **Great Salt Lake** is also a good place to study Utah's version of the Biblical Dead Sea. Is it scenic? You be the

Birds take flight beyond the refuge's reeds.

judge. Pretty, it certainly is not. But it no doubt deserves the title "Great." Directly across the water, the long barren ridge of the Promontory Mountains defines the western horizon. To the south stretches 50 miles of briny water baking in the sun. With a salt content as high as 27 percent, the lake is five times as salty as the ocean. Of all the bodies of water on Earth, only the Dead Sea is saltier than the Great Salt Lake.

The cause of the lake's salinity is fairly obvious if you look at a map. The lake receives water from numerous streams and rivers, yet it has no outlet. It is, in effect, a broad evaporation pond. Although it is, on average, 70 miles long and 30 miles across, it averages only about 13 feet in depth and is, on average, only 33 feet at its deepest. The amount of land it covers varies greatly, depending on climate—in the past 50 years alone, it has ranged from 950 to 3,300 square miles. As moisture is lost to evaporation, the mineral salts washed into the lake remain. This process has been going on since at least the last Ice Age, when most of western Utah and parts of Idaho and Nevada were covered by prehistoric Lake Bonneville, of which the Great Salt Lake is a remnant.

Due to the high salt content, nothing lives in the lake except for tiny brine shrimp that are harvested as fish food (or for use as low-maintenance aquarium pets called "sea monkeys"). So what do all the waterfowl who live here permanently and visit annually eat? The marsh grasses and mudflats here are a great breeding ground for a wide variety of insects, which the birds consume with gusto. The mudflats at the edge of the water are also popular with frogs, a favorite food for herons and egrets. And there are plenty of fish in the mouth of the Bear River to keep the pelicans and other fish-eaters happy.

In fact, there is a waterfowl management area at each point where a large source of freshwater flows into the salty lake: at the mouths of the Bear, Weber, Ogden, and Jordan Rivers. These must have long ago been established as prime "buffet spots" for the migratory birds. The large inflow of fresh river water also supports the variety of marsh grasses that grow in these places, on a lake that is otherwise conspicuous for its lack of vegetation.

Ducks banded at the Bear River Refuge have been found in 31 states and 5 foreign countries, from Siberia to Colombia, from Maryland to Palmyra Island. One of the most interesting stories regarding the refuge's temporary winged visitors is of a pintail duck, banded and treated for botulism in 1942, who was found 83 days later on Palmyra Island—3,500 miles from here. The bird was described as being in an exhausted state. I guess I would be, too.

27

Logan Canyon's Lively Hills

Logan to Bear Lake

General Description: A 55-mile canyon and alpine drive from Logan to scenic Bear Lake.

Special Attractions: Wasatch-Cache National Forest, dramatic canyon scenery, Jardine Juniper, Ricks Spring, Tony Grove, Bear Lake, rock climbing, raspberry milk shakes.

Location: Northeast Utah, primarily in the Wasatch National Forest. The drive starts at Logan, east of I-15, and runs to the southern tip of Bear Lake, on the Utah/Idaho state line.

Drive Route Numbers & Names: US 89/ Highway 30, Logan Canyon Scenic Byway/ Bear Lake 30 Scenic Byway.

Travel Season: Year-round, though roads may be slick during winter. Autumn colors can be outstanding in Logan Canyon.

Camping: There are 10 national forest campgrounds along the Logan Canyon Scenic Byway, 4 state park campgrounds at Bear Lake, and commercial campgrounds around Bear Lake and at Beaver Mountain Ski Resort in summer.

Services: All services in Logan; most services in Garden City.

Nearby Attractions: Mount Naomi Wilderness Area, Old Ephraim's Grave, Hardware Ranch Scenic Backway.

The Drive

This drive combines two designated scenic byways in a single excursion. The entire drive could be completed (one-way) in just an hour and a half, though more time is recommended for stops and side trips in the car or on foot.

The Logan Canyon Scenic Byway runs east along US 89 from the backyard of Utah State University in Logan, up the narrow gorge of Logan Canyon, and over the Bear River Mountains to the resort town of Garden City on the banks of scenic Bear Lake. This 40-mile alpine/canyon drive passes beneath imposing limestone cliffs carved by the Logan River and through lush green forest on its 3,000-foot climb to Bear Lake Summit. A second designated scenic byway continues for 15 miles from Garden City to Laketown, at the southern end of the lake.

The roads on this drive are in excellent condition, and there are no inordinately steep grades. The upper part of Logan Canyon and the road over the summit receive heavy snow in winter; snow tires or chains will be helpful. This is also the coldest part of the state. Bring more clothes than you think you'll need, even in summer, and carry emergency gear—warm clothes, spare food and water, even sleeping bags—if driving in this region during winter.

Logan Canyon's Lively Hills

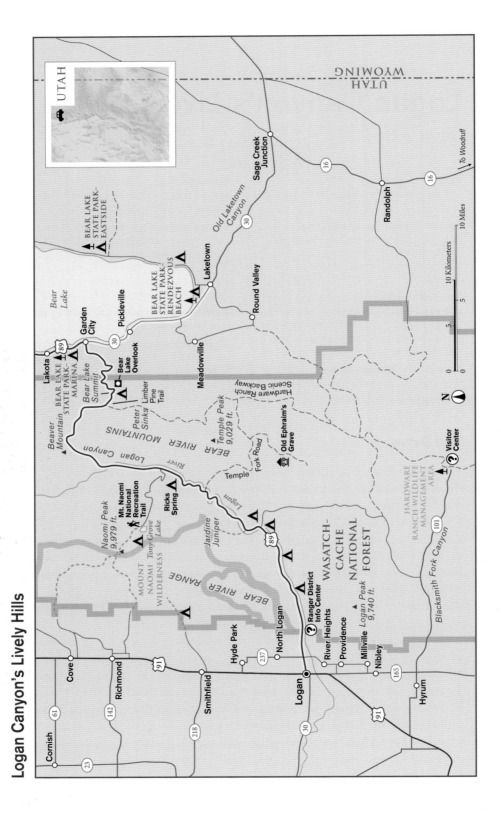

College Town

The drive begins in **Logan,** a university town and the regional center for northern Utah. Stop in at the regional tourism office, in a beautiful restored building at 199 North Main in the center of town, to get any brochures, maps, or other information you may want about northern Utah.

Also worth viewing in town are the **Logan LDS Temple** (200 North 200 East) and nearby **Logan Tabernacle.** The modified gothic-style temple, built between 1877 and 1884, is the second-oldest temple in Utah (after St. George) and justifiably considered one of the most beautiful religious buildings in the West. Logan's main claim to fame today is **Utah State University,** which sits practically at the mouth of Logan Canyon.

From downtown Logan, 400 North is also US 89. Once east of the university you are pretty much out of town. As with the drives farther south, as soon as you

The Cache Valley visitor information center in downtown Logan, in a restored former courthouse, is one of the state's most attractive tourism offices.

enter the mouth of the canyon, just past the **Forest Service Information Office,** you are in the mountains. Visit the very helpful Forest Service office (open 8 a.m. to 4:30 p.m., Mon through Fri) on your way out of town, especially if you plan on returning via the unpaved **Hardware Ranch Scenic Backway.** This is also the best place to pick up a Logan Canyon driving-tour guide or information on hikes from Logan Canyon trailheads.

As with other canyons within commuting distance of Utah's larger urban areas (Ogden Canyon and the Cottonwoods), there are a number of private homes here, although much better hidden than in Ogden Canyon. Most are tucked away in the trees, or even behind locked gates, and you will barely catch a glimpse of them. Keep in mind that this is the backyard of Utah State University, so watch for bicyclists. If you are driving slowly, use the pull-outs to let traffic pass.

One mile up the canyon, the **Stokes Nature Center,** which runs education and stewardship programs for students and adults, is on the left (open Wed through Sat during the summer). Slightly more than 3 miles from the mouth of the canyon are **Bridger and Spring Hollow Campgrounds.** At about mile 4 the canyon opens up a little, and some nice fishing ponds have formed along the Logan River. Also here is **Guinavah Campground.** The campgrounds, as well as several picnic areas, are all on the right, beside the river. **Logan Canyon,** particularly between miles 9 and 12, is popular with rock climbers, so you might see folks climbing right beside the road.

At around mile 11 watch on the left for **Wood Camp Campground,** which is also the start of the trail leading to the 1,500-year-old **Jardine Juniper.** This ancient tree is thought to be the oldest juniper in the Rocky Mountains. The trail gains nearly 2,000 feet in about 5.5 miles (for a total of about 11 miles, round-trip) and leads through a beautiful alpine landscape.

Another mile or two up the canyon is the turnoff on the right for Temple Fork Road and **Old Ephraim's Grave.** The fork is named for the wood harvested here for use in the Logan Temple and tabernacle. Ephraim was the name given to a huge grizzly bear (some say 9 feet tall, some say 11) who lived in the Cache National Forest and who dined on cattle and sheep from around 1911 until he was shot in 1923. Local Boy Scouts erected the current marker to the legendary beast, whose skull was sent to the Smithsonian in Washington, DC, but is now housed at Utah State University's **Merrill Library.** It's a 9-mile drive on rocky unpaved road that is often very rough and is suitable only for high-clearance vehicles; go right at the major fork at the summit of this drive.

Old Ephraim's memorial is at the end of a steep, rocky dirt road.

IN MEMORIAM

THIS RUGGED FOUR AND ONE HALF TON NATIVE
STONE IS SYMBOLIC OF A GREAT GRIZZLY BEAR
CALLED OLD EPHRAIM WHO RANGED THIS AREA
FOR MANY YEARS KILLING SHEEP, CATTLE AND
GAME. HE WAS TRAPPED, SHOT, AND BURIED NEAR
HERE AUG. 1923. BY FRANK CLARK OF MALAD, IDAHO.

STANDING UPRIGHT HE EQUALED THE HEIGHT OF
THIS MONUMENT (9 FT. 11 IN.) AND WEIGHED
ABOUT 1100 LBS. SMITHSONIAN INSTITUTE,
WASHINGTON D.C. HAS HIS SKULL.

ERECTED BY LOCAL SCOUTS AND SCOUTERS
AUG. 22,1966

OLD EPHRAIM, OLD EPHRAIM, YOUR DEEDS WERE SO WRONG
YET WE BUILD YOU THIS MARKER AND SING YOU THIS SONG.
TO THE KING OF THE FOREST SO MIGHTY AND TALL,
WE SALUTE YOU, OLD EPHRAIM THE KING OF THEM ALL.
                                    NEPHI J. BOTT

Just up the canyon, watch for well-marked **Ricks Spring,** a flow of crystal-clear water—actually a diversion, through a fault in the rock, of the Logan River—that issues from a cave on the left of the road. A nice pathway less than 20 yards from the road leads to the cave. Note the pioneer signatures on the rock, just above the point where the water issues forth (sadly, it's not suitable for drinking).

Alpine Drive

Beyond Ricks Spring, the road runs up and out of the well-defined canyon and takes on the aspect of a mountain drive. The stream still flows on the right, but the canyon has widened greatly, the views are more open, and the predominant tree is now aspen. About 4 miles beyond Ricks Spring is the turnoff on the left for **Tony Grove Lake Recreation Area.** Paved FR 003 leads 7 miles up to the lake, at 8,050 feet. Note the small building near the turnoff: Built in 1907, it housed the canyon's first forest ranger and later served as a Civilian Conservation Corps building.

On a weekday, you might find a space in the lovely campground here, set in an aspen, spruce, and fir grove beside this extremely beautiful glacial lake. Most who camp here reserve spots well in advance. This is also a popular picnic area with a nature trail and a starting point for hikes into the **Mount Naomi Wilderness,** including the 4-mile (each way) **Mount Naomi Peak National Recreation Trail.** There's a day-use fee of $7 to use the site; whether you're camping or hiking, bring your own water. If the campground is full, there are two other campgrounds near the intersection of FR 003 and US 89.

The turnoff for the family-owned **Beaver Mountain ski area** is about 5 miles farther up the canyon. During the summer, the resort operates a full-service campground and RV park. Go to bookthebeav.com for information. Six miles past Beaver Mountain is **Limber Pine Trail,** on the right, which is about the high point of this drive.

The turnoff for the **Hardware Ranch Scenic Backway** is just before Limber Pine. The first half of this roughly 50-mile mountain backway, from US 89 to Hardware Ranch Wildlife Management Area, is unpaved, often rough, and impassable when wet. Ask about the road in Logan or Garden City. The route from Hardware Ranch to Hyrum, just south of Logan (Blacksmith Fork Canyon Road) is paved, so for those in low-clearance vehicles, the best bet to reach the ranch is to go out and back from Hyrum.

Because of unique atmospheric conditions, the coldest winter temperature ever recorded in the lower 48 was at **Peter Sinks,** between here and Hardware Ranch (minus 69 degrees in 1985).

Blue-Water Playground

Half a mile in descent from the summit is **Sunrise Campground** and a fine scenic overlook with a great view of **Bear Lake.** From this height you get some idea of why the lake has been called "the Caribbean of the Rockies," for it really is a remarkable shade of blue, ringed with sandy beaches. This color is sometimes attributed to limestone particles carried into the lake from the surrounding hills, or to the lake's sandy white bottom and relative shallowness—208 feet at its deepest. The lake is 20 miles long, 8 miles wide, and it sits in a graben (a valley depression created by two faults). Like the Great Salt Lake, Bear Lake has no surface outlet. But unlike the briny Great Salt Lake, Bear Lake loses most of its waters through percolation or subsurface flow through the earth itself. These waters later resurface as springs.

Descend steeply to **Garden City,** the main resort community on Bear Lake. Once you leave the national forest and as you approach town, you pass through significant property development.

The steepness of this descent might suggest a different return route for drivers of large vehicles: either through Woodruff to reach I-80 at Evanston, Wyoming, or via Highway 39 from Woodruff to Ogden (reversing Drive 25 from this guide).

In 1827 and 1828 Bear Lake was the site of the annual rendezvous held by regional fur trappers. The lake basin had been a popular Shoshone Indian gathering place for many years before Donald Mackenzie, a Scottish-Canadian trapper, first saw it in 1819 and named it Black Bear Lake.

Although early maps of the Oregon Trail indicate it passed considerably north of here, there is evidence that at least some of the earlier emigrants (ca. 1830) passed along the south shore

It's easy to reach Ricks Spring, just off Highway 89 in Logan Canyon. Don't drink the water: this is not a true spring.

of Bear Lake and then went up through canyons to the northwest. Old wagon ruts from this period and stories of early settlers and Native Americans support this claim. This makes logistical sense, since the important rendezvous held here in 1827 and 1828 would have made Bear Lake well known to all early travelers through the region.

Despite the lake's notoriety among early trappers and explorers, no year-round settlement occurred until the mid-1860s, when cabins were built at current Garden City. The old settlement has since spread up and down the west side of the lake in typical resort development fashion.

Bear Lake is a water-sports center for northern Utah, southeastern Idaho, and southwestern Wyoming. While this may sound like it draws an awful lot of people, these sparsely populated regions don't have that many folks even when combined. Summer weekends are fairly busy, but this is hardly a destination resort, so weekdays are nice and slow. Boating, camping, and picnicking facilities are provided around the lake at state-run parks including three areas of **Bear Lake State Park** (Marina, Eastside, and **Rendezvous Beach**).

The designated Logan Canyon Scenic Byway continues north from Garden City to the Idaho state line (about 4 miles). This part of the lakefront probably *was* scenic before it was all sectioned off and developed. There is no real reason to drive north unless you want to visit the historic LDS towns of Paris and Montpelier in Idaho. Otherwise, I recommend turning south here or returning to Logan.

Before leaving Garden City, don't fail to partake of the raspberry treats for which this place is famous. The town probably has more drive-in restaurants per capita than anywhere in the West, and they all specialize in fresh raspberry shakes.

About 3 miles south of Garden City is the **Pickleville Playhouse,** with its summertime theater specializing in family-friendly comedy and melodrama. This is also the site of atrociously ugly rabbit-warren condominium development. Just past Pickleville the lakefront development ends, and the drive actually becomes scenic again, with the big lake to the left and scrub-covered hills on the right. This is private land; development has already begun to creep up the hillsides.

Eight miles south of Garden City is **Bear Lake State Park–Rendezvous Beach**. It is 1.5 miles farther to the rustic village of **Laketown** (which isn't quite on the lake at all), where you have several options. You can return to Logan. You can continue south to Woodruff and on to Evanston, Wyoming, and hop on the interstate back to the Salt Lake Valley. Or you can do Drive 25 in reverse to Ogden. If you want to make this a multiday excursion, you might even consider driving south from Evanston and doing the Mirror Lake drive (21) in reverse.

Laketown to Woodruff is 30 miles of virtual wilderness punctuated by just one real settlement at Randolph. The landscape here is rough but primitive and unspoiled. At Sage Creek Junction, 12 miles past Lakeside, turn right on Highway

16 and drive 9 miles south to **Randolph.** With a population of about 500, Randolph must surely be one of the nation's smaller county seats. The town does have a cute little courthouse, a nice pink brick LDS church, at least one gas station, a mechanic, and two restaurants.

    Woodruff, with a gas station/convenience store, is 10 miles south; Evanston, Wyoming, is 25 miles farther.

Northwest Railroad Trail Expedition

Snowville to Grouse Creek to Golden Spike to Corinne

General Description: A long excursion into the desert and grasslands of Utah's neglected northwest corner.

Special Attractions: Great Basin views, remote ranching communities, old Central Pacific rail line, Golden Spike National Historic Site, rocket display at ATK, Corinne, monumental art.

Location: Northwestern Utah.

Drive Route Numbers & Names: Highway 30, Highway 83, Transcontinental Railroad Backcountry Byway (also known as Central Pacific Railroad Trail Scenic Backway).

Travel Season: Year-round, though it's sun-baked in summer and drifting snow can be a winter problem.

Camping: Limited. There are no developed campsites along this route, but primitive camping is allowed along much of it.

Services: Basic services at Snowville and Corinne; gas and groceries at Montello, Nevada. There are no services along the 88-mile Transcontinental Railroad Backcountry Byway.

Nearby Attractions: City of Rocks, Sawtooth National Forest, Bear River Bird Refuge (Drive 26).

The Drive

While God may not necessarily have forsaken this corner of Utah, man certainly has. Apart from a handful of isolated ranch communities, the entire northwest corner of the state, from the Great Salt Lake to the Idaho and Nevada borders, is a vast, empty quarter.

For about 40 years, from 1869 until just after the turn of the century, the main track of the transcontinental rail line passed through this remote desert grassland. In a peculiar way, the lifeline of as many as 10 trains per day, supporting and supported by railroad towns along the way, meant this empty land was more populous, more lively, and much less lonely 100 years ago than it is today. Today only the landscape and a few relics remain.

Regional attractions for the modern traveler focus on **railroad history** and wide-open spaces. This is a big area, and the drive is potentially very long; some serious decisions need to be made regarding itinerary. Snowville to the farming hamlet of Grouse Creek is 104 miles. The backway return along the old railroad bed from Lucin to Golden Spike is 88 (very slow and potentially hazardous) miles, then it's another 25 miles to Corinne. If you intend to do the entire loop, it is *technically* possible to do this in a single marathon day, presuming an early start from

Northwest Railroad Trail Expedition

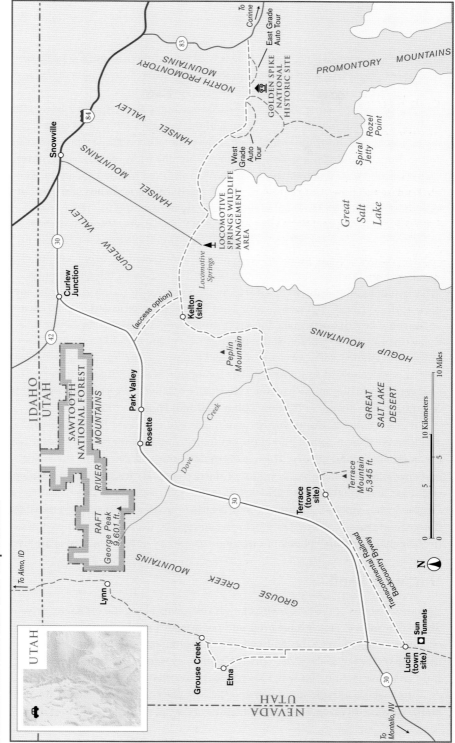

Snowville and no dawdling. The problem with extending this into a slower, more relaxed overnight trip is that there is practically no place to overnight, apart from camping on the abundant BLM-administered public lands.

The drive back along the old rail bed, designated a BLM National Backcountry Byway in 1994, follows the last stretch of the Central Pacific line before it met the Union Pacific at Promontory Summit. The old railroad grade—narrow, rutted, and without shoulders—is a slow drive in any rig; the BLM recommends nothing longer than 30 feet. The roadway is also strewn with old railroad spikes, broken glass, nails, and other tire-popping hazards; the BLM recommends you bring at least one spare tire and preferably more. Because driving speeds are so slow, it will take at least 4 hours to do the rail bed alone. Those who object to the idea of changing tires in the middle of the desert should skip this backway or drive just a short stretch of it. Cell phone service is almost nonexistent, so bring a paper map.

There are three reasonable options for getting a sense of the nature of the drive without committing to its entire length: Start east from Lucin, then escape back north to paved Highway 30 on one of several good dirt roads (mentioned in the route description); make the short drive from Highway 30 to Kelton and follow the rail bed to Golden Spike; or drive west along the old grade for a few miles from Golden Spike, perhaps as far as Locomotive Springs or the cemetery at Kelton, then return to Promontory. The last option is safest, since it traverses the least remote portion of the backway. No matter what you do, plan to spend a bit of time reliving history at **Golden Spike National Historic Site.**

It could come down to whether you're more in the mood for a taste of remote and unspoiled farm country and how enthralled you are with backcountry driving and remnants of rail history. These sorts of decisions will determine the length and character of your drive. The start of the drive, on Highway 30, is in excellent condition and suitable for all vehicles, as is the well-maintained gravel road up to Grouse Creek. Anyone attempting to drive the railroad bed must be prepared for desert conditions: Summer temperatures can top 100 degrees, and winter lows can drop below zero. Carry plenty of extra food and water and a couple of spare tires.

Untamed Land

This drive begins at the **Snowville** exit on I-84. Even along the interstate drive to Snowville you will get a pretty good sense of this area's grand desolation. Because of the detachment from the landscape that the interstate imposes on the traveler, this may not promise to be particularly "scenic," but just wait: This is land you must get close to, and you will once you leave the interstate behind.

Snowville is a truck-stop town and the best place to fill your tank before embarking on this long desert drive. A final logistical warning is in order here:

If you have a large-capacity tank (or if you plan only to go to Grouse Creek and back on Highway 30), you can easily do this entire trip on one tank. If you intend to drive the length of the old railroad grade, carry gas just to be safe or plan to drive across the Nevada border to Montello to refuel. The truck stop at Snowville is open all night, and there is a small motel. Snowville also has a classic western cafe: **Mollie's Cafe** is just past the couple of gas stations that make up the greater Snowville commercial district.

From Snowville, follow I-84 west about 2 miles to the first exit, marked Highway 30 and signed for Park Valley. You cross back over the highway on the two-lane, signed here also for Elko, and you're on your way to a driving adventure.

The road runs west, straight as an arrow, toward the **Raft River Mountains.** The first 10 miles pass through fairly monotonous irrigated farmland that gradually turns to dry sagebrush prairie. It's fascinating to contemplate the vastness of this land and the scarcity of people here. About 15 miles from the interstate, you will reach the point shown on the map as **Curlew Junction.** There is no town here, just a fork in the road. Straight ahead is Highway 42; left is the continuation of Highway 30. Take this left, signed for Park Valley, Montello, and Elko.

Small Towns, Big Hearts

Here the road strikes out to the southwest, and the land becomes increasingly more remote. At this point, something increases this sense of remoteness: You leave the power line behind for a while, so only the sparse traffic along this road reminds you of civilization.

This is **Great Basin desert**—much rougher and less "scenic" in conventional terms than the sandstone plateau country and rugged alpine terrain to the south and east. The land here has a hard, unfriendly look, and it is resistant to Man's attempts to subdue it. This is one of the most unpopulated regions in America, precisely because the land is so uninviting.

The few folks who inhabit the region are, however, anything but inhospitable. As in other remote ranching districts of the American West, passing motorists still wave to one another out here, a tradition that hopefully will endure. There are many things about this corner of Utah that suggest times past, reinforcing the sense that this place is still tied to pioneer traditions of friendliness mixed with cowboy independence.

A few miles past the major direction change at Curlew Junction, if you look off ahead and to the left you may just catch a glimpse of the sun glinting off the Great Salt Lake. Also note that off to the left/south is approximately the route of the return option along the old railroad bed. About 10 miles past Curlew Junction is the turnoff on the left for Kelton, a good dirt road leading down to the ghost town described in the rail-bed return option. (If you plan on missing the rail line return, you may want to make a side trip here to see the site of Kelton.)

In another few miles, note the occasional field under cultivation, indicating that you're approaching the ranching community of **Park Valley.** It contains little other than the ubiquitous LDS church (quite a cute little LDS church, in fact).

It is 4 more miles to the tiny hamlet of **Rosette,** home to more horses than people and without services. Other than Park Valley and Rosette, there are no real communities out here; most of the road signs at the side roads are for private family ranches rather than for towns. As you drive south/southwest from Rosette, look straight ahead in the distance to see the extremely remote Silver Island Mountains, far to the south near the Bonneville Salt Flats. A designated scenic backway (on dirt roads) encircles these fascinating peaks, but this drive is best accessed from I-80, west of Salt Lake, just before the Nevada state line at Wendover. Driving south from Lucin is not advised unless you're prepared for rough conditions.

About 38 miles past Park Valley, note the concrete structure on the right (the work of those clever folks at AT&T), the first man-made edifice since Rosette. Just 5 miles farther, note the picturesque old US Department of Interior sign for **Rabbit Springs**, on the left, indicating the use of these springs by grazing livestock. Forty-six miles west of Park Valley is the obvious intersection with a substantial gravel road: north to Grouse Creek, south to Lucin.

It is 20 miles of good gravel road to **Grouse Creek.** It may be useful to know that the land to the east of this road is mostly public (at least for the first 12 miles), where you may camp, provided you are self-sufficient and practice no-impact camping techniques. (This area, especially north of Grouse Creek, is more pleasant than camping along the totally treeless railroad grade, your other option on this trip.) The land on the west side of the road is almost entirely private property. A couple of local ranches rent out rooms or cabins, especially during hunting season. Go to the town's homespun website, grousecreek.com, for information—or just ask anyone you meet in town.

Grouse Creek is an attractive town in a pretty, relatively well-watered valley. There is an imposing stone elementary school, a large LDS church, and one of the most picturesque little rodeo arenas in all of Utah. If you happen to be here the weekend of or before July Fourth, stay for the **community rodeo** that has a long tradition in this traditional ranch country.

From Grouse Creek, the 34-mile drive up to **Almo, Idaho,** is scenic and leads to the stone jumble at **City of Rocks National Reserve.** Almo also has services, including a hotel. Ask in Grouse Creek about the condition of the road, which can be difficult when wet. To return to the intersection with Highway 30, one option is the loop through neighboring **Etna** from Grouse Creek. While well maintained, this gravel road is narrow, so RVs and trailers should probably return south on the main gravel road. This alternate return doesn't look much different from the main road (Etna is just a handful of ranches and a closed school), but it does give a slight change of scenery.

At the intersection with Highway 30, you must decide whether to do the rail-bed drive or return to Snowville on Highway 30. If you do return to Snowville on Highway 30, by all means rejoin this drive at Golden Spike National Historic Site. The easiest way to get there from Snowville is to take I-84 to exit 26 (Howell/Highway 83) and follow Highway 83 south for 14 miles to the well-marked turn on the right (just past the ATK rocket display).

Rail Trail

For those game to drive the rail line (or for those who want to see the remnants of Lucin before rejoining Highway 30), cross Highway 30 and drive 5 miles south to the start of the **Transcontinental Railroad Backcountry Byway.** It includes both the little bit of the Union Pacific line in Golden Spike (see below) and the Central Pacific line.

You'll have to detour around the decrepit old trestles on the Transcontinental Railroad route.

Set your odometer to zero: mileages here are from the start of the backway.

One of the most significant events in the history of American transportation took place on May 10, 1869, 88 miles east of here at Promontory, when the driving of the **Golden Spike** joined the Union Pacific and Central Pacific railroad lines and completed the nation's first transcontinental line. It was, at the time, an event of the same magnitude and public interest as that which took place almost exactly a century later: the landing of a man on the moon. The two stops at the end of this drive—the Golden Spike site and the ATK rocket-building plant—symbolize these two eras nicely.

This drive runs right along the old railroad grade, the final stretch of the Transcontinental's 800-mile line from California. You may wonder why there is no longer a rail line here today (nor is there a town of Lucin, for that matter). In 1904 the **Lucin Cutoff,** still in use, was completed south of here, crossing the lake by trestle. This shortened the route to Ogden by 40 miles and eliminated some of the difficult grades you will see later along the old line.

As soon as the main line shifted south, the old towns along the original line began to die, and many buildings were taken down and moved to more important sites in the lumber-poor desert. Regular traffic ceased completely in 1938, and in 1942 the rails were removed so the steel could be used in the war effort.

At one time there were vibrant railroad towns strung along this now-abandoned line. Nothing remains from that era but desert, a very few building foundations, and the occasional human artifact from the trash piles that remained when the towns disappeared. That, and one more thing: the old trace of the railroad bed, which gives us this level surface on which to drive across the desert.

The deserted (even ignored) character of this region made it a perfect setting for monumental art pieces created by two prominent figures in the 1970s arts movement sometimes referred to as *earthworks.* These artists created pieces in outdoor settings to engage the landscape and to comment on our relationship to physical environments. One of these grand-scale pieces lies at the very western end of the old railroad grade, the other close to the eastern terminus. It is also of some interest that each was produced, separately, by husband and wife.

Sun Tunnels was created between 1973 and 1976 by Nancy Holt on the barren desert floor 4 miles from **Lucin.** The "tunnels" are actually four huge concrete pipes laid out to mark sunrises and sunsets at the winter and summer solstices. To find the artwork (hard to miss in this empty plain), cross the rail line at the deceased town of Lucin and follow the dirt road 4 miles to the southeast. You can see the piece from the site of Lucin.

The site inspires some viewers to contemplate the complexity of these open, empty spaces; others may find these terse concrete pipes as evocative as highway

The railroad bed chugs up and down, and sometimes through, the hilly terrain, as seen here on the monument's East Grade drive.

construction debris. At the far end of the rail line, you will have the opportunity to see the somewhat more famous *Spiral Jetty*, created by Holt's husband, Robert Smithson.

This is not exactly a sandy desert. Depending on how much moisture there has been, the landscape can be quite luxuriant with desert grasses. There are also a number of old volcanic rock piles along the drive. Spaced along the old rail bed are brown BLM historical markers describing important places along the old line. It is impossible to miss these markers in this treeless landscape. Please heed the frequent written warnings not to collect souvenirs or vandalize the few remaining ruins and artifacts, or soon nothing will be left for future visitors. The BLM requests that anyone witnessing the disturbance of any site here contact them at (801) 977-4300 or the Box Elder County sheriff's office at (435)734-3800. Get a license number and vehicle description if you can.

Watch your speed along the old grade: 25 mph is about right for most vehicles. The road is smooth enough in places that you may want to speed up—but you'll be sorry when you hit the inevitable rut or railroad spike, many of which have been sharpened over time by the elements. Keep your eyes on the road. There are also numerous creek beds to cross on old wooden bridges and many small deviations around bridges deemed too weak to support vehicle traffic.

The old rail line, just barely wider than your vehicle, is elevated slightly, giving you a heightened sense of being out in the middle of the desert—which, in fact, you are. No-impact camping is permitted along the railroad grade, though no facilities, water, or shade are available anywhere.

Deserted Towns

At mile 22 you reach the site of **Terrace,** the largest of the Central Pacific towns built in Utah, which lasted from 1869 until around 1910. The town had 1,000 people, a 16-stall roundhouse, and an 8-track switching yard and boasted many businesses, a school, a library, a Wells Fargo office, a public bath, and even a justice of the peace. Most of the commercial buildings were north of the tracks; residential neighborhoods were to the south. There was a nice town square, and the streets were lined with trees watered with water brought in by train. With the completion of the Lucin Cutoff, most of the buildings were transported to Carlin, Nevada, and the town of Terrace died.

Not much remains of the town, but if you stroll around, you can find brick foundations and traces of the old railyard. From the town site, note on the right that the old ties (without the track) are still in place. The cemetery site is well marked about half a mile farther along. The cemetery was in pretty good condition until 1986, when vandals stole most of the remaining headstones.

At mile 25 is a good escape route up to Highway 30 (8 miles north), at a well-marked intersection. This might also be a good place to start the railroad-bed drive, avoiding many of the hazards on the Lucin end of the road. At just under mile 27 the road begins to climb up into the hills, becoming more rocky.

At about mile 40 there is a view off to the left and down onto where **Dove Creek** forms either a pond or a mudflat, depending on the season. Also here is the rough road on the right to the very remote **Hogup Mountains**. Artifacts found in a cave there are from the Desert Archaic period of proto-Indian culture, dating back 10,000 years. At just under mile 45 there is a nice view ahead and to the right of the lake, which has been elusive to this point.

At just past mile 45, the railroad grade takes a jog to the left. Here there are a couple of the by-now familiar signs for deviations from the grade. There is also a prominent road descending on the right, signed for Kelton. Take this road, as the road along the grade dies shortly past here. The dirt road drops down onto the desert flat, while the rail line clings to the rocky hillside, clearly visible above and to the left. Drive slowly down on these flats, as there may be occasional washed-out sections. At just under mile 49, you will intersect a major dirt road, signed for Kelton, to the left. Take this obvious left, continuing in the same general northeast direction as the rail line, visible on the hillside to your left.

At just past mile 50, you will re-cross the old grade, which has been closed off. At mile 52, intersect another good dirt road and trend to the right (northeast), signed for Kelton. Two and a half miles farther, note on the right the **Kelton cemetery,** which served the residents of Kelton until it was abandoned in 1942. Sadly, this picturesque old graveyard has been badly vandalized.

Continue on to the prominent historic markers for the town of **Kelton,** clearly visible to the northeast. Kelton (also known as Indian Creek) survived until 1942, partly due to its importance as a transportation hub. There was evidently a very substantial town here (about 700 people), where the stage from Oregon Territory to the north made the rail connection. This northern stage line was reportedly the most-robbed stage in the West, usually robbed weekly, sometimes daily.

At this point you can rejoin the railroad grade, which is better maintained from here east and signed for Golden Spike National Historic Site. If you're completely tired of the desert driving, you can also follow the good road north to rejoin Highway 30, although at this point that option provides no real advantage.

At mile 65 is the important intersection with the good road north to Snowville (again, no point taking this unless your tank is close to empty). Also here is **Locomotive Springs,** a series of springs and ponds that serve as a bird refuge. It makes a decent place to camp, provided you need no facilities and the bugs aren't too vicious.

The railroad bed continues to Golden Spike (mileages from here are taken from Locomotive Springs). East of Locomotive Springs, the road can be pretty rough; at any rate, at mile 3.5 you will have to exit to the good dirt road on the left. You're best off getting on this road right from Locomotive Springs: It runs parallel to the rail line, about 30 yards to its left. At just under 8 miles from Locomotive Springs take the prominent right fork (signs around here may be missing or badly shot-up, but the route is obvious—just stay on the main road, avoiding deviations to the left).

At mile 13 is a good opportunity to return to the railroad grade. The only advantages to driving the old grade from here are the better views of the lake, off to the right, along with a few more historical markers.

Golden Spike

A prominent BLM backcountry drive sign indicates your arrival at **Golden Spike National Historic Site.** At this sign, go left about 10 yards, then turn right to drive along the designated West Grade Auto Tour. It is about 5 miles from here to the visitor center on a road parallel to the railbed gate.

Exhibits, films, and literature at the visitor center describe both the momentous Golden Spike event and its profound impact on the subsequent history of the American West. A short section of track has been re-laid at precisely the spot where the two lines met, and exact replicas of the Transcontinental's "Jupiter" and the Union Pacific's "119" make scheduled appearances during the summer season.

There are also two very nice short driving tours with interpretive signs—which will probably seem rather tame to those who have just finished the old rail-bed drive from Lucin. For those who opted not to drive east along the old rail bed, this is a fine opportunity for an abbreviated introduction to this fascinating and important slice of American history. The 14-mile west tour loop passes the spot where Union Pacific workers, rushing to keep on schedule, laid 10 miles of track in one day. The 2-mile east loop passes a couple of trailheads for short hikes to the railroad grade and lets you drive on the steepest mile of railroad grade in Utah.

The visitor center is open 9 a.m. until 5 p.m. daily (closed Thanksgiving, Christmas, and New Year's Day). The locomotives reappear for reenactments at 11 a.m. and 1 p.m. on Sat and holidays. No camping or services are available at Golden Spike.

Now for the second installment on the Northwest Utah Arts Tour. **Spiral Jetty,** Robert Smithson's odd embellishment of the salty shores of the Great Salt Lake, is a 15-mile drive southwest on uneven dirt roads from Golden Spike. It is definitely worth a visit, but check first with the folks at Golden Spike on the status of the road into the site and get directions (the route, through private property, is not well marked). It gets interestingly rough as you near the lake; the determined can park and walk the last bit if necessary. The jetty is past an old commercial venture of some sort that has its own (straight) jetty.

Spiral Jetty has a genuinely archaeological look to it, as if it somehow belongs there or might have performed some arcane function, either nautical or spiritual, in the distant past. Constructed in 1970, it disappeared under the rising waters of the lake two years later. It remained submerged in the briny depths until 1994, when the lake receded. Recent weather patterns will determine whether it's dry or partly submerged, but it's easy to see either way.

It is precisely what the name suggests: a grand spiral jetty winding its way off-shore. Built of earth and rock, like some sort of monumental hippie-era hallucino-genic road-building scheme, it will surely cause you to ponder deeply significant questions like: Why? One thing seems certain. If it belongs anywhere, to quote Brigham one final time: Surely, this is the place.

To continue on to Corinne from Golden Spike, follow the paved road from Golden Spike about 8 miles to the intersection with Highway 83. As you near the intersection, note the extensive research, testing, and production facilities of **ATK** (formerly Thiokol Corporation). To visit the company's very nice **outdoor rocket display,** complete with explanatory panels, turn left/north and drive just under 2 miles. This is definitely worth the quick detour, especially if you have kids with you—when they see these real-live rockets, they will no doubt forget all about

The Spiral Jetty is one of two earthwork art installations in this part of Utah visible via unpaved side trips.

concrete pipes and earthen causeways. It does seem appropriate that a company that builds space exploration vehicles should choose to do its testing and development in this extraterrestrial landscape.

It is 17 miles from the Highway 83 intersection to Corinne. This attractive but rough landscape—alkali salt flats to the right, rough scrub hills to the left—serves as a final reminder that this is land upon which humanity cannot impose its will. Tracts of marshland along the road are home to myriad forms of bird life.

The final 6 miles to **Corinne** pass through peaceful, productive farmland that belies the town's roughneck past. As the two rail lines pushed toward this area from east and west, non-Mormon speculators rushed in to promote the rowdy shanty town and freight relay station of Corinne as the future transportation hub of the Intermountain West. They assumed that the joining of the rails, along with the important freighting needs of the new Montana and Idaho mining districts to the north and the newly formed Tintic district to the south, would make Corinne's position ideal. The town grew to a very boisterous and decidedly anti-Mormon 1,500, with boosters claiming Corinne would eclipse Salt Lake City and become the new territorial capital.

PLEASE DO
NOT CLIMB
INTO THE
NOZZLE

Corinne's first disappointment came when Promontory was selected for the joining of the lines, and her bubble ultimately burst when Ogden was chosen for the regional rail center. The boosters slunk off, the community gradually dissolved, and Corinne was finally "resettled" as a conventional Mormon town. Though at one time there were 29 saloons and two dance halls here, not much remains of Corinne's heyday. One lasting reminder of its non-Mormon character is the **Corinne Methodist-Episcopal Church,** dedicated in 1870—the oldest existing Protestant church building in Utah. The town also has a restaurant or two and at least one bar.

It is 2.5 miles from Corinne to I-15 and another 4 miles to Brigham City.

Don't forget to stop by the ATK rocket display, which brings visitors close to real components used in space launches.

Appendix:
More Information

For more information on lands and events, please contact the following agencies and organizations.

Statewide

Utah Office of Tourism
Council Hall/Capitol Hill
300 North State St.
Salt Lake City, UT 84114
(800) 200-1160
visitutah.com

Utah State Parks and Recreation
Administrative Office
1594 West North Temple, Suite 116
Salt Lake City, UT 84114
(801) 538-7220
stateparks.utah.gov

National Park Service
nps.gov/state/ut/index.htm

Bureau of Land Management
Utah State Office
440 West 200 South, Suite 500
Salt Lake City, UT 84101
(801) 539-4001
blm.gov/office/utah-state-office

US Forest Service
Intermountain Region
Federal Office Building
324 25th St.
Ogden, UT 84401
(801) 625-5605
fs.fed.us/r4

Drive 1

St. George Tourism Office
20 North Main St., Suite 105
St. George, UT 84770
(435) 634-5747
visitstgeorge.com

Dixie National Forest
Pine Valley Ranger District
196 East Tabernacle St., Room 38
St. George, UT 84770
(435) 652-3100
fs.usda.gov/recarea/dixie/

Bureau of Land Management
Color Country District Office
176 East D.L. Sargent Drive
Cedar City, UT 84721
(435) 865-3000
blm.gov/office/color-country-district
-office

Drive 2

St. George Tourism Office
20 North Main St., Suite 105
St. George, UT 84770
(435) 634-5747
visitstgeorge.com

Zion Canyon Visitors Bureau
(435) 772-3434
zionpark.com

Zion National Park
Springdale, UT 84767
(435) 772-3256
nps.gov/zion

Drive 3

Kolob Canyons Visitor Center
(435) 586-9548
nps.gov/zion

Drive 4

Kane County Information Center
78 South 100 East
Kanab, UT 84741
(435) 644-5033
visitsouthernutah.com

**Bureau of Land Management
Grand Staircase-Escalante National
Monument Office**
669 South Highway 89A
Kanab, UT 84741
(435) 644-1200
blm.gov/office/grand-staircase
-escalante-national-monument

Drive 5

**Cedar City/Brian Head Tourism
& Convention Bureau**
581 North Main St.
Cedar City, UT 84721
(435) 586-5124
visitcedarcity.com

**Dixie National Forest
Cedar City Ranger District**
1789 North Wedgewood Lane
Cedar City, UT 84721
(435) 865-3700
fs.usda.gov/dixie

**Dixie National Forest
Powell Ranger District**
225 East Center St.
Panguitch, UT 84759
(435) 676-9300
fs.usda.gov/dixie

Drive 6

**Cedar City/Brian Head Tourism
& Convention Bureau**
581 North Main St.
Cedar City, UT 84721
(435) 586-5124
visitcedarcity.com

Bryce Canyon National Park
Bryce Canyon, UT 84717
(435) 834-5322
nps.gov/brca

**Dixie National Forest
Escalante Ranger District**
Escalante Interagency Federal Building
755 West Main St.
Escalante, UT 84726
(435) 826-5400
fs.usda.gov/dixie

Drive 7

Capitol Reef Travel Council
PO Box 7
Teasdale, UT 84773
(435) 425-3365
capitolreef.travel

Dixie National Forest
Escalante Ranger District
Escalante Interagency Federal Building
755 West Main St.
Escalante, UT 84726
(435) 826-5400
fs.usda.gov/dixie

Dixie National Forest
Loa/Teasdale Ranger District
138 East Main
Teasdale, UT 84773
(435) 425-9500
fs.usda.gov/dixie

Bureau of Land Management
Grand Staircase-Escalante National
Monument Office
669 South Highway 89A
Kanab, UT 84741
(435) 644-1200
blm.gov/office/grand-staircase
-escalante-national-monument

Drive 8

Capitol Reef Travel Council
PO Box 189
Loa, UT 84747
(800) 858-7951
capitolreef.org

Capitol Reef National Park
Torrey, UT 84775
(435) 425-3791
nps.gov/care

Dixie National Forest
Fremont River Ranger District
138 East Main
Teasdale, UT 84773
(435) 425-9500
fs.usda.gov/dixie

Drive 9

Bureau of Land Management
Hanksville Office
380 South 100 West
Hanksville, UT 84734
(435) 542-3461
blm.gov/office/henry-mountains-field
-station

Natural Bridges National Monument
HC-60 Box 1
Lake Powell, UT 84533
(435) 692-1234
nps.gov/nabr

Blanding Visitor Center/Pioneer
Museum
13 North Grayson Pkwy.
Blanding, UT 84511
(435) 678-3662
blandingutah.org

San Juan County Tourism
117 South Main St.
Monticello, UT 84535
(800) 574-4386
utahscanyoncountry.com

Drive 10

San Juan County Tourism
117 South Main St.
Monticello, UT 84535
(800) 574-4386
utahscanyoncountry.com

Monument Valley Navajo Tribal Park
PO Box 360289
Monument Valley, UT 84536
(435) 727-5874
navajonationparks.org/tribal-parks/
monument-valley

Hovenweep National Monument
McElmo Route
Cortez, CO 81321
(970) 562-4282
nps.gov/hove

Drive 11

San Juan County Tourism
117 South Main St.
Monticello, UT 84535
(800) 574-4386
utahscanyoncountry.com

Canyonlands National Park
2282 Southwest Resource Blvd.
Moab, UT 84532
(435) 719-2313
nps.gov/cany

Drive 12

Canyonlands National Park
2282 Southwest Resource Blvd.
Moab, UT 84532
(435) 719-2313
nps.gov/cany

Arches National Park
PO Box 907
Moab, UT 84532
(435) 719-2299
nps.gov/arch

Moab Travel Information
Center and Main Streets
Moab, UT 84532
(435) 259-8825
discovermoab.com

Drive 13

Moab Travel Information
Center and Main Streets
Moab, UT 84532
(435) 259-8825
discovermoab.com

**Bureau of Land Management
Moab District Office**
82 East Dogwood
Moab, UT 84532
(435) 259-2100
blm.gov/office/canyon-country-district
-office
(Please review the BLM's "Canyon
Country Minimum Impact Practices"
brochure while visiting this area.)

**Green River Information Center
John Wesley Powell River History
Museum**
885 East Main St.
Green River, UT 84525
(435) 564-3427
johnwesleypowell.com

**Manti-LaSal National Forest
Moab Ranger District**
62 East 100 North
Moab, UT 84532
(435) 259-7155
fs.usda.gov/main/mantilasal

Drive 14

Capitol Reef Travel Council
PO Box 189
Loa, UT 84747
(800) 858-7951
capitolreef.org

Sevier County Tourism
250 North Main, B16
Richfield, UT 84701
(435) 893-0457
trailcountry.com

Dixie National Forest
Fremont River Ranger District
138 East Main
Teasdale, UT 84773
(435) 425-9500
fs.usda.gov/dixie

Fishlake National Forest
Richfield Ranger District
115 East 900 North
Richfield, UT 84701
(435) 896-9233
fs.usda.gov/fishlake

Drive 15

Beaver County Travel Council
105 East Center
Beaver, UT 84713
(435) 438-6482
beavercountry.com/visit

Piute County Travel
Piute County Courthouse
Junction, UT 84740
(435) 577-2949
piutecounty.org

Sevier County Tourism
250 North Main, B16
Richfield, UT 84701
(435) 893-0457
trailcountry.com

Fishlake National Forest
Beaver Ranger District
575 South Main St.
Beaver, UT 84713
(435) 438-2436
fs.usda.gov/fishlake

Drive 16

Juab Travel Council
4 South Main St.
Nephi, UT 84648
(800) 748-4361
juabtravel.com

Millard County Tourism
Delta Visitor Center
75 West Main St.
Delta, UT 84624
(435) 864-4316
millardcountytravel.com

Topaz Museum
55 West Main St.
Delta, UT
(435) 864-2514
topazmuseum.org/

Bureau of Land Management
West Desert District Office
2370 South Decker Lake Blvd.
West Valley, UT 84119
(801) 977-4300
blm.gov/office/west-desert-district
-office

Drive 17

Juab Travel Council
4 South Main St.
Nephi, UT 84648
(800) 748-4361
juabtravel.com

**Uinta-Wasatch-Cache National Forest
Spanish Fork Ranger District**
44 West 400 North
Spanish Fork, UT 84660
(801) 798-3571
fs.usda.gov/main/uwcnf

**Uinta-Wasatch-Cache National Forest
Nephi Office**
635 South Main
Nephi, UT 84648
(435) 623-2735
fs.usda.gov/main/uwcnf

Drive 18

**Manti-La Sal National Forest
Sanpete Ranger District**
540 North Main St.
Ephraim, UT 84627
(435) 283-4151
fs.usda.gov/main/mantilasal/

**Castle Country Regional Information
Center**
751 East 100 North
Price, Utah 84501
(435) 636-3701
castlecountry.com

**San Rafael Country/Emery County
Travel Bureau**
75 East Main St.
Castle Dale, UT 84513
(888) 564-3600
emerycounty.com/travel

Drive 19

**Castle Country Regional Information
Center**
751 East 100 North
Price, Utah 84501
(435) 636-3701
castlecountry.com

**Ashley National Forest
Duchesne Ranger District**
85 West Main St.
Duchesne, UT 84021
(435) 738-2482
fs.usda.gov/ashley

**Manti-La Sal National Forest
Price Ranger District**
599 West Price River Drive
Price, UT 84501
(435) 637-2817
fs.usda.gov/main/mantilasal

Drive 20

Dinosaurland Regional Travel Office
55 East Main St.
Vernal, UT 84078
(800) 477-5558
dinoland.com

Flaming Gorge Tourism
PO Box 122
Manila, UT 84046
(435) 277-0709
flaminggorgecountry.com

Dinosaur National Monument
4545 East Hwy. 40
Dinosaur, CO 81610-9724
(435) 781-7700
nps.gov/dino

Ashley National Forest
Vernal Ranger District
355 North Vernal Ave.
Vernal, UT 84078
(435) 789-1181
fs.usda.gov/ashley

Bureau of Land Management
Green River District
170 South 500 East
Vernal, UT 84078
(435) 781-4400

Flaming Gorge National Recreation Area
Flaming Gorge Ranger District
25 West Hwy. 43
Manila, UT 84046
(435) 784-3445
fs.usda.gov/ashley

Drive 21

Uinta-Wasatch-Cache National Forest
Kamas Ranger District
50 East Center St.
Kamas, UT 84036
(435) 783-4338
fs.usda.gov/main/uwcnf

Uinta-Wasatch-Cache National Forest
Evanston Ranger District
Evanston, WY 82931
(307) 789-3194
fs.usda.gov/main/uwcnf

Drive 22

Utah Valley Convention and Visitors Bureau
220 West Center St., Suite 100
Provo, UT 84601
(801) 851-2100
utahvalley.org

Uinta-Wasatch-Cache National Forest
Pleasant Grove Ranger District
390 North 100 East
Pleasant Grove, UT 84062
(801) 785-3563
fs.usda.gov/main/uwcnf

Timpanogos Cave National Monument
R.R. 3, Box 200
American Fork, UT 84003
Visitor Center (summer only): (801) 756-5238
Headquarters: (801) 756-5239
nps.gov/tica

Heber Valley Chamber of Commerce
475 N Main St.
Heber, UT 84032
(435) 654-3666
gohebervalley.com/

Drive 23

Salt Lake Convention & Visitors Bureau
90 South West Temple
Salt Lake City, UT 84101
(800) 541-4900
visitsaltlake.com

**Bureau of Land Management
West Desert District Office**
2370 South Decker Lake Blvd.
West Valley, UT 84119
(801) 977-4300
blm.gov/office/west-desert-district
-office

**Pony Express National Historic Trail
National Park Service National Trails
Intermountain Region**
50 W. Broadway, Suite 950
Salt Lake City, Utah 84101
(801) 741-1012
nps.gov/poex

**Uinta-Wasatch-Cache National Forest
Salt Lake Ranger District**
6944 South 3000 East
Salt Lake City, UT 84121
(801) 733-2660
fs.usda.gov/main/uwcnf

Drive 24

**Uinta-Wasatch-Cache National Forest
Salt Lake Ranger District**
6944 South 3000 East
Salt Lake City, UT 84121
(801) 733-2660
fs.usda.gov/main/uwcnf

**Salt Lake Convention & Visitors
Bureau**
90 South West Temple
Salt Lake City, UT 84101
(800) 541-4900
visitsaltlake.com

Drive 25

**Uinta-Wasatch-Cache National Forest,
Ogden Ranger District**
507 25th St., Suite 103
Ogden, UT 84401
(801) 625-5112
fs.usda.gov/main/uwcnf

Ogden Convention & Visitors Bureau
2438 Washington Blvd.
Ogden, UT 84401
(800) 867-8824
visitogden.com

Drive 26

Bear River Migratory Bird Refuge
2155 West Forest St.
Brigham City, UT 84302
(435) 723-5887
fws.gov/refuge/bear_river_migratory_
bird_refuge

Box Elder County Tourism
1 South Main St.
Brigham City, UT 84302
(435) 734-3300
boxeldercounty.org/visiting.htm

Drive 27

Cache Valley Visitors Bureau
199 North Main St.
Logan, UT 84321
(800) 882-4433
explorelogan.com

**Uinta-Wasatch-Cache National Forest
Logan Ranger District**
1500 East Hwy. 89
Logan, UT 84321
(435) 755-3620
fs.usda.gov/main/uwcnf

Drive 28

Box Elder County Tourism
1 South Main St.
Brigham City, UT 84302
(435) 734-3300
boxeldercounty.org/visiting.htm

Bureau of Land Management West Desert District Office
2370 South Decker Lake Blvd.
West Valley, UT 84119
(801) 977-4300
blm.gov/office/west-desert-district
-office

Golden Spike National Historic Site
PO Box 897
Brigham City, UT 84302
(435) 471-2209
nps.gov/gosp

Index